① Still the Wild River Runs

Still the Wild River Runs

Congress, the Sierra Club, and the Fight to Save Grand Canyon

Byron E. Pearson

The University of Arizona Press ⓓ Tucson

The University of Arizona Press
© 2002 Arizona Board of Regents
All rights reserved
♾ This book is printed on acid-free, archival-quality paper.
Jacket and text design by Chelsea Cloeter
Manufactured in the United States of America
First Printing

07 06 05 04 03 02   6 5 4 3 2 1

Library of Congress Cataloging-in-Publication Data
Pearson, Byron E., 1960–
    Still the wild river runs : Congress, the Sierra Club, and the fight to save
Grand Canyon / Byron E. Pearson.
       p.   cm.
    Includes bibliographical references and index.
    ISBN 0-8165-2058-5 (cloth : alk. paper)
    1. Dams—Political aspects—Arizona—Grand Canyon. 2. Dams—Ari-
zona—Grand Canyon—Public opinion. 3. Public opinion—United States.
4. Sierra Club. 5. Environmental policy—United States. I. Title.
  TC557.A62 G737 2002
  333.91'62'0979132—dc21

                                       2002001549

British Library Cataloguing-in-Publication Data
A catalogue record for this book is available from the British Library.

For Paula, Nate, and Josh

Contents

① figures

① maps

⑦ Acknowledgments

I could never have completed this project without the guidance, help, and patience of some very special people. From the University of Arizona Department of History, I wish to thank Dr. Douglas Weiner, my mentor and friend, for challenging me intellectually, for sharing his expertise in environmental history, his enthusiasm about this topic, and his sense of humor, which helped keep me grounded. I am also indebted to Dr. Katherine Morrissey for her rigorous and constructive critiques of my ideas and writing style, as well as her willingness to share her insights about Western history. Likewise, Dr. Juan Garcia has not only contributed his insights and knowledge about twentieth-century American history, but sets a standard for teaching which I hope someday to emulate. Dr. George Lubick, Dr. Valeen Avery, and Dr. Robert Baron of the Northern Arizona University Department of History have also played important roles in the evolution of this manuscript and have given me much needed direction at critical points in time. It has been my privilege to work with each of them.

I have also benefited from many archivists whose knowledge of source materials has opened new and varied paths for me to research. Peter Steere, former curator of the Morris and Stewart Udall Papers at the University of Arizona, helped me immeasurably as I mined these immense resources. Joe Schwartz of the National Archives in College Park, Maryland, pointed me to National Park Service and Interior Department records, while Barbara Walton of the Conservation Archives in Denver introduced me to the Wilderness Society and Richard Bradley collections. The archival staffs at the Denver Federal Records Center and National Archives, Indiana University of Pennsylvania, Arizona State University, Northern Arizona University, American Heritage Center at the University of Wyoming, Clemson University, and the Bancroft Library at U.C. Berkeley all helped me utilize the resources held in these repositories, while Colleen Hyde and Carolyn Richards of the Grand Canyon National Park Museum helped me to maximize my time at the canyon. Additionally, I would like to thank the editors of the *Journal of the Southwest* and the *Western Historical Quarterly* for permitting me to republish portions of two of my articles in chapters 1, 5, and 6. A special thanks to the Bancroft Library for granting me permission to quote from oral histories conducted through the Regional Oral History office. I would also like to salute Dr. James Hallmark, Dean of the Graduate College at West Texas A&M, who procured financial support for the final stages of this project.

I would also like to thank the many individuals with whom I have corresponded and whom I have interviewed. In particular I wish to acknowledge Dr. Stephen Jett of U.C. Davis, and Dr. Barbara Brower of Portland State University. I wish also to thank the following people who granted me personal or telephonic interviews: Stewart Udall, Jeff Ingram, Sharon Francis, Frank Gregg, Floyd Dominy, George Hartzog, John Carver, Orren Beaty, and the late David Brower. Each of these individuals enabled me to break free of the documentary record, and experience history as they lived and shaped it.

Finally, I wish to thank my parents, Ben and Kathryn Pearson, for their love and support, my wife, Paula, for her patience, and my sons, Nathaniel and Joshua, who with their smiles, remind me of what is really important in this life. Most important, I wish to thank my lord Jesus whose sacrifice and love gives us hope in all things and brings purpose to human existence. Although all of the aforementioned people have facilitated the writing of this book, I am responsible for assessing and presenting the evidence upon which these conclusions are based. Therefore, any inadequacies of interpretation, style or argument the reader may find are mine and mine alone.

① Introduction

Translucent in the shadows of the late afternoon, the great river slipped smoothly through walls of black schist accented with streamers of red granite. A raft appeared in the narrow chasm, drawn along by the inexorable tug of the Colorado, chief excavating agent of Grand Canyon. As the river continued on its erosive mission, the proverbial irresistible force meeting a not quite immovable object, the sound of a contentious debate emanated from the depths.

The year was 1969, and David Brower, former executive director of the Sierra Club, held court before the small captive audience of river runners. Also on board and seated near Brower was Floyd Dominy, commissioner of the federal Bureau of Reclamation and Brower's chief antagonist over the development of water resources in the American West for the past decade. The topic of discussion—the recent battle over the construction of dams in Grand Canyon for the generation of hydroelectric power—weighed heavily upon all present. Although these dams had recently been defeated in Congress, Brower and Dominy, riding the river at the behest of author John McPhee, argued their respective positions so stridently it appeared as though the issue was still very much in doubt.

The group was fresh from a tour of Lake Powell, and Glen Canyon Dam, where Dominy had extolled the beauty of the reservoir and benefits of power generation, a tour during which he had swayed more than a few of the people present. Now it was Brower's turn and while the expedition careened through thunderous rapids and glided across tranquil stretches, Brower said relatively little, instead allowing Grand Canyon itself to persuade the audience with the power of its visual eloquence. Finally, almost 150 miles into the Canyon, Brower began to speak unexpectedly. "We are now entering the reservoir," he said. When asked to clarify his meaning, Brower asserted that here, at mile 144.5, the group had now reached the point in the Canyon where the living river would have ended and the still water of a reservoir would have begun had Bridge Canyon Dam been constructed. In response to questions from the audience, Dominy could only agree that Brower was correct. After a period of silence as the magnitude of what Brower had said was absorbed by the audience and accented by the natural spectacle surrounding them, one traveler queried the commissioner again. "Do you mean the reservoir would cover Upset Rapid? Havasu Creek? Lava Falls? all the places we are coming to?" Pulling on the visor of his Lake Powell cap, Dominy replied, "Yes." "I'd have to think about that," the man said thoughtfully.[1]

The above exchange constitutes, in microcosm, an accurate reflection of the most public part of the struggle over the Grand Canyon dams that occurred between 1963 and 1968, one of the most bitter environmental debates in American history. Dominy, as well as politicians from the state of Arizona and other supporters of western water development, fought environmentalists, whose most public persona was David Brower, in the court of American public opinion. After five years of tumultuous debate and intrigue, at the height of one of the most politically and socially charged decades of the twentieth century, Congress decided to delete the dams from the proposed legislation. David Brower emerged from the struggle having added to his already formidable reputation as an environmental advocate, while the Sierra Club attained the status as the leading environmental organization in the United States and perhaps the world, at a time when environmentalism had become a mainstream issue. As a result of its having gained an enormous national constituency during the controversy, the Sierra Club was able to parlay its reputation as the savior of Grand Canyon into influence at the policymaking level, where it continues to wield power as an activist environmental organization today.

Although the Grand Canyon dam controversy is directly linked to the Central Arizona Project, this book is not a comprehensive discussion of the Central Arizona Project (CAP). Rather, this analysis examines the environmental debates related to the most controversial aspects of the CAP within the context of the policymaking process, grassroots activism, and shifting public perceptions of land use from the period 1963 to 1968. The CAP was under consideration long before the 1960s, and private, state, and federal dam proposals affecting Grand Canyon had been considered since the turn of the twentieth century. Conflicts between the State of Arizona and Native Americans over resources during the 1950s also set the stage for the federal/American Indian conflicts that appear in this narrative. This background material will appear in another book-length analysis that will cover the period 1900–1963. However, the present study contains references to relevant historical antecedents so that the events that occurred after 1963 are contextualized.

Very little has been written about the Grand Canyon dam controversy. Popular writers have written primarily from the pro–Sierra Club perspective and contend that the club is responsible for "saving" Grand Canyon. The few environmental historians who have discussed the controversy have also focused primarily upon the Sierra Club's successful mobilization of public opinion that resulted in one of the largest outpourings of public sentiment in American history when measured by the number of letters written to Congress, federal officials, and agencies. Although the number is difficult to tabulate, it appears as though hundreds of thousands of people wrote Congress protesting the proposed damming of Grand Canyon. These historians argue that this tremendous public outcry the Sierra Club generated translated into changes in policy, and that Interior Secretary Stewart Udall, a strong proponent of the Grand Canyon dams initially, changed his mind as a result of this public reaction, and that after experiencing a shift in his own environmental consciousness, he worked within the political process and helped the environmentalists to prevail.[2]

However, these arguments consider inadequately the intricate and complex nature of the political aspects of the controversy and instead assign undue weight to the actions and influence of the Sierra Club and other environmental organizations, as well as the influence public opinion had upon the formation of policy in the late 1960s. This book will analyze the Grand Canyon dam controversy in the context of shifting political agendas, technological advancements, and social tumult during the period historians recognize as the genesis of the modern environmental movement. I have attempted to illuminate the complexity of the controversy at many levels within these pages, and have had a wealth of documentary and oral history sources upon which to rely, as well as a topic rich in intrigue and personality about which to write.

The Grand Canyon dam controversy occurred on two levels: in the court of public opinion, and within the political process. In this analysis I will investigate the development and interrelationship between these two levels of the debate, and evaluate the effect that the public outcry had upon the formulation of policy. I will also assess the place and meaning of the Grand Canyon dam controversy within the context of U.S. environmental history after 1945, and explore the linkages between it and other western environmental controversies, in particular, the debate over the Echo Park dams that occurred ten years previously which has been interpreted by leading historians such as Roderick Nash and Stephen Fox as a reversal of the harmful precedent of invading national parks for water development begun during the Hetch Hetchy debates of 1905–1913.[3]

The Grand Canyon dam controversy took place in a complex political context and offers fertile ground for the scholar interested in examining the policy-making process during the formative years of the modern environmental movement. To the delight of the historian and researcher, the story is dominated by a fascinating and eclectic cast of characters such as: Arizona's shrewd representatives Morris Udall and John Rhodes; powerful Arizona Senator Carl Hayden; Wayne Aspinall of Colorado, the "prickly" House Interior Committee Chairman; Washington's uncompromising Senator Henry Jackson; Floyd Dominy, Reclamation commissioner and, according to environmentalists, an environmental exploiter without peer; the ingenious legal strategist Northcutt Ely of California; David Brower, Sierra Club executive director and strident environmental advocate; and the pragmatic interior secretary and former Arizona congressman Stewart Udall, all of whom influenced the eventual outcome of the controversy.

Although each of these individuals played important roles during the controversy, this book is in no way a biographical sketch. As of this writing, there are at least two biographies of Wayne Aspinall and one of Stewart Udall under review, as well as recent, published biographies of Morris Udall and Carl Hayden. These books should be examined by interested readers in order to gain insights into how and why these prominent players in the current analysis made the decisions and shaped policy in the manner they did.

The debate over the Grand Canyon dams that took place between 1963 and 1968 was also shaped by the bitter dispute between the states of Arizona and California over Colorado River water that had gone on since the signing of the Colorado River Compact in 1922. Between 1922 and 1963, Arizona and California had battled in the Congress and the courts and almost exchanged gunfire on at least one occasion over the development of the Colorado River.

From the 1920s through 1963, California won three Supreme Court cases, and shepherded legislation through Congress that enabled it to utilize not only its own share of the river, but almost one million acre feet of water Arizona claimed.

Arizona was not without influence, however, and in 1950–1951 Arizona senator Carl Hayden obtained Senate approval of a federally constructed Central Arizona Project, only to see the legislation defeated in the House Interior Committee because of the strident opposition of California's congressional representatives. The enmity between the two states grew when these same California congressmen pushed legislation through Congress in 1952 throwing the entire issue of lower Colorado Basin water rights into the U.S. Supreme Court. Thwarted at the federal level, the State of Arizona even tried to "go it alone" and sought to construct the project as a state-sponsored endeavor between 1957 and 1963, only to see these efforts dissolve in a bitter and ironic feud between advocates of the state proposal and Carl Hayden and Interior Secretary Stewart Udall, a former Arizona congressman who blocked Arizona's proposal hoping to obtain federal backing for the project instead.

In 1963, after the longest and most voluminous litigation in United States history, the Supreme Court decided in favor of Arizona. Yet the California opposition continued, and gaining California's support became an obsession of virtually every Arizona politician with the exception of Senator Hayden, who believed he possessed the power to obtain congressional passage of the Central Arizona Project in the wake of the Supreme Court decision.

Stewart Udall, who was named interior secretary by President Kennedy in 1960, formulated a regional water plan designed to gain California's political backing for the Central Arizona Project and he introduced it amid great fanfare immediately after the Supreme Court handed down its ruling. However, after three years of tumultuous and sometimes bitter debate within the Congress, and among Arizona's own water advocates, the regional scheme was defeated in 1966, undone by the very political deals Udall had hoped would ensure its passage. After the failure of his grandiose proposal in September of 1966, Stewart Udall and Senator Hayden pushed a bare-bones Central Arizona Project without dams in Grand Canyon through Congress that President Lyndon Johnson signed into law on 30 September 1968.

Udall's role in the controversy is important, not only because of the prominent political office he held and the influence he wielded, but because for much of the debate he struggled to reconcile his own loyalties to Arizona with his ethical responsibilities to the people of the United States and his preservationist leanings with his own belief in western water development. Udall, one of the most public figures during the Kennedy administration, personified the aura of the young president. Like Kennedy, Udall was handsome, athletic, and was willing to try new approaches to old problems. Realizing that the nation's natural resources and natural grandeur had come under siege in the years following World War II, Udall believed that scientific advances would enable Americans to have their cake and eat it too, that America could continue as a materialistic, consumer society while at the same time it would be possible to preserve many of the nation's environmental treasures that had not yet been destroyed.

Udall's ideas were publicized in his classic 1963 book *The Quiet Crisis*, the publication of which occupies a prominent position among the events of the 1960s that, historians argue, helped facilitate the emergence of modern environmentalism. Yet ironically, it appears as though its author had not completely reached a modern environmental consciousness himself by the time the book was published. At the height of the dam controversy, Udall received hundreds of letters from opponents of the dams that questioned how the author of such an important argument in favor of preservation could support the construction of dams in the greatest natural wonder of them all. It is a question that Udall was never able to answer to the satisfaction of his critics as the controversy raged.

Many of the environmental historians whom I have cited previously have argued that Udall was ultimately swayed by the arguments of the environmentalists and that in the summer of 1966 he changed his mind, perhaps the pivotal development in the campaign against the Grand Canyon dams. Yet the documentary record and Udall's own personal recollections support a conclusion that he made his decision out of political pragmatism to gain the support of Washington Senator Henry Jackson, who, as chairman of the Senate Interior Committee, had opposed the dams because they were the primary means of financing the importation of water into the Colorado River Basin from the Pacific Northwest. By removing the dams from the Central Arizona Project bill in early 1967, Udall gained Jackson's backing and virtually assured that the Senate would approve the scheme.

I believe that the evidence supports my premise that Stewart Udall would

have supported the construction of the Grand Canyon dams had congressional support for them existed in late 1966. Hence, I will argue throughout
this book that despite the preservationists' national publicity campaign, it
appears as though the Grand Canyon dams were eliminated because of the
aggregate effects of the political intrigue between Arizona and California and
Stewart Udall's political pragmatism, rather than as a result of the environmentalists' ability to influence Congress.

Yet environmental groups did play an important role in the debate over the
Grand Canyon dams, and none was as important as the Sierra Club. At the
beginning of the controversy, the Sierra Club was but one of several environmental advocacy organizations that had taken the lead in attempting to change
the nation's environmental consciousness. Groups such as the Wilderness
Society, National Parks Association, Izaak Walton League and others had
joined the Sierra Club during the successful battle to defeat dams proposed
for Dinosaur National Monument in the 1950s. Thus, there were several
groups that placed themselves in a position to lead the cause of preservationism into the next decade. One question I attempt to shed light upon is why the
Sierra Club emerged from the 1960s as the leading environmental advocacy
organization instead of one of these other groups?

The answer, I believe, lies in the fact that of all the influential conservation
organizations, the Sierra Club's leadership made a conscious decision to challenge IRS prohibitions on lobbying in the wake of a landmark 1954 Supreme
Court ruling in *United States v Harriss*, which upheld the constitutionality of
the Federal Regulation of Lobbying Act of 1946. This holding had a chilling
effect upon the lobbying efforts of other conservation organizations because
their leaders feared the loss of their groups' tax-deductible status, a development that had the potential of greatly reducing contributions from private citizens. Alone of all of these conservation groups, the Sierra Club chose to
defend its rights of free speech and petition enumerated within the First
Amendment. Thus, its advocacy against the Grand Canyon dams, in particular the letter-writing campaign it encouraged and the national advertising it
sponsored, had a two-fold effect. First, it placed the Sierra Club at risk of
incurring sanctions imposed by the Internal Revenue Service, an eventuality
that was actually realized in June of 1966. Second, because it was the only
group willing to challenge governmental erosion of fundamental constitutional principles, the Sierra Club stood apart from all other organizations in terms

of the lengths it was willing to go to defend the environment.[4]

Consequently, in 1963, when the Grand Canyon dam controversy began, other organizations looked to the club for guidance, and it solidified this position of leadership as the controversy unfolded by making appeals to the American public through the mass media. When the IRS revoked the Sierra Club's tax-deductible status in June of 1966 after David Brower placed ads condemning the proposed damming of Grand Canyon in national newspapers; it precipitated a wave of public sympathy for the club from people concerned with civil liberties issues and created a broad constituency from which the club's leadership drew strength to push its environmental agenda in subsequent environmental debates. By taking a stand on constitutional grounds, the Sierra Club placed itself in the position of possibly losing a battle—the revocation of its tax-deductible status—but the winning of a much larger war in the form of sympathy from an American public already whipped into a fervor over civil liberties issues in the wake of the Civil Rights and antiwar movements. The Sierra Club emerged from the fight to save Grand Canyon, bloody, martyred, but unbowed, with an enormous public constituency behind it.

Historians Roderick Nash and Marc Reisner contend that the environmental movement "came of age" during the controversy because environmentalists were able to apply enough pressure to convince Congress to delete the dams from the legislation.[5] Although my argument opposes this mainstream interpretation, because I believe the evidence demonstrates just the opposite, it is not my intent to minimize the impact that the controversy had upon the growing strength of the environmental movement, and particularly upon the emergence of the Sierra Club as the leading environmental organization. As the following pages will show, the evidence suggests that although the Sierra Club did not wield the ability to effect actual changes in policy in the case of Grand Canyon, its ability to mobilize public opinion during this campaign catapulted the organization into the undisputed leadership of the environmental movement at almost the exact instant that Congress granted environmentalists unprecedented access to the policymaking process through the passage of the National Environmental Policy Act (NEPA) in 1969.[6] Hence, in a very real sense, the Grand Canyon dam controversy represents the point at which the Sierra Club "came of age" as an activist organization because of the position of preeminence it had gained within the environmental movement.

A brief clarification of some terms used in the text is appropriate here. With the emergence of modern environmentalism after World War II, the meaning and usage of certain terms has shifted over time. In this discussion, "conservation," "preservation," and "environmentalism" are used interchangeably because of changes in meaning that have occurred over the last fifty years. For example, historians writing of "conservation" organizations in the 1950s would use the term "environmental" organizations to describe these same groups currently.

Likewise, advocates of Pinchotian resource management also referred to themselves as "conservationists," and modern environmentalists often use "conservationists" as a pejorative term to describe proponents of wise-use today. Because the term "conservation(ist)" has held dual meanings for much of the twentieth century, I have used appropriate modifiers throughout this narrative to clarify its meaning for the modern reader. Likewise, the meanings American society has associated with the term "wilderness" have also evolved since the British colonized the Virginia tidewater region in 1607, and I have used this word to refer to places twentieth-century environmentalists thought it important to protect for scenic and psychological reasons, rather than to refer to an idealized pristine landscape untouched by human development.

I also make references to the "public" throughout this narrative, and in doing so, I refer to the large numbers of people who expressed their opposition to the Grand Canyon dams through letters or other means of protest rather than to the American public at large. However, I would caution the reader to be aware that the positions taken by these letter writers is not necessarily a representative sample of public opinion as a whole. One thing that is striking about the environmentalists' anti-dam campaign is the large number of letters written by persons holding advanced degrees. How and why this was the case is beyond the scope of the current analysis; however, one must be cognizant both of the prominent role played by educated elites during the campaign as well as of how small a segment of the American people actually felt motivated enough to express their concern.

A note on organization is also appropriate. This book is organized chronologically for several reasons. First, much of this analysis focuses upon the evolution of ideas, political and social transformations, and legal authority, all of which have changed over time. One cannot isolate the Grand Canyon dam controversy from the changing political and social context of the post–World

War II period. Consequently, a chronological approach is necessitated because I have used policy formation as a prism through which to view the controversy. Congresses meet for two years at a time, and events that affect one Congress may have little or no effect upon another. Consequently, one encounters factors that may affect the Grand Canyon debate during one Congress that have little bearing upon it in the next. One prominent example is Stewart Udall's increasing concern over his own and Carl Hayden's retirements in 1969. Though not a paramount concern during the first session of the 89th Congress in 1965, by the 90th Congress of 1967–1968, with a Republican presidency becoming ever more likely and the elderly Senator Hayden in failing health, Udall was forced to find a solution to the dilemma while Arizona still possessed enough political strength to obtain passage of the proposal. Thus, the Grand Canyon dam controversy took place against, and was affected by, a larger backdrop of shifting, unpredictable political currents that waxed and waned over time.

I have organized the chapters as follows. In chapter 1, I discuss the important events of the twentieth century leading up to the Grand Canyon dam controversy of the 1960s including the Hetch Hetchy dispute and its precedent, the creation of Grand Canyon National Park, the Arizona/California water fight, the importance of the Dinosaur controversy, the emergence of a vocal environmentalist movement, and the key political and environmentalist leaders who played important roles during the 1960s. The year 1963, the focus of chapter 2, is critical for it is during this year that Stewart Udall introduced the Pacific Southwest Water Plan, and gained the tentative blessing of both California and Wayne Aspinall. Carl Hayden's renewed efforts to gain a barebones project in the wake of Arizona's victory in the Supreme Court in 1963, and the initiation of the environmentalists' opposition campaign are also discussed. Chapter 3 covers the rift between Hayden and Udall, the problems of presidential politics during the 1964 election year, Udall's pragmatic decision to pursue a high Bridge Canyon Dam, the Columbia River diversion—and its ramifications—and the preservationists' attempts to publicize the growing threat to Grand Canyon.

In chapter 4, I discuss the context in which the controversy was unfolding, particularly the social concerns of the 1960s over threats to civil liberties, free speech, and civil rights, as well as the 1965 House hearings in the Irrigation and Reclamation Subcommittee, and the preservationists' realization that their legal and technical arguments were not powerful enough to change reclamation policy. As a result, David Brower of the Sierra Club, and Richard Bradley of the Colorado Open Space Coordinating Council mounted a campaign to attain access to the national media, and in chapter 5, I discuss their efforts and eventual success, the steps the pro-dam interests took to counter them, and the unfolding drama in the House Interior Committee hearings of May 1966. In chapter 6, I analyze the results of the Sierra Club's national media campaign, including the public reaction to the IRS revocation and the complex political intrigue that caused the regional plan to unravel in the House Rules Committee when on the brink of success. Interior Secretary Udall's practical decision to pursue a bill without dams in Grand Canyon, a strategy that led to the passage of CAP legislation in 1968, is also treated in this chapter, as are the hardball political maneuvers Carl Hayden used to gain the backing of a reluctant Wayne Aspinall in the House. In chapter 7, I analyze how academic and popular historians have presented the controversy in the literature, and how these interpretations have shaped public perceptions. The formulation of the Sierra Club's reputation as the savior of Grand Canyon is also discussed, along with how this reputation enabled the club to gain a national constituency and thus become the spearhead of the modern environmental movement.

The Grand Canyon dam controversy, one of the most important environmental debates in American history, constitutes an important case study for modern policymakers seeking historical precedents for environmental policy decisions as well as for historians who desire to analyze how the congressional system works from a practical rather than a theoretical perspective. Although I argue that the Sierra Club had relatively little influence within the political process during the debate over Grand Canyon, nevertheless, the tactics it used to mobilize public opinion, and the success it had in doing so proved important as environmentalists gained entree to the levers of real political power after the passage of NEPA in 1969. After the enactment of NEPA, Congress could no longer afford to ignore public reaction as it had during the Grand Canyon dam controversy because environmental advocates and the organizations they supported now possessed access to the political process.

The Sierra Club, having attained the reputation as the leading activist organization by virtue of its having "saved" Grand Canyon in 1968, commanded an enormous constituency that it was able to mobilize to fight future environmental battles. Although one can argue that the mere preservation of natural phenomena had become anachronistic by the close of the 1960s, and hence, that the Grand Canyon dam debate constituted the last major campaign of John Muir–style preservationism, it also represents an important transition as preservationist organizations such as the Sierra Club, having gained a large national audience during the Grand Canyon debate, began to espouse a more ecologically based environmentalism to this new constituency. Perhaps this is the most important legacy of the Grand Canyon dam controversy, for in leading the last great fight in favor of old-style preservationism, the Sierra Club gained a reputation for environmental activism and the public and congressional recognition that enabled it to transcend the John Muir tradition and espouse a less anthropocentric environmental message to a nation that was now willing to listen.

① Still the Wild River Runs

1

"A Profitless Locality"

[I]n the interest of the country...keep this great
wonder of nature as it is now...Leave it as it is.
You cannot improve on it. The ages have been at work
on it, and man can only mar it.

—Theodore Roosevelt, *New York Sun*, May 1903

Looking westward along the Potomac River in the late eighteenth century, Thomas Jefferson described where the river passed through the Blue
Ridge Mountains as "one of the most stupendous scenes in nature," a
sight so spectacular that it would be worth a "voyage across the Atlantic just to
gaze upon it."[1] One of the first American writers to break free of utilitarian
views of the natural world, Jefferson also lamented that few of his fellow citizens held an aesthetic appreciation of wild nature. As president, Jefferson
helped launch America's fixation with the trans–Mississippi West by acquir-
ing the Louisiana Purchase and sponsoring the Lewis and Clark Expedition
to explore it. By 1848, the United States, building on Jefferson's precedent, had
acquired most of its present territory by virtue of its victory in the Mexican
War. Included within this vast region were scenic wonders that would inspire
ever increasing migrations of people who would cross continents and oceans
to view them. Among these wonders of the American West were Yosemite
Valley, the Yellowstone region of Wyoming, Mount Rainier of Washington
and the Grand Canyon of the Colorado River where it flows through northern Arizona.

Drawn by the promise of gold and other economic opportunities, tens of thousands of individuals moved into the new territories of the Southwest which, for the first half of the nineteenth century remained a blank spot marked "unexplored" on most maps of the period. Rumors of enormous mineral wealth and spectacular works of nature soon piqued the interest of eastern politicians. In 1857, the United States War Department commissioned Lieutenant Joseph Christmas Ives to lead an expedition up the lower reaches of the Colorado River. The purpose of the mission was to ascertain the navigability of the river, upstream from the Gulf of California. Ives launched his stern-wheeled paddle boat, *Explorer*, in December and managed to pilot his craft nearly four hundred miles upriver to the mouth of Black Canyon, where the boat collided with a submerged rock and incurred severe damage. Ives and half of his men set out on foot eventually reaching Grand Canyon, while the remainder effected repairs. Though the grandeur of the Canyon impressed Ives, he evaluated it in utilitarian terms stating:

> The region last explored is, of course, altogether valueless. It can be approached only from the south, and after entering it there is nothing to do but to leave. Ours has been the first, and will doubtless be the last, party of whites to visit this profitless locality. It seems intended by nature that the Colorado River, along the greater portion of its lonely and majestic way, shall be forever unvisited and undisturbed.[2]

But Ives' prediction soon proved incorrect. Although the Colorado River bisects one of the most arid regions in the American West, the soil is fertile. Consequently, by the turn of the twentieth century, agricultural interests from California and Arizona had placed a high priority upon harnessing this untamed, yet potentially beneficial, natural resource. The failure of private irrigation ventures in the region made it painfully clear that construction of projects of the scale necessary to stabilize the Colorado's erratic flow was beyond the capability of individuals, corporations and even states. Faced with explosive population growth and with thousands of square miles of potentially rich agricultural land lying fallow, politicians from the western states began lobbying for federal assistance. Congress passed the Newlands Reclamation Act of 1902 creating the Federal Reclamation Service, and charged the new bureau with the task of opening vast areas of the West to agriculture through the construction of massive water projects.[3] Although the Reclamation Service initiated water development throughout much of the region, initially it all but ignored the lower Colorado River.

The early twentieth century also witnessed the initiation of a legal struggle over how to prioritize between the preservation of natural scenery and economic values. As early as 1900 pro–water development interests in the city of San Francisco had begun advocating for the construction of a dam in the Hetch Hetchy Valley located in a remote corner of Yosemite National Park. John Muir and the Sierra Club advocated its preservation, while Gifford Pinchot, founder of the U.S. Forest Service contended that the valley should be used as a reservoir site. Pinchot, the father of scientific resource management in the United States, espoused a policy of resource conservation that stressed efficiency over aesthetics, and stated that resource management should exist "for the greatest good to the greatest number for the longest time." Pinchot and Muir, good friends at one point, parted over the issue of preservation versus conservation. After 1905, this break became more and more acute as preservationists and conservationists fought this, the first important environmental battle of the twentieth century.[4]

Eventually, the preservationists' lack of vigilance during the early years of the controversy proved fatal and the water project passed both houses of Congress with substantial majorities in fall 1913. Politically outgunned and outnumbered, the Sierra Club lost this battle and on December 19, 1913, President Woodrow Wilson signed the Raker Act, granting San Francisco all water rights in the valley. Embittered and heartbroken by the loss, John Muir died the following year.[5]

The Hetch Hetchy debate gave rise to two oppositional political impulses that had immediate effects upon Grand Canyon. By passing the Raker Act, Congress established a precedent that economic concerns would supersede preservationist values even within national parks ostensibly created to protect areas of natural splendor from exploitation. But the lost cause of Hetch Hetchy also motivated the Sierra Club and influential preservationists such as Frederick Law Olmsted Jr., Stephen T. Mather, and Horace Albright to press Congress for increased federal protection of national parks. This campaign bore fruit in 1916 when Congress established the National Park Service.[6]

Theodore Roosevelt, a disciple of Pinchotian conservation, was so awed by Grand Canyon's stark, yet beautiful topography, that he admonished potential developers to "leave it as it is" upon seeing it for the first time in 1903. In 1908, Roosevelt, in a liberal construction of the 1906 Antiquities Act, set aside approximately 100 miles of the Canyon as a national monument.[7] Yet the Canyon, and the river that flowed through it, also held the potential of vast wealth, and boosters and promoters ignored Roosevelt's admonition. The Colorado River falls 1,930 feet as it flows through the 277-mile length of Grand Canyon, making it one of the most ideal locations for the generation of hydro-electric power in the continental United States. Consequently, federal agencies and the states of the Colorado Basin began to envision the future development of the lower Colorado River for reclamation and irrigation, and sponsored a bas-inwide dam-site study in 1916 conducted by E. C. La Rue, the chief hydrologist of the United States Geological Survey (USGS). La Rue identified several dam sites within Marble and Grand Canyons (geologists considered the former as a part of the latter), but he was unable to conduct a comprehensive analysis. Despite incomplete data, he suggested that the power potential of the river could be utilized by constructing thirteen dams in the Canyon, writing that, "foundations suitable for high masonry dams can probably be found."[8]

Arizona politicians also eyed the Colorado River in Grand Canyon and sought to utilize it. Arizona Representative Carl Hayden introduced a bill in 1918 that, when signed on 26 February 1919, converted the national monument Roosevelt created into Grand Canyon National Park. Although the park boundaries included approximately 100 miles of river, they did not encompass the entire Grand Canyon system, which was defined by geologists as extending from Lee's Ferry, through Marble and Grand Canyons to the Grand Wash Cliffs, a distance of 277 miles (map 1). Thus, park protection did not extend to all of Grand Canyon. Since the National Park Act of 1916 prohibited water development in parks and monuments, Hayden, reflecting the desires of his water-hungry constituents, inserted a special provision within the Establishment Act, granting the secretary of the interior the power to authorize reclamation projects within the park at his/her discretion.[9]

The pertinent language in the Grand Canyon National Park Establishment Act reads: "That whenever consistent with the primary purpose of said park, the Secretary of the Interior is authorized to permit the utilization of areas therein which may be necessary for the development and maintenance of a Government [sic] reclamation project." Though scarcely debated, this reclamation provision constituted a pivot point for the disputes that followed, for

Figure 1. A winter photo of the Marble Canyon Dam site looking downstream. *Courtesy of the National Archives, Denver Federal Records Center.*

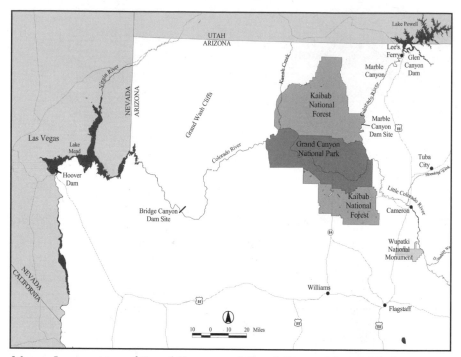

Map 1. Juxtaposition of Grand Canyon, and Grand Canyon National Park in 1919, including the Bridge and Marble Canyon dam sites. *(Map created by Gary Christopherson and Peter Johnson, Center for Applied Spatial Analysis, University of Arizona.)*

it established congressional endorsement of water projects within the park itself, and the Park Service was powerless to do anything about it. Carl Hayden, anticipating the water needs of his native state, astutely provided the legal foundation necessary for the future utilization of both the power and water resources within Grand Canyon.

Arizona, however, was not the only state that sought to lay claim to the Colorado River. The other six states of the Colorado River Basin also desired to put the water to use. California, the most politically powerful state in the Southwest, initiated efforts to gain approval of a large dam designed to eliminate the flood peaks that made farming in the lower Colorado River Basin difficult. But the other six states refused to support California's efforts until all legal water rights in the basin had been determined. In 1922, representatives of the seven basin states met in Santa Fe, New Mexico, under the leadership of Herbert Hoover, the secretary of commerce, and after much haggling, signed the Colorado River Compact, laying the legal foundation for all future reclamation projects proposed within the basin.[10] However, Arizona's legislature refused to ratify the Compact, setting the stage for more than a half century of legal battles, fought primarily between Arizona and California.

The Compact arbitrarily divided the river into upper and lower basins at Lee's Ferry, Arizona, just south of the Utah border. On the basis of an annual estimated flow of 17.5 million acre feet, it allocated 7.5 million to the upper-basin states of Wyoming, Colorado, Utah, and New Mexico and 7.5 million to the three lower-basin states of Arizona, Nevada, and California. Mexico was allotted 1.5 million acre feet and the surplus of one million was given, albeit reluctantly, to the lower basin in years of excess flow. The Compact did not include agreements between the individual states of each basin; they were left to argue among themselves.[11]

Arizona and California immediately began to formulate plans for the development of the lower reach of the river. In 1923, E. C. La Rue embarked upon the first comprehensive dam-site survey of the Canyon, an expedition commissioned by California Edison. Unlike La Rue's previous survey, this expedition navigated the tempestuous river from Lee's Ferry through the entire length of Grand Canyon. Colonel Claude Birdseye led the death-defying adventure, and the voyage received extensive coverage in both eastern and western newspapers. La Rue employed Emery Kolb, the famous Grand Canyon photographer and river runner, as a guide, and apparently Kolb and Birdseye almost came to blows on several occasions.

Despite the threat of hostilities, La Rue obtained geological data confirming his earlier conclusion that rock formations of suitable strength and hardness for the construction of high dams existed in the Canyon. He investigated sites, including two that would become the focus of preservationists and water interests alike for the next several decades: Marble and Bridge Canyons. Bridge Canyon was located about seventy-eight miles below the western boundary of the park while Marble Canyon, initially referred to as the Red-Wall site, lay twelve miles upstream of it (map 1; fig. 1).[12]

Armed with this comprehensive dam-site study, California water officials negotiated with the other basin states, hoping to gain approval of a large main stem dam. After agreeing to limit its annual consumption to 4.4 million acre feet per year, California gained congressional support in 1928 over Arizona's objections.[13]

The construction of Boulder Dam commenced in 1930, initiating a thirty-year period of unprecedented water project development in the American West. While Arizona's water leaders chafed, the rest of the nation, mired in the depths of the Great Depression, watched the unfolding drama with a mixture of awe and pride as the shimmering white concrete plug rose from the bowels of Black Canyon. Scarcely four and one-half years after the initiation of construction, President Franklin Delano Roosevelt dedicated the gigantic edifice, proclaiming: "This morning I came, I saw, and I was conquered as everyone will be who sees for the first time this great feat of mankind." Boulder Dam, perhaps the most important structure ever built in the United States, had tamed the untamable Colorado at a cost of $48,890,955 and the lives of 110 men.[14]

The significance of Boulder Dam cannot be overstated. It was by far the largest dam built up to that time, and its engineers pioneered construction processes that were used later on other huge projects. It constituted the first major effort by the Bureau of Reclamation (the Reclamation Service had been renamed in 1928) and provided power to drive the great defense industry of Southern California that played such an important role in the Allies' victory in World War II. Finally, by stabilizing the river's unpredictable flow, it ensured a dependable water supply for agricultural interests and safeguarded downstream irrigation works, ensuring the viability of farming along the lower reach of the river.

The federal government soon considered additional plans for the development of the lower Colorado River. By 1930, the Bureau of Reclamation considered Bridge Canyon one of the most desirable power sites on the Colorado River, now that Boulder Dam was well on its way to completion, and it proposed to construct a 570-foot dam that would back water to the western boundary of the park. When President Herbert Hoover proclaimed a new Grand Canyon National Monument downstream of the national park on 22 December 1932, it caused immediate concern within the Bureau because any dam constructed to maximize the power potential of the Bridge Canyon site would now back water through the new monument (map 2). Though it appeared that legally, the monument did not pose an obstacle to the construction of a dam at Bridge Canyon, the Bureau wished to avoid a conflict with the Park Service.[15]

In anticipation of Hoover's action, Dr. Elwood Mead, the commissioner of

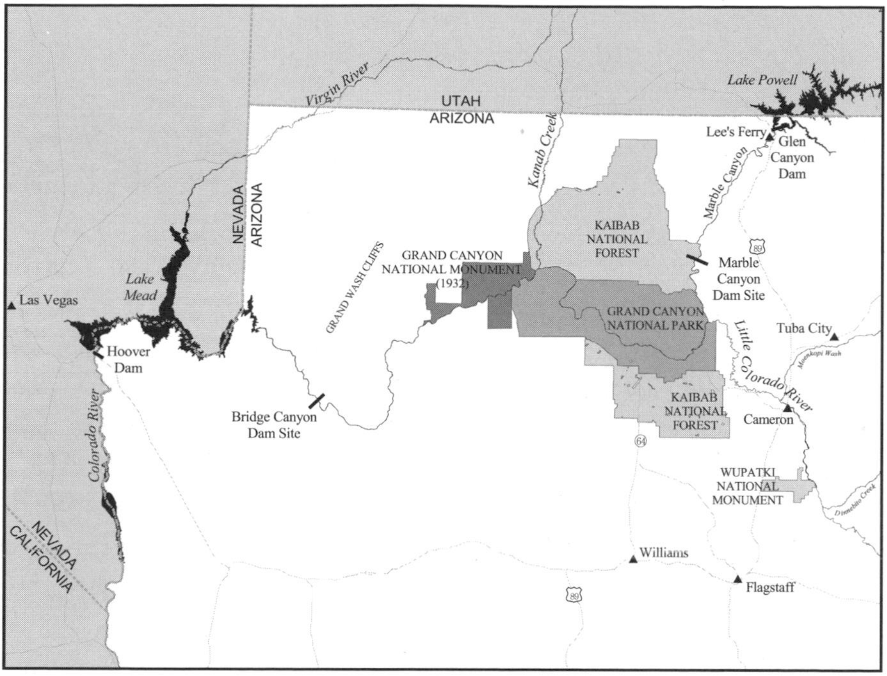

Map 2. Grand Canyon National Park and Grand Canyon National Monument as created in 1932. *(Map created by Gary Christopherson and Peter Johnson, Center for Applied Spatial Analysis, University of Arizona.)*

the Bureau of Reclamation, wrote Park Service Director Horace Albright during the summer of 1932 and asked him whether the Park Service would object to a dam at Bridge Canyon that would back water through the proposed monument. Albright, in turn, polled his subordinates, and Roger Toll, superintendent of Yellowstone Park who had previously undertaken a comprehensive study of the lower reaches of Grand Canyon, responded, arguing that the "only objection would be one of precedent" and stated further that a lake would make the lower reaches of the Canyon more accessible to tourists. Albright wrote Mead on 11 January 1933 after Hoover's proclamation, outlining the Park Service position:

> As I see it, the Bridge Canyon Project is in no way affected by the Grand Canyon National Monument proclamation and the area insofar as power development is concerned is under the jurisdiction of the Federal Power Commission, so far as the granting of a power license is concerned. The power withdrawals are intact. *We have had in mind all the time the Bridge*

Canyon Project. . . . As a matter of fact . . . there can be no necessity for the Reclamation Service seeking the approval of the Park Service on this project.[16] (Emphasis mine)

This exchange reveals much about intra-agency relations within the Department of the Interior at the time when the Bureau of Reclamation first began to consider the construction of dams in Grand Canyon. A feeling of cordiality existed between Mead and Albright, unlike interactions that occurred after 1940, when different individuals occupied these offices. It also reveals the pervasiveness of the Hetch Hetchy precedent well into the 1930s. The reason why Toll and Albright did not object to the idea of a lake backing water into Grand Canyon National Monument is because most Park Service officials had resigned themselves to the fact that when push came to shove, water development within parks and monuments would be approved by the Interior Department and Congress. In the case of Grand Canyon, congressional intent was crystal clear, for the establishment act had specifically reserved the right of the government to build dams in the park itself.

The Great Depression and World War II halted temporarily these plans to build Bridge Canyon Dam. But the conclusion of the war ended the constraints upon western water development. After the war, the population of the United States began a second westward migration as millions of people moved to the Southwest, placing an unprecedented strain upon existing municipal infrastructures. Faced with burgeoning populations, Arizona and California once again looked to the Colorado River to provide water and power to sustain this new oasis civilization. The Bureau of Reclamation, freed from wartime constraints, now embarked upon another extraordinary period of dam building.[17]

The Bureau published a report in March 1946 entitled, *The Colorado River, a National Menace Becomes a Natural Resource,* outlining its comprehensive plan for the development of the lower Colorado River Basin. The analysis included a high Bridge Canyon Dam which would back water through the monument and into Grand Canyon National Park, as well as a scheme called the Marble Canyon–Kanab Creek Project (MCKC). This plan contemplated the construction of a dam in Marble Canyon that could stand alone as a separate project, twelve miles upstream of the park. The primary feature of this proposal was a forty-five-mile-long tunnel from Marble Canyon Reservoir underneath the north rim of the canyon to Kanab Creek that would, in effect, straighten the course of the river by diverting most of its flow around the national park,

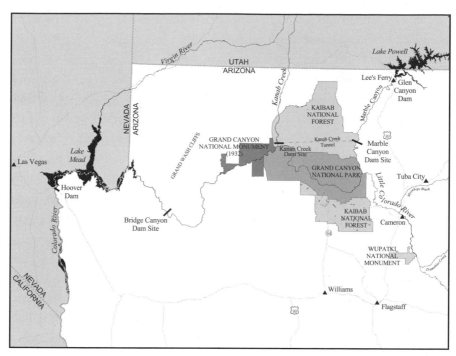

Map 3. Grand Canyon National Park, and the proposed Marble Canyon/Kanab Creek Project. *(Map created by Gary Christopherson and Peter Johnson, Center for Applied Spatial Analysis, University of Arizona.)*

while leaving a trickle of water in the river for "scenic purposes" (map 3).[18]

Park Service officials were horrified when they learned of this proposal and yet, unlikely as it may seem, the Bureau conceived of this project in an attempt to avoid conflict with the Park Service and other groups interested in the preservation of Grand Canyon. The MCKC plan was designed to utilize every cubic foot of water and the entire 950-foot drop of the river within the park without building dams there. The Bureau estimated the MCKC project's power output at over 6.6 billion kilowatts per year.[19]

These proposals raised the ire of Newton Drury, who had become director of the National Park Service in 1940. Drury, a staunch preservationist and astute legal tactician, had determined that the integrity of the national park system must be protected from further encroachments if the natural wonders contained within the parks were to be protected for future generations. Consequently, Drury began to focus upon reversing the precedent of park exploitation begun during the Hetch Hetchy debate, and in 1942 the director drew the line at which he would defend the integrity of the park system at the western boundary of Grand Canyon National Park.[20]

By 1946, Drury confronted threats to the Colorado River and its tributaries involving two national monuments as well as Grand Canyon National Park. Although geologists included Marble Canyon as a part of the Grand Canyon system, this spectacular gorge remained unprotected, and so Drury believed he could not successfully oppose a dam there. He also believed he stood little chance of defeating a low Bridge Canyon Dam that would only back water into the monument, the project to which his agency had previously acquiesced. However, none of his predecessors agreed to an invasion of the park itself. This is why Drury drew his last line of defense at the western boundary of Grand Canyon National Park and remained against a high Bridge Canyon Dam despite the friction he knew this position would create within the Interior Department. Drury also opposed the Marble Canyon–Kanab Creek project because he feared that the Kanab Creek power plant and its transmission lines would be visible from the south rim, and that the reduction in flow below Marble Canyon Dam would result in a great loss of scenic values. At a time when the Bureau's momentum was accelerating and politicians such as Arizona Representative John Murdock were speculating that Bridge Canyon Dam should be raised to 1000 feet above the river, Drury was forced to fight battles where he believed that he had a reasonable chance to prevail.[21]

Drury's dilemma was compounded by the fact that he did not have much support from conservation organizations outside the Interior Department, none of which had gone on record as opposing either the high Bridge Canyon Dam or the MCKC project. Many of these groups, such as the Sierra Club and the Wilderness Society, had been formed to pursue single issues or to protect local areas of natural beauty. Having lost the Hetch Hetchy battle at the turn of the century, these conservation organizations rarely entered the public arena until after the Second World War. It was only after 1945 that many of these groups would become advocates for nature preservation on a national scale. As postwar development pressures began to center upon the canyon country of the American West, groups such as the Sierra Club struggled to reinvent themselves, a process that was not yet complete by the late 1940s.

Consequently, it would not be until May of 1949 that Drury would gain his first steadfast ally in the struggle against the high Bridge Canyon Dam, when the National Parks Association (NPA) began publishing a series of articles written by field secretary Fred Packard opposing the Bridge Canyon and MCKC projects in its bi-monthly *National Parks* magazine. Historically, the Association had been one of the Park Service's most vocal critics since its founder, Robert Sterling Yard, and the first Park Service Director, Steven Mather, had split over the Service's promotion of a carnival-like atmosphere at Yosemite and other national parks. Now the NPA became the first conservation organization to try to influence public opinion to support Drury in his fight to return the Service to its founding principles by opposing reclamation projects in Grand Canyon in a national publication.[22]

Drury continued to try to sway the leaders of important conservation groups to join him in his fight against the high Bridge Canyon Dam. In July, the Wilderness Society's Executive Council held its annual meeting at Olympic National Park and passed a resolution asking the Interior Secretary to reexamine the entire project and initiate new intradepartmental studies. In the fall, both Ira Gabrielson of the Wildlife Management Institute and Harlean James of the American Planning and Civic Association had sided with Drury's attempt to limit the height of Bridge Canyon Dam.[23] By late autumn of 1949, it was becoming apparent that the leaders of some influential conservation organizations were at last aroused that the Interior Department had approved a dam and reservoir that would intrude upon Grand Canyon National Park. Hoping to gain another important base of support, Drury awaited the November meeting of the Sierra Club Board of Directors, at which the club's leadership planned to take a definitive position on the height of Bridge Canyon Dam.

On 12 November 1949, the Sierra Club directors met. Richard Leonard read a letter from new Interior Secretary Julius Krug in which the secretary stated he had canceled the MCKC project and pledged to limit the elevation of Bridge Canyon Dam to 1877 feet above sea level, a height that would create a small reservoir encroachment into the park and which Drury had been forced to officially endorse. After some discussion, Sierra Club President Bestor Robinson took the floor and offered the following proposals:

1. Bridge Canyon Dam should not be authorized unless the Bureau constructed silt retention structures on the Little Colorado and upstream on the main stem of the Colorado River first.
2. The reclamation provision within the Grand Canyon National Park establishment act should be repealed prior to the authorization of Bridge Canyon Dam.

3. The boundaries of the park should be adjusted to exclude the reservoir, and that the national monument should be abolished.

4. Bridge Canyon Dam should be constructed so as not to impound water *above Tapeats Creek, two thousand feet above sea level.*

5. The water level in the reservoir should be maintained at a stable level to avoid scarring of the canyon walls between the high and low water marks. (Emphasis mine)

After discussing these recommendations, the board of directors, including Richard Leonard and David Brower, voted unanimously to adopt them as the official position of the Sierra Club.[24]

Improbable as it may seem, the Sierra Club leadership unanimously approved proposals that would: eliminate Grand Canyon National Monument; flood part of Wupatki National Monument on the Little Colorado River; shift the boundaries of Grand Canyon National Park to accommodate a reservoir project; and allow Bridge Canyon Dam to be constructed to an elevation of almost 2000 feet, 70 feet higher than any previous Bureau proposal, and over 120 feet higher than the dam it was most likely to build.

Newton Drury reacted with shock and dismay. He wrote Richard Leonard and communicated his disappointment in no uncertain terms:

> That the Sierra Club, founded by John Muir for the protection of the national parks, should adopt a resolution approving of a reservoir which would back water more than 30 miles into Grand Canyon National Park is somewhat of a shock. *Administrators sometimes have to reconcile themselves to something less that the ideal, but conservation organizations are under no such necessity.* This action of the club greatly weakens our defense of the park and is confusing to many other conservation organizations. (Emphasis mine)

Regarding the suggested boundary shift, Drury continued:

> I feel sure you will agree that it would be establishing a very dangerous precedent to embark upon a program of shifting national park boundaries to accommodate reservoir projects. If that were undertaken, it would be only a matter of a few years before there wouldn't be any national parks worthy of the name.[25]

Though perhaps unimaginable to a modern reader, the Sierra Club's position in the winter of 1949 is indicative of the deep philosophical divisions the leadership of many conservation organizations faced at this time. Strong future preservation advocates such as Richard Leonard and David Brower had approved of the Bureau's plan to create a reservoir in Grand Canyon National Park and Monument, a position entirely in congruence with the attitudes many Americans held toward their natural environment in the mid twentieth century. Why not build a water highway that would open up the lower reaches of the Canyon to sightseers? Why not improve upon nature? Indeed, the club would find itself in the embarrassing situation of having these same arguments used against them in hearings over Bridge Canyon Dam a decade later by none other than Reclamation Commissioner Floyd Dominy himself. Yet by the early 1960s, these same arguments would be an anathema to environmentalists fighting to preserve Grand Canyon. The 1950s were a time of great ideological change, a period when, at least in the minds of many environmental advocates, encouraging the development of the recreational potential of park lands would give way to viewing parks as the most available means to preserve wilderness. The preservationist impulse would crystallize as a result of important environmental controversies and social and political transformations that occurred during this critical decade.[26] It is from this inauspicious position of having approved of dams in Grand Canyon in 1949 that the Sierra Club would slowly emerge as one of the most vocal and successful advocates in favor of wilderness preservation and defending the integrity of the national park system during the last half of the twentieth century.

In February of 1950, the political forces in favor of the CAP swung into action, and the United States Senate took up the debate. Carl Hayden, who had moved over from the House in 1928, and Arizona Senator Earnest McFarland, who was now the majority leader, overcame California's opposition and on 21 February 1950, the Senate voted 55–28 in favor of the Central Arizona Project with a high Bridge Canyon Dam.[27] Though relieved, Hayden knew that the real battleground was in the House of Representatives, where California's large bloc of representatives wielded substantial influence. Hayden's fears were soon realized as the House began debating the bill in August. Despite the efforts of Arizona's delegation, the House Interior Committee addressed the CAP question in closed sessions and adjourned without taking action in early September because of the upcoming congressional elections, sealing the fate of the CAP in the Eighty-first Congress.[28]

Meanwhile, as the CAP debate got underway, the Bureau proposed to build still more dams that would encroach upon national parks and monuments. As the post–World War II economic and population boom continued in the American West, representatives from states in the upper Colorado River Basin began to agitate for federal development of the water resources in their region. By 1949, the Bureau had conducted watershed studies and was close to obtaining Interior Department approval of a scheme it called the Colorado River Storage Project (CRSP). Breathtaking in scope, this proposal called for the construction of ten major dams on the Colorado and its tributaries within the upper basin. The Bureau argued that revenues from hydropower would pay for this massive endeavor, whose total storage capacity of 48.5 million acre feet was greater than that of all the existing reservoirs on the main stem of the Colorado and its tributaries. The most important features of the plan included dams in Flaming Gorge in Wyoming, Echo Park in Colorado, and Glen Canyon in northern Arizona.[29] The dam at Echo Park, at the confluence of the Green and Yampa Rivers, as well as another, Split Mountain Dam, located downstream in Utah, were both slated for construction within Dinosaur National Monument.

Faced with this new peril to the integrity of the national park system, conservationists began to focus upon the impending threat to Dinosaur National Monument. Newton Drury was so adamant in his opposition to the Dinosaur dams that he pressured new Interior Secretary Oscar Chapman into scheduling public hearings so that all views could be articulated. On 3 April 1950, representatives of conservation organizations, the Bureau of Reclamation, and members of Congress all testified at the Interior Department hearings, an important event simply because it is indicative that opposition to proposed violations of the national park system had now risen to such a level that the interior secretary believed it necessary to debate the issue in a public forum.[30] But despite the vocal opposition of conservationists, Interior Secretary Chapman gave his assent to the construction of the two dams planned for Dinosaur National Monument.

The secretary's approval of the Dinosaur dams reinforced a growing suspicion among conservationists that the Bureau of Reclamation would always have the last word when it came to water development policy. In September of 1950, the Sierra Club Board discussed Dinosaur and Bridge Canyon Dam at its fall board meeting and resolved to oppose vigorously a dam in Dinosaur National Monument and to unite with other conservation societies in doing so. Then, revisiting the threat to Grand Canyon, the Sierra Club's leaders voted to repudiate unanimously their 1949 approval of the high Bridge Canyon Dam, and instead took the official position of being against any intrusion into Grand Canyon National Monument.[31] Now all of the major conservation organizations stood against a high Bridge Canyon Dam and had extended Drury's last line of defense to include national monuments as well.

During the fall of 1950 the mounting tension between Newton Drury and Interior Secretary Chapman reached its peak. Infuriated by a scathing article by Bernard DeVoto of *Harper's Magazine* entitled, "Shall We Let Them Ruin Our National Parks," published in the 22 July edition of the *Saturday Evening Post*, Reclamation Commissioner Michael Straus claimed that Drury, a close friend of the cantankerous *Harper's* columnist, had coauthored the piece, a charge Drury denied. Chapman, having approved of the dam at Echo Park, and weary of the constant sniping between his Park Service director and commissioner of Reclamation, asked Drury to relinquish his directorship for an advisory position without authority and at a decrease in salary. Drury refused and tendered his resignation, effective April 1, 1951.[32]

Although Dinosaur may have been the final straw, Drury had been a thorn in the Bureau's side for the better part of a decade while opposing a high Bridge Canyon Dam. When reflecting upon these events, David Brower contended that Drury's opposition to the high dam also contributed to his ouster, an explanation that, though it defies absolute proof, is certainly in line with the series of events just described.[33] Whatever the reasons, preservationists would miss Drury, an articulate, tenacious proponent of the national park ideal, and his removal served to heighten the resolve of preservationists to continue the struggle he had begun.

Meanwhile Arizona's congressional representatives introduced new CAP bills in both houses of Congress in January 1951. The proposals were essentially the same as those debated during the previous year, with one notable difference from a Park Service point of view—the bills included a height limitation of 1877 feet. Hayden and McFarland reintroduced the bill in the Senate Interior Committee and on 30 January the committee favorably reported it, recommending that it should be passed. But because the 1950 House Interior Committee debates had been conducted in such an acrimonious tone, the two senators decided to wait and see what would happen in the House before scheduling the bill for floor debate in the Senate.[34]

The House debate began in February 1951 in the Interior and Insular

Affairs Committee and it soon became apparent that great animosity between California and Arizona's representatives still existed. California had also gained strength in the 1950 election and now held three seats on the committee to Arizona's one. Furious exchanges occurred in February and March of 1951, with most of the debate centered upon the question of whether the Supreme Court should adjudicate the water rights of the lower-basin states prior to committee approval of the bill.

Arizona argued that a cause of action did not exist because Congress had yet to pass a bill and that House passage must occur before Supreme Court review. California contended that a justiciable issue did exist because the three lower-basin states had not entered into a contract as stipulated by the Compact of 1922, and that it did not make sense to approve a water project while water rights were still in dispute. After twenty-three sessions during which accusations of water stealing flew across geographical and party lines, Congressman John Saylor, Republican from Pennsylvania, introduced a motion on 18 March endorsing the California position, and called for a moratorium upon CAP legislation until the Supreme Court had determined the water rights of California, Arizona, and Nevada. The committee approved the motion over Arizona's vociferous objections. Now federal construction of Bridge Canyon Dam as a part of the CAP was delayed indefinitely.[35]

Although proponents of hydroprojects in Grand Canyon had been thwarted temporarily, conservationists could not afford to relax because of the imminent threat to Dinosaur National Monument. After Drury's resignation in April 1951, conservationists intensified their protests about the Dinosaur situation to Interior Secretary Chapman who, after considering strong arguments from the Army Corps of Engineers attacking the project's economic feasibility, reversed his earlier endorsement of the Echo Park Dam in December of 1952. After the Eisenhower administration assumed office in January of 1953, senators from the upper-basin states began to lobby Douglas McKay, the new interior secretary, to reinstate the Dinosaur dams into the Colorado Storage Project legislation. In December of 1953, McKay assented, and the conservation organizations began to prepare for the CRSP congressional hearings scheduled for January of 1954.

The year 1954 constitutes a watershed in the history of American environmentalism because it was during this year that conservation organizations formed a coalition to fight the Dinosaur dams and developed strategies

designed to influence legislation. Their assault consisted of two thrusts: a publicity drive designed to stimulate public opposition, which they hoped would
be manifested in letters to Congress; and testimony at congressional hearings
in which the witnesses would attack the dams on aesthetic and technical
grounds. In January, conservation leaders, including Ira Gabrielson, now of the
Emergency Committee on Natural Resources, Fred Packard of the NPA,
David Brower of the Sierra Club, and General Ulysses Grant III of the American Planning and Civic Association and formerly of the Army Corps of Engineers, testified before the Senate Interior Committee. During the hearings,
Grant and Brower attacked the evaporation figures that the Bureau had used
to rebut arguments that dams built at alternate sites could produce the same
amount of power generation and water storage by discovering fundamental
arithmetical errors in the Bureau's calculations. Brower argued that if the
dam already planned for Glen Canyon were raised thirty-five feet, it could
provide essentially the same storage capacity as that provided by Echo Park and
Split Mountain Dams. The Bureau's experts challenged these arguments,
stating that the enlarged Glen Canyon Reservoir would result in much greater
evaporation losses than the Dinosaur projects.

However, Richard Bradley, a Cornell University physics professor whom
Brower had enlisted in the fight, was startled to receive a letter from Assistant Reclamation Commissioner Floyd Dominy in April of 1954 providing figures that substantiated Brower's claims. Brower then issued a press release
that was picked up by national newspapers, and the resulting publicity shat-
tered the myth of the Bureau's expertise in water engineering. By the end of
1954 the battle had not yet been won, but environmentalists had made significant gains.[36] This two-pronged approach of generating public support to
apply pressure from outside, and obtaining expert opinions to challenge the
technical and economic justification of reclamation projects, first developed
during the Echo Park campaign, would provide a strategic foundation for environmentalists fighting to save Grand Canyon in the years ahead.

The Dinosaur controversy entered its climactic phase during 1955 as a
parade of opposition witnesses testified against the dams. In an attempt to gain
even more public support the Sierra Club published *This Is Dinosaur*, the first
of its Exhibit Format books, filled with stunning color photographs of the
monument's canyons and essays by prominent environmental writers. The
book was designed as a propaganda piece against the Dinosaur dams, and it sig-

naled the entry of conservation organizations into the lobbying arena which would soon precipitate consequences for the environmental movement as a whole.

When the CRSP came before the Interior Committees of both Houses in 1955, opponents testified not only against the dams planned for the Echo Park and Split Mountain sites but also addressed the broader question of how the construction of these dams would affect the national park system. Fred Packard of the NPA testified during the Senate committee hearings in March that more than sixteen dam proposals currently hung over the system, and he argued that reclamation interests would use congressional permission to construct dams in Dinosaur as "the entering wedge" to open the rest of the parks and monuments to resource exploitation.[37] Now more twenty conservation organizations stood united against a dam in any national park or monument.

Representative Stewart Udall of Arizona, who had just been elected to Congress during the midterm elections of 1954, closely watched these Senate hearings and paid particular attention to both the content of the conservationists' testimony and the treatment the witnesses received from committee members. Udall managed to garner a seat on the key House Committee on Interior and Insular affairs, and he, like most Arizona politicians, viewed the CAP as essential for the state's economy. He had closely followed the CAP debates of 1950–1951 and was aware that the record contained no evidence of conservationists' opposition. Surprised by Packard's testimony regarding Bridge Canyon Dam, Udall prepared to elicit more information from Packard about the conservationists' position on the CAP when the CRSP came before the House.

Hearings before the House Subcommittee on Irrigation and Reclamation began in March 1955, and conservationists once again voiced their concerns about the precedent that would be set if Congress approved of a reclamation project in Dinosaur National Monument. Under questioning from Udall and Subcommittee Chairman Wayne Aspinall, four prominent conservationists, Fred Packard, General Ulysses S. Grant III, Howard Zahniser of the Wilderness Society, and David Brower of the Sierra Club, all testified that their organizations would oppose Bridge Canyon Dam the next time it came before Congress. A "thunderstruck" Udall pressed Brower further and asked if his organization would be willing to compromise and accept a dam that would not affect the national park. After Brower's affirmative reply, Udall, anticipating future CAP hearings, then stated prophetically: "That is something I know both of us will be interested in and might have a collision of our own on some day."[38]

A few days later, Udall raised the issue of compromise once again, this time with Fred Packard, trying to discern whether the NPA would object to a small invasion of a national monument. Basing his argument on the legal doctrine of *de minimis*, where the law overlooks "trifling" violations, Udall asked Packard whether his organization would object to an invasion of only a "few feet." Packard responded that while the NPA opposed all invasions of the national park system, including national monuments, one also had to use "common sense" in these matters. Satisfied, Udall now believed that conservationists would be willing to compromise in the case of Grand Canyon National Park and Monument.[39]

In 1956, after passage by both Houses of Congress, President Eisenhower signed the Colorado River Storage Project bill into law without the controversial Dinosaur dams. For the first time in American history, environmentalists had forced Congress to delete a water project from a reclamation bill proposal because it would have intruded upon a unit of the national park system. But unfortunately for preservationists, they had predicated their defense of Dinosaur upon the contingency that alternative dam sites existed, and they had argued in favor of those alternatives before going there and looking them over. Split Mountain and Echo Park Dams had been removed from the Colorado River Storage Project in favor of raising Glen Canyon Dam, the largest and most important part of the project in terms of water storage and power production. In 1956, Glen Canyon remained unprotected and few environmentalists had ever visited it. Only after agreeing to withdraw opposition for the CRSP with a high Glen Canyon Dam, did conservationists begin to visit the area in significant numbers, and they soon discovered, to their chagrin, that Glen Canyon was arguably more spectacular than the canyons for which it had been sacrificed.

The high Glen Canyon Dam posed another problem in addition to the inundation of a canyon that some felt worthy of national park status. The reservoir it would create threatened to back water into Rainbow Bridge National Monument just north of the Arizona-Utah border. Newton Drury had voiced concern about this possibility as early as 1949, and environmentalists feared that the water would undermine the sandstone foundation of the arch, the largest freestanding natural bridge in the world. As a result, Congress inserted a provision within the CRSP act calling for the construction of a small dam to protect this monument from encroachment.[40]

Additionally, the increasing activism of the environmentalists began to attract attention from the Internal Revenue Service, which had established code provisions governing the political activities of nonprofit organizations based upon the Federal Regulation of Lobbying Act of 1946. The relevant provisions of the tax code stipulated that so long as an organization's "primary purpose" was not to engage in "substantial" efforts to influence legislation, contributions made to that organization would be tax deductible. Further, the Lobbying Act stated that persons and organizations that engaged in lobbying without registering with Congress would be held criminally liable.[41]

During the Dinosaur controversy organizations such as the Wilderness Society and the Sierra Club found themselves in the public arena, stridently attempting to influence legislation through fund-raising and propaganda. David Brower's tactics included exhorting private citizens to write their congressional representatives directly to communicate their opposition to the Dinosaur dams. In addition to *This Is Dinosaur*, the Sierra Club and other preservation advocates published pamphlets, distributed leaflets, and produced a movie, all designed to sway public and congressional opinion. By entering the public arena for the purpose of influencing legislation, conservation organizations now found themselves coming dangerously close to the provisions of the Internal Revenue Code, although what constituted "substantial" in the case of conservation organizations had not yet been clarified by the courts.[42]

Most conservationists remained unaware that their increased advocacy had the potential to bring about an IRS investigation. However, two constitutional issues were about to collide in the U.S. Supreme Court: the citizens' rights of free speech and petition guaranteed by the First Amendment; and the government's enumerated power to guard against the manipulation of the legislative process by special interest groups. In *U.S. v Harriss*, decided in June of 1954, the Supreme Court in a 5–3 decision upheld the constitutionality of the Federal Lobbying Act of 1946 because it was intended to limit the ability of special interest groups to influence Congress. Chief Justice Earl Warren, newly appointed to the bench, established a three-part test to determine whether a "person" engaged in political activism—defined by the statute to include nonprofit organizations—would be subject to the act. The Court wrote that in order for a "person" to come under its provisions: (1) they must solicit or receive funds; (2) one of the "main purposes" of either the "person" or funds was to influence legislation; and (3) the "person" must have encouraged "direct" contact with members of Congress. The Court cited specifically "artificial letter-writing campaigns" as well as the Internal Revenue Code provisions governing the tax deductibility of contributions to nonprofit organizations in arriving at this test.[43]

A close examination of the majority holding reveals that in *Harriss*, the Court clarified the meaning of the Internal Revenue Code provision pertaining to "substantial" attempts to influence legislation. Simply put, if a substantial portion of a contribution was used to facilitate direct contact with congressmen *or*, if the organization to which the contribution was made engaged in lobbying as one of its "main activities," then the contribution would not be tax deductible.[44]

The Sierra Club and other organizations had encouraged the public to write their representatives, used membership dues and contributions to print propaganda, and participated in hearings attempting to defeat the Dinosaur dams, actions that the Court had cited specifically as "substantial" attempts to influence legislation. As a result, the Supreme Court's decision threw the leadership of these organizations into a panic. After consulting with colleagues in the legal profession who urged that the Sierra Club retreat from the lobbying arena and after reading case precedent that supported this argument, Sierra Club member Richard Leonard, a tax attorney by trade, began to discuss with other conservation leaders the problem of how to continue advocacy without risking the tax deductibility of funds needed to finance lobbying efforts.[45]

Leonard's solution was to create a lobbying organization, the Trustees for Conservation, in autumn of 1954, registered with Congress and the IRS to solicit funds to be specifically used to campaign against the Dinosaur dams. Other conservation leaders formed two other organizations, the Citizens' Committee on Conservation and the Council of Conservationists, for the same purpose, and together with the Trustees, they constituted the primary lobbying effort for the remainder of the Dinosaur campaign. Even though prominent leaders such as Howard Zahniser, Leonard, and David Brower served these associations in an official capacity, they were only marginally successful in generating funds for the conservationists' cause.[46]

Brower and Zahniser believed that even though these organizations provided a legal bulwark for the conservation lobby, they affected detrimentally the solicitation of funds. The American people looked to the Sierra Club, Wilderness Society, National Parks Association, and other conservation groups as the standard-bearers for the preservation movement. Brower and Zahniser feared that the public would not be able to understand the legal necessity behind creating these lobbying agencies and would perceive the established organizations as too cowardly to lead the fight to protect the national park system, a public perception that did not bode favorably for future campaigns.[47]

Ironically, as the Dinosaur victory was being won, most conservation leaders, fearful of losing the large gifts and bequests that provided a substantial part of their funding, began to pull their organizations back from the legislative arena in light of the *Harriss* decision. However, after debating the merits of continuing to try to influence legislative activity, the Sierra Club decided to adopt a policy of "calculated risk," as its directors felt that the statute did not clearly outline the extent of permissible legislative activity.[48] So even while Richard Leonard advised other conservation societies to curtail their legislative efforts, the Sierra Club remained a "fighting organization" and continued to advocate publicly in favor of wilderness preservation in this climate of legal uncertainty.[49]

A climate of political uncertainty also existed in the United States at the close of the 1950s. President Eisenhower's administration, though supportive of the Colorado River Storage Project, had instituted a policy of "no new starts" with regard to reclamation projects. Seeking western support, both John F. Kennedy and Lyndon Johnson campaigned for the Democratic nomination promising to reverse this policy. Although Kennedy entered the campaign's final weeks with a relatively large lead in state delegates, Democratic Party strategists still questioned Kennedy's inexperience, and some predicted that he would not win the nomination on the first ballot at the Democratic National Convention, to be held in Los Angeles in July 1960. Johnson tailored his tactics to that effect and intensified his attacks on Kennedy during the days leading up to the convention where, Johnson believed, his close relations with House Speaker Sam Rayburn and Senator Carl Hayden might prove to be decisive in capturing a second ballot nomination.[50]

At the Democratic National Convention, Arizona congressman Stewart Udall maneuvered behind the scenes to convince Arizona's delegation to support Kennedy unanimously rather than to split between the two candidates. The tactic worked, and Kennedy stole Arizona's vote from beneath the nose of

Carl Hayden, the senior member of the Senate and a strong Johnson support-er. Though Kennedy later won in a landslide, he claimed afterward that because Arizona's delegation was one of the first to record its vote, Stewart Udall's ploy initiated a shift of support from Johnson that swept the Massa-chusetts Senator to a first-ballot nomination. After defeating Richard Nixon during the November presidential election, Kennedy rewarded the Arizona congressman by naming him secretary of the interior. Udall's ideas about con-servation impressed the president-elect greatly, and Kennedy's first conserva-tion message to Congress, delivered on 23 February 1961, reflected Udall's philosophy. Handsome, athletic, and with a penchant for the outdoors, Udall exuded the youthful aura of the new administration and became a great favorite of the new president.[51]

At first blush it appeared that Arizona was now in a strong political posi-tion to obtain authorization to build the Central Arizona Project, with Stewart Udall as the head of the all-important Interior Department. However, Udall's triumph also came at a cost, for not only did he antagonize Senator Hayden with his pre-election antics, he also created two other potential enemies: Lyn-don Johnson, who as the former Senate majority leader understood the nature of practical politics better than perhaps any political pragmatist on the Hill, Udall included; and Wayne Aspinall, the House Interior Committee chair-man, who had also aspired to become interior secretary and believed himself the best available candidate.[52] But in the afterglow of the election of 1960, with Johnson confined to the vice-presidency and with Kennedy's support, Stew-art Udall now contemplated how to solve the political infighting that had thus far prevented Arizona from obtaining authorization of the Central Ari-zona Project.

Environmental advocates viewed Udall's appointment as interior secretary with great optimism, and Sierra Club historian Michael Cohen suggests that David Brower pushed actively for his nomination. Wallace Stegner, author and Sierra Club member, writing for the Outdoor Recreation Resources Review Commission in 1961, articulated what many preservationists were trying to grasp—an argument to rebut charges of elitism levied against wilderness preservation efforts. Stegner conceptualized that wilderness as an idea—just the knowledge that it existed somewhere—provided comfort and reassurance to people unable to experience it, and that it constituted a "geography of hope," for the great mass of the population. Udall became entranced with the idea and the phrase, and he asked Stegner and an expatriate from the Wilderness Society named Sharon Francis to collaborate with him in articulating a philosophical foundation for the new style of environmentalism that was beginning to crystallize in the early 1960s.[53]

The resulting book, *The Quiet Crisis*, published in 1963, established Udall as a leader in the emerging environmental movement. Artfully written, *Quiet Crisis* called upon Americans to reassess their industrial materialistic society in light of the environmental depredations it caused. Udall argued that scientific advances would enable Americans to achieve harmony with the natural world while allowing them to retain their high standard of living, and he called upon "modern Muirs" to influence the legislative process to arrest environmental exploitation and "despoilment."[54] Little did he know that he was soon to get his wish in the form of David Brower and others who were soon to confront him over the proposed construction of dams in Grand Canyon.

Yet, despite his lofty rhetoric, Udall remained a political pragmatist at heart, and this is also evidenced in the *Quiet Crisis*. Though he articulated strong support for wilderness preservation, Udall also adhered to the Pinchotian tradition of efficiency, and he called for "regional planning...and transmountain diversions of water" to arid lands—in other words, maximum utilization. Environmental leaders who had initially hailed his appointment with great optimism soon found themselves disillusioned as Udall acquiesced in the inundation of Glen Canyon and refused to order the construction of protective dams to stop the invasion of Rainbow Bridge by the rising waters of Lake Powell. But Udall had cut his teeth as an Arizona politician, where opposition to reclamation projects was considered political suicide. Buoyed by the release of Special Master[55] Simon H. Rifkind's preliminary opinion in December 1960, in which he recommended that the Supreme Court find in favor of Arizona in its lawsuit against California, thus anticipating a favorable holding by the Supreme Court as a whole, Udall as interior secretary began to conceive of a strategy designed to obtain federal approval of the CAP.[56]

Meanwhile, conservation organizations still struggled over how active a role they should take in the face of IRS threats. In December of 1959 the Sierra Club board voted to place strict curbs upon the activities of David Brower, now its executive director and most public persona, despite its previous approval of a policy of "calculated risk" with regard to lobbying. Though the Sierra Club continued to advocate in the public arena, especially in favor of a national wilderness system, it did so cautiously, keeping its 25,000 members apprised of Grand Canyon developments in its bi-monthly publication, the *Sierra Club Bulletin*. Unlike the Echo Park fight, the club did not encourage its members to write to their congressional representatives nor did it print literature designed to influence legislation. Brower chafed under these restrictions, and he feared that the club would no longer be able to face the environmental challenges he felt sure it would have to confront during the next decade.[57]

Brower became exasperated as the Trustees for Conservation and other lobbying organizations failed to generate the funding and publicity needed for major campaigns. In the spring of 1960, with threats looming over Rainbow Bridge and the North Cascades, and with the Wilderness Bill in trouble, Brower once again appealed to the club's executive committee and suggested that the club form a "Sierra Club Foundation" to carry on the club's scientific and educational work. The foundation would free the club to lobby, while shielding the majority of the club's income in the event that the IRS revoked its tax status. As Brower passionately argued his case, Richard Leonard became convinced that a Sierra Club Foundation was the best alternative, and he agreed to draft the requisite paperwork to create it. With Leonard now in support of the idea, the rest of the board acquiesced and agreed to "let Dave lobby as effectively as he wanted to." Now the Sierra Club was free to enter the political arena with a contingency plan in place should its lobbying efforts evoke a response from the IRS. If the latter were to occur, Leonard believed that the club would have a good chance to challenge the IRS in court on constitutional grounds.[58]

Attempting to weigh potential sources of opposition and support, Stewart Udall wrote to his brother Morris, who had recently been elected to his old congressional seat, stating that he believed the conservationists were in "an ugly mood" as a result of the Rainbow Bridge "fiasco" and were "spoiling for a fight."[59] But Udall also believed he could fashion a solution to the Southwest's water problems, overcome any opposition the environmentalists might pose, and gain California's support for the CAP. Surveying the political situation in the wake of the election of 1960, Udall believed that Arizona was in a strong position with himself as interior secretary and Hayden in the Senate. In addition, two of the state's representatives, Republican John Rhodes, a quiet but effective coalition builder, and Udall's brother Morris, a Democrat and shrewd political strategist, carried the CAP banner in the House. However, this position of political strength would crumble if the increasingly frail Hay-den, now in his mid-eighties, died or was forced to retire.[60]

Ultimately, Udall formulated his proposal within the context of political pragmatism. Although it appeared that the Supreme Court was going to rule in Arizona's favor on the basis of Special Master Rifkind's report, the secretary also saw that several obstacles could still possibly interfere with congression-al passage of the CAP. First, California's congressional representatives now numbered thirty-eight and posed an even more powerful obstacle to over-come than they had when Hayden had futilely attempted to obtain approval of a CAP measure the previous decade. Second, the frequently irascible Wayne Aspinall, from the upper-basin state of Colorado, now chaired the key House Interior Committee at a time when the upper-basin states were becoming increasingly apprehensive about the possibility of additional projects in the lower basin preempting their entitlements under the 1922 Compact. Udall realized that the support of California and Aspinall were essential to obtain-ing congressional approval of the CAP. Finally, Udall knew that Senator Hay-den sought to introduce bills calling for essentially the same project debated in 1950–1951, a proposal that offered nothing for either California or Aspinall's constituency. Consequently, Udall believed Hayden's CAP bills stood little chance of passage because they would be opposed by California and Aspinall.[61]

Therefore, Udall began to consider alternatives that offered at least the possibility of eliminating the political cleavages and infighting that had doomed Arizona's previous efforts. By the early 1960s, Nobel Laureate Glen Seaborg, an eminent atomic physicist and the discoverer of plutonium, had guaranteed that power generated by fusion reactors would be practicable by 1970, and Atomic Energy Commissioner John von Neumann had predicted that by 1980 energy would be so cheap as to be virtually free. The seeming omnipotence of modern science created an aura that captured the nation's imagination, and Udall along with much of the American populace believed that in science lay the means to overcome the world's heretofore finite limitations. Already the secretary had directed Commissioner Dominy to open a dialogue with the Atomic Energy Commission about coordinating the federal reclamation pro-gram with the construction of nuclear-powered desalinization plants, and he had created the position of Science Advisor within his department to keep abreast of other technological advances. Udall also pushed for an enormous expansion of the federal saline water program, begun in 1952, asking Congress in 1961 to appropriate $100 million over the next five years. Buoyed by the possibility of solving the Southwest's water crisis in autumn of 1962, Udall began to query Wayne Aspinall about what the chairman would require for his committee to report a CAP bill favorably to the House floor for debate.[62]

In November Aspinall wrote Udall and emphasized that only through "thoughtful discussion" between states could the problems of the lower basin be resolved. Aspinall held up the CRSP as an example of effective intrabasin cooperation, suggested that Udall use it as a model for lower-basin legislation, and asked for a statement of the Interior Department's basin studies outlining ideas for a comprehensive lower-basin plan. Most important, although Aspinall understood that representatives from the southwestern states intended to introduce water project legislation immediately after the Supreme Court handed down its ruling, the chairman emphasized that only legislation based upon mutual cooperation among the lower-basin states would receive his blessing. To Udall, the ramifications were clear—projects that served only local interests, such as the CAP, stood little chance of making it out of the Interior Committee. Aspinall ruled his committee with an iron fist, and members who hoped to obtain favors from the "prickly" chairman dared not oppose him, particularly on legislation with potential ramifications for his home state of Colorado.[63]

Stewart Udall responded to Aspinall in January of 1963, and outlined his first ideas about basinwide water resource planning. Udall viewed the Compact of 1922 as a straitjacket, particularly because its allocations were based upon a great overestimation of the Colorado's annual flow. Thus, projects based upon this estimate would inherently overdevelop the river. Udall intimated to Aspinall that the impending Supreme Court decision was of secondary importance because he believed that no matter what the ruling, the lower Colorado did not contain enough water to meet the Southwest's needs. The solution lay in more efficient usage of water still available in the river for the short term and in "developing additional supplies" to meet the inevitable shortages caused by utilization of all available surface water and groundwater overdrafts.

Udall suggested that additional supplies of water could be obtained from nuclear-powered desalinization plants and interbasin water transfers, particularly from rivers in northern California, a suggestion that was sure to anger the Southern California water interests. In order to placate Arizona water advocates such as Hayden, Udall argued that the CAP should be incorporated into the overall plan and be one of the first projects constructed. The sale of hydroelectric power would provide the bulk of the financing, and generating plants at Hoover and Parker Dams would be incorporated into the scheme, along with additional powerplants "to be constructed on the Colorado River at Marble Canyon, Bridge Canyon and *wherever else such plants on the Colorado may prove feasible*" (Emphasis mine). As the only remaining undeveloped stretch of the lower Colorado River, apart from the Bridge and Marble Canyon Dam sites, lay within Grand Canyon National Park and Monument, it appears as though Udall was now beginning to contemplate at least a high Bridge Canyon Dam, and possibly the MCKC project for power generation.[64]

By 1963, Interior Secretary Stewart Udall had conceived of a broad scheme designed to cut across regional and political differences, an ominous development from the perspective of environmental organizations concerned with keeping Grand Canyon free of hydroelectric projects. In early 1963, the Supreme Court of the United States stood on the verge of ruling on the water rights of the lower-basin states after almost twelve years of litigation. Senator Hayden and his allies looked forward to reintroducing the CAP in essentially the same form as the project debated in 1950–1951, believing that a holding favorable to Arizona would create enough momentum that they could then drive a bill quickly through the House. But Udall, the student of practical politics whose bold ideas had captured the imagination of both the conservationists and President Kennedy, could see that potentially fatal obstacles, some old and some new, had arisen since the CAP debates of the early 1950s. A powerful conservationist lobby, California's growing congressional delegation, and Interior Committee Chairman Wayne Aspinall would in all likelihood pose grave threats to the ultimate success of the Hayden proposal.

Secretary Udall believed that in nuclear power and desalinization, along with intrabasin cooperation, lay the means to solve the present water crisis and heal the bitter wounds of conflicts past. "The hour for water statesmanship in the Pacific Southwest has arrived," Udall would write in June of 1963, to the governors of Arizona, California, and Nevada.[65] Young, vigorous, and with absolute faith in scientific progress, the secretary eagerly anticipated taking the lead in implementing a bold new framework for conservation, based upon maximum efficiency and technological advances he believed were just over the horizon.

Udall also knew that successful realization of these solutions would fall short if the attempt was made half-heartedly or if political differences brought about by shortsightedness prevented their implementation. The ideas of the past and the politicians who had promoted them had already been given a chance, and they had failed. Both, he believed, would fail again if they tried to follow the strategy of 1950, even if the Supreme Court rendered a favorable decision, because California still stood in the way of House approval. Though Arizona held a strong political position on Capitol Hill owing to the influence of its senior senator, this position was growing ever more precarious with each passing year. Udall believed there was only one way for Arizona to gain authorization of the project it had long dreamed of, and that was to formulate a revolutionary new proposal designed to break the political logjam and gain the support of California, the upper basin, and, if possible, the conservationists. While most of Arizona's federal water advocates planned to introduce bare-bones CAP legislation in the wake of a favorable Supreme Court ruling, Udall had already concluded, on the basis of his assessment of the political landscape, that these renewed efforts would be in vain. A bold, new approach was needed, one that reflected the persona and philosophy of the Kennedy administration. This was not a time for archaic ideas that had already been proven unsuccessful in the harsh realm of western water politics. It was time, Udall believed, to "think big!"[66]

2

Think Big!

Today, we are told, technology carries in its hands
the keys to a kingdom of abundance, and sound
solutions to many conservation problems rest largely
on adequate research and efficient management.

—Stewart Udall, *The Quiet Crisis*

On the morning of 21 January 1963, David Brower, the executive director of the Sierra Club waited nervously in the outer office of the secretary of the interior of the United States. Brower's mood was one of urgency as he hoped that he could convince the occupant of that office, Stewart Udall, to refrain from closing the valves on the recently completed Glen Canyon Dam. Although the high Glen Canyon Dam was the product of a complex political agreement brokered during the Dinosaur controversy a few years previously, Brower blamed himself for the impending loss of Glen Canyon, which contained some of the most spectacular scenery in the world. Convinced that his suggestion to raise the height of Glen Canyon Dam in exchange for the deletion of the Dinosaur dams constituted an egregious mistake, David Brower appealed to Stewart Udall's preservationist instincts, seeking to persuade him to intervene and delay the filling of Lake Powell. Brower hoped to convince the interior secretary that the dam was not needed in the twentieth century and that it should only be utilized after Lake Mead filled with silt. By the time that occurred, Brower believed, alternative energy sources would be available and Glen Canyon could be spared. But Brower waited in vain, for Stewart Udall gave his assent, Reclamation Commissioner Floyd Dominy ordered his personnel at the site to close the valves, and the Colorado River began to create Lake Powell—water playground for millions, pride of the Bureau of Reclamation, and a source of revulsion in the minds of many environmentalists.[1]

The loss of Glen Canyon haunted conservationists once they realized that their efforts at Echo Park had resulted in the destruction of a canyon more beautiful than the one they had saved. Though they viewed it as a tragic mistake, Brower and his followers learned a hard lesson from the Echo Park compromise, one equally as important as what preservationists had learned from the Hetch Hetchy dispute. In agreeing not to oppose the construction of a high Glen Canyon Dam in exchange for the deletion of the dams at Echo Park, environmentalists left themselves without recourse when they discovered that Glen Canyon should also be protected. Rendered powerless by his own compromise, Brower agonized as construction neared completion, and he pleaded eloquently with Interior Secretary Stewart Udall to spare this spectacular canyon he believed was worthy of national park status. When Glen Canyon Dam's steel gates slammed shut in 1963, Brower cried over what would soon be destroyed. Interviewed twenty-five years later, he could scarcely speak, still despondent over so great a loss.[2]

The controversies over Glen Canyon and Hetch Hetchy closely parallel one another, though separated by more than sixty years. Both involved the destruction of indescribable beauty by dams whose opponents claimed were not necessary because, in both instances, other sources of water and power were available. The Hetch Hetchy and Glen Canyon defeats devastated the respective executive officers of the Sierra Club—the heartbroken Muir died the year after Congress gave San Francisco the authorization to flood Hetch Hetchy Valley, while Brower's friends feared he might take his own life in the wake of losing Glen Canyon.[3] Both controversies awakened the Sierra Club from relatively lengthy periods of complacency and spurred it into activism. And, most important, each contest taught tactics needed for future conflicts: Hetch Hetchy—the necessity of political awareness; Glen Canyon—that entering into agreements without fully investigating their ramifications can endanger other wilderness areas. The bitter fruits of the Echo Park compromise, and the perception that the interior secretary had abdicated his responsibility to preserve Rainbow Bridge, served to strengthen the resolve of many environmentalists to prevent a similar situation from occurring in the case of Grand Canyon.

The same day he authorized the filling of Lake Powell, Stewart Udall held a press conference, which Brower attended, to publicize that the Interior Department was in the process of formulating studies of a massive regional water plan for the southwestern United States, combining the importation of water with the construction of desalinization plants to meet the needs of the lower Colorado Basin. "Piecemeal development cannot do the job," the secretary said, and he stressed that both nuclear and conventional generating plants would provide power for the immense proposal—including hydroelectric projects at the Bridge and Marble Canyon sites in Grand Canyon. Udall also lobbied for congressional authorization of the construction of the world's largest nuclear plant at Hanford, Washington, a potential power source for the regional water plan he was now beginning to conceptualize. Udall stressed that revenue from existing hydroprojects such as Hoover and Parker Dams, combined with the sales of power from Bridge, Marble, and other feasible Colorado River developments, would finance the rest of the plan, including the transbasin diversions the proposal depended upon to augment the Colorado River.[4]

Udall believed it imperative to construct the hydroelectric generating plants as the first phase of the proposal because revenue from power sales would flow into a basin account, and the funds from that account would then be used to construct the rest of the project. According to the secretary's plan, this development account constituted the key to gaining the political support of California and the other basin states, because it represented tangible evidence that these states also stood to gain from the proposal. Obtaining this trust was of utmost importance because Udall contemplated the construction of the CAP as the major portion of the first phase, both to put the revenue-generating dams in place as quickly as possible, and to placate Arizona's water interests. The regional plan offered something for virtually everyone in the Pacific Southwest, and California's representatives reacted positively to the scheme. Encouraged, Udall pressed forward.[5]

Udall conceived of the regional proposal after touring hydroelectric facilities within the Soviet Union in the summer of 1962. At one point during the secretary's trip, Premier Khrushchev promised Udall that the Soviet Union would "overtake" the United States in an "energy race," a contest Udall enthusiastically supported, for it offered the United States a chance to demonstrate its technological prowess before the rest of the world. In January of 1963, the United States needed such an opportunity, for, despite President Kennedy's bold challenge of a lunar mission by 1969, the Soviets held the lead in the space race and used it to argue the superiority of Communism before a global audience. As Udall later recalled, the early 1960s were a time of "the space program, atomic power, big technologies. We [the Interior Department] are left out of the big picture except for our program, water desalting." In 1962, Kennedy declared that the desalinization of seawater constituted the single most promising scientific breakthrough, even more important than the moon mission, because the rest of the world would "look to the nation" that developed it. As an exponent of the New Frontier, Udall believed that conservation of water resources and the development of desalinization offered the Interior Department the chance to develop peaceful technology that the United States could share with the rest of the world.[6] While the secretary grappled with the complexities of reconciling reclamation and preservation in the context of the cold war and scientific advances, Brower, defeated in his attempt to save Glen Canyon and discouraged by the new Interior Department proposal, returned to California, unsure of the effect that Udall's regional plan would have upon Grand Canyon.

Ever the practical politician, Udall hedged his bets in January of 1963, and did not specify as to the height of the latest dams proposed for the Colorado River gorge.[7] However, the political support of California and the rest of the basin states rested upon the promised lower-basin account, and contractual agreements controlled the revenues from Parker and Hoover Dams; thus, these projects would not be available to contribute to the account for several decades. Hoover, the largest existing hydroelectric producer, could not be utilized to contribute revenue to the basin fund until 1990.[8] Construction of the power dams at Bridge and Marble Canyons constituted the only means readily available to provide revenue for the basin account and the rest of the project in the foreseeable future.

According to a 1962 Bureau of Reclamation analysis of three possible heights for the Bridge Canyon project, the agency found that a dam sufficiently low to avoid backing water into the national monument would not be justifiable from an economic standpoint. Next, the Bureau compared a low dam that would back water through the length of the monument to a high dam that would back water through both the monument and encroach upon the park.

Though they found both to be feasible, Bureau engineers estimated that the high dam would generate 250,000 more kilowatts annually than the low dam, while the best option to maximize revenues, according to Commissioner Dominy, would be to construct a high Bridge Canyon Dam in conjunction with a dam at Marble Canyon.[9]

Stewart Udall confronted the dilemma of having to decide between kilowatts and wilderness preservation as he sought to gain support for his regional proposal. Previously, Udall had only considered the construction of a low Bridge Canyon Dam and Marble together to avoid conservationist opposition; however, Dominy's analysis suggested a means to maximize revenue generation that would, in all likelihood, appeal to water interests throughout the region, including California officials and Wayne Aspinall, the all-important House Interior Committee chairman. Though Dominy's proposal would most certainly precipitate strident objections from the conservation interests, this opposition might be more than offset by the support of California's representatives, who would almost certainly favor the high dam because of its revenue potential. Capital generated by a high Bridge Canyon Dam in concert with Marble promised a much greater and more rapid increase in the basin development fund than any other option and hence, the commencement of water importation that much sooner. If his new political allies from California and the rest of the Colorado Basin states insisted upon maximum power and revenue production, Stewart Udall would be forced to choose between their support, which could be measured in actual votes gained in the House, and the support of conservation organizations whose influence, though potentially powerful, as demonstrated by the Echo Park outcome, could not be assessed in conventional political terms, and who, with the exception of the Sierra Club, appeared to be more interested in preserving their tax-deductible status than in further environmental lobbying.

Additionally, California and the conservationists had united against the CRSP, and California water interests, according to Brower, helped finance the Sierra Club's opposition campaign against the Echo Park dams,[10] a situation that would not occur again if Udall could induce California to support the Pacific Southwest Water Plan (PSWP) with a high dam. Conservationists had not initiated a national opposition campaign other than Dinosaur since the Supreme Court's affirmation of the Federal Lobbying Act in its 1954 *Harriss* decision, creating the appearance that the holding had caused them to withdraw from the political arena in the light of potential IRS threats. Though the secretary purchased some time by not revealing publicly which proposition he favored, there would soon come a day when he would no longer have that luxury, and Udall would have to decide whose political support he could afford to lose and whose he deemed indispensable.

Although the secretary spoke boldly in favor of a regional river basin development for the lower Colorado, in January of 1963, Stewart Udall based his proposal more upon rhetoric than definitive studies; in fact the Bureau of Reclamation had not even released an updated CAP report, and it had not yet begun to initiate investigations of the interbasin water transfers required by a regional proposal of the magnitude Udall had outlined. Additionally, the Arizona Power Authority (APA), an organization empowered by Arizona to build a state-sponsored project, had gained approval from the Federal Power Commission (FPC) in 1962 to construct a dam at the Marble Canyon site on its own. The success of the APA's license application before the FPC took many advocates of a federal project, Udall included, by surprise, and he now feared that the APA's proposal would interfere with his own broadly conceived plans. Although Udall's opposition created resentment among some state interests, the APA was about to encounter a far more serious challenge from the state's chief water advocate himself, Senator Carl Hayden.[11] Hayden believed that the APA was jeopardizing his ability to obtain a federally funded CAP by attempting to build Marble Canyon Dam alone. The senator, acting in what he believed were the long-term best interests of his native state, made the painful decision to delay the APA's construction of Marble Canyon Dam because he hoped soon to obtain congressional approval for federal construction of the CAP.[12]

Three days after Udall announced the Interior Department's regional proposal, Senator Hayden introduced S. 502, a bill to prevent the FPC from licensing any power projects on the Colorado River from Glen Canyon Dam to Lake Mead until 31 December 1966. This action created a rift between Hayden and his Senate colleague, the volatile Barry Goldwater, who "hit the ceiling" when he learned of the measure. Goldwater, a strong proponent of the APA proposal, was taken completely by surprise because Hayden had not consulted him prior to the bill's introduction. Stewart Udall welcomed the effect of Hayden's bill because it would delay the APA's attempt to construct the dam and provided his department with the time needed to formulate a regional proposal on paper. However, Udall and Hayden did not pursue this objective in tandem because Hayden intended to introduce virtually the same proposal that Congress defeated in 1950–1951, and he made it clear to Udall that he only supported a regional plan if it included the CAP as the first project in line for authorization.[13] Scarcely one month into 1963, Arizona's water advocates had broken into three distinct factions whose internecine dispute now threatened to derail the CAP.

Water officials who advocated these differing strategies met on 6 February 1963 in Senator Hayden's Washington office to discuss the Marble Canyon project, the CAP, and other issues of concern including the conservation movement. All of Arizona's prominent politicians and water advocates attended, including Interior Secretary Stewart Udall, Senators Carl Hayden and Barry Goldwater, Representatives John Rhodes, Morris Udall, and George Senner, and Governor Paul Fannin. Among the others present were: Floyd Dominy, the commissioner of the Bureau of Reclamation; Wayne Akin, chairman of the Arizona Interstate Stream Commission; John Smith, chairman of the APA; and Rich Johnson, executive director of the CAP Association.[14]

Senator Hayden opened the meeting with a statement favoring a bare-bones CAP proposal, and afterward a lively discussion ensued. Goldwater suggested that perhaps Hayden should withdraw S. 502, but Hayden, with support from Stewart Udall, declined, stating that the only way to prevent California's congressional delegation from torpedoing future CAP proposals was to "get them with us." Therefore, he supported a moratorium on the issuance of FPC licenses for the disputed stretch of river, hoping that if Arizona relinquished its APA victory it would entice California to negotiate. Hayden then revealed that he intended to introduce a CAP bill immediately after the Supreme Court ruled on *Arizona v California*, a holding that would finally resolve the dispute between the lower-basin states over their allocations from the Colorado River.[15]

Stewart Udall argued in favor of his regional proposal, and stated that Arizona's best chance of obtaining the CAP was to support a regional development that included it as a key component. Contending that with five states working together, a proposal for a high dam at Bridge Canyon would have a better than 50 percent chance of passing the House, he articulated that Arizona's best chance of congressional approval of the CAP lay in "treat[ing] the river as a common asset of all the states." Noting that California's representatives had reacted positively to the proposal, Udall stated that ultimately, "it boils down to the art of the possible—what can we get through the House?" Goldwater and Rhodes disagreed with Udall, and argued that a regional approach would not garner enough votes to win congressional approval.[16]

Hayden and Stewart Udall also discussed the conservation movement. Hayden, reiterating his support of a high dam at Bridge Canyon, stated that "my point is that for our purposes Bridge Canyon is the desirable site, but it backs water into Grand Canyon." While reviewing the recent events at Echo Park that led to the elimination of the proposed dam there, he said "the wildlifers, bird-watchers, etc., stood up on their hind legs and beat it." Turning to face Udall, he said emphatically, "we have to get the bird-watchers in line, and, by the way, the very nature lover we want to get in line is your National Park Service Director," referring to Director Conrad Wirth's recent testimony at the FPC hearings in which he had testified against the construction of dams in Grand Canyon. Udall replied, "we are working on that." Hayden again emphasized that his sole objective was to obtain the CAP, and that he desired the flexibility to use Marble Canyon Dam in the event that the preservationists stopped the high Bridge Canyon Dam.[17]

Floyd Dominy then broached the subject of the Marble Canyon–Kanab Creek project, stating that the reach of the river through Grand Canyon National Park held the most promise for hydroelectric development in the lower forty-eight states. Goldwater gave the proposal a "snowball's chance in hell" of ever being built. But the secretary contended that while it was doubtful that the project would be built in the near future, eventually water shortages would reach the point where "we can put people above scenery." Goldwater derisively replied that, "that would be a change in your thinking too, wouldn't it," referring to Udall's emerging leadership position within the environmental movement.[18] The meeting adjourned, the feuding sides having failed to reach an agreement with regard to strategy, guaranteeing that Arizona's water interests would continue to pursue separate agendas for the foreseeable future.

This dialogue reveals a great deal about what was going through the minds of Arizona's water leaders immediately after Stewart Udall's introduction of the regional plan. Udall sought to gain the support of the rest of Arizona's water advocates by describing California's favorable initial reaction to it. Every person in the room understood the significance of this development, for they had all fought unsuccessfully to overcome California's opposition in the House a decade earlier. Since the passage of any House bill required a tally of at least 218 votes, California's 38 representatives often controlled the destiny of reclamation projects, which typically passed the House by narrow margins. California also held a powerful position on the vital House Interior Committee, and it now controlled five seats to Arizona's one, occupied by Morris Udall.

Stewart Udall also disclosed that all options were now on the table, including future consideration of the MCKC project and a high Bridge Canyon Dam. By putting "people above scenery," Udall revealed in the case of Grand Canyon that he ultimately subscribed to Gifford Pinchot's philosophy of wise use for the "greatest good to the greatest number." In February of 1963, Udall had not yet taken a public position about the height of the dam; however, this meeting reveals that privately, in consultation with other water leaders, Stewart Udall now considered using the high dam to gain the support of California and the other basin states despite the conservationist opposition this would undoubtedly create.

Conversely, Carl Hayden sought to guarantee enough power for the CAP only, and so he had adopted the position Udall had advocated previously. If the conservationists refused to "get in line" and proved potent enough to stop the high dam, the senator was willing to compromise by building a low Bridge Canyon Dam in concert with Marble. Hayden believed Marble must be held in reserve to assure that the CAP would be feasible. Hayden and Udall, though outwardly united in favor of federal construction, pursued strategies that had the potential to bring them into conflict, for while Hayden's primary concern was to obtain the CAP, Udall sought to obtain California's backing, which in his mind was becoming more and more associated with the construction of a high dam. If California should demand construction of the high dam for its revenue potential in the face of increasing conservationist opposition, it would place Udall in the position of threatening Hayden's avenue of retreat, a situation not likely to sit well with Hayden, who had spearheaded Arizona's water strategy since the early 1940s.

Complicating matters even further, the APA continued to seek a license from the FPC to construct Marble Canyon Dam despite Udall's and Hayden's opposition, and this so angered the senator that he rarely spoke with APA representatives after February of 1963. Stewart Udall was also displeased with the APA's efforts, which exacerbated the tensions between Arizona's competing water interests. Udall also had another worry, for despite his dramatic announcement of the regional plan, the Interior Department had not yet drafted a proposal to that effect. With the APA's continuing advocacy before the FPC and knowing that Senator Hayden intended to introduce CAP legislation after the Supreme Court decision, Udall instructed his assistant secretary for Water and Power, Kenneth Holum, on May 1 to create a committee to draw up the regional plan, a task that Udall deemed so urgent that he instructed Holum to treat it as though it were a "crash effort" and to complete the preliminary draft of the enormous project in only one month.[19]

The Sierra Club also undertook a crash effort of sorts in the spring of 1963. Angry at the Interior Department for its refusal to reconsider the filling of Lake Powell, and at himself for the part he had played in the raising of Glen Canyon Dam, David Brower contemplated different means to raise public awareness of the threats the Bureau's plans posed to western wilderness. He decided that visual imagery would have the greatest public impact, and he had already dispatched Eliot Porter, a skilled photographer, to capture Glen Canyon on film in 1961 and 1962 before its inundation. Brower himself filmed Glen Canyon for a forthcoming movie. The resulting book, *The Place No One Knew*, presented haunting imagery combined with the writings of prominent wilderness advocates. Sierra Club historian Michael Cohen argues that it was the "greatest" and "saddest" of the exhibit format books, a book so elegantly written and photographed that Wayne Aspinall, the crusty Interior Committee Chairman who had supported the construction of Glen Canyon Dam, wept when he read it.[20]

Presented as a requiem for Glen Canyon, *The Place No One Knew* also warned of future proposals that were "well underway to eradicate the finest miracles left on the Colorado" and that alternative energy sources such as fossil fuel or nuclear power could be used in the place of hydropower. Brower wrote in his foreword:

> Glen Canyon died in 1963 and I was partly responsible for its needless death. So were you. Neither you nor I, nor anyone else, knew it well enough to insist that at all costs it should endure.... The rest will go the way Glen Canyon did unless enough people begin to feel uneasy about the current interpretation of what progress consists of—unless they are willing to ask if progress has really served good purpose if it wipes out so many of the things that make life worthwhile.[21]

Though the book argued against future development of the Colorado River, the first edition of *The Place No One Knew* was also remarkably restrained, for the Sierra Club had yet to adopt an official position on Udall's regional water plan. Other than admonishing people to become aware that important decisions about wilderness preservation were being made without public input, the book did not appeal for an outpouring of letters or other public efforts to try and influence Congress. Though beautifully photographed and skillfully edited, *The Place No One Knew* is also notable for what it did not include; nowhere are Grand Canyon or the proposed dams mentioned by name. In a very real sense, the book reflects the Sierra Club's continuing uncertainty about how politically active it should become; it was one thing to mourn what was already lost, it was quite another to enter the legislative arena to prevent future destruction.

The Sierra Club now stood at an important crossroads in its evolution as an environmental organization. Though it had adopted as a matter of official policy in 1957 a resolution to oppose any more water projects on the lower Colorado River, the club's leadership had not actually entered the arena, giving the appearance of indifference or retreat. Now, with Glen Canyon going under, with the Interior Department formulating a regional water plan predicated upon dams in Grand Canyon, and with the Supreme Court's ruling in *Arizona v California* imminent, the club could no longer avoid taking a public stand.

The Sierra Club board of directors met on 4 May 1963 to discuss what position the club should take with regard to these latest Grand Canyon dam proposals. Bestor Robinson, now Sierra Club vice president, still wielded great influence among the leadership, and just as he had in 1949, Robinson argued for compromise. Robinson made a strong case for the recreation potential of Marble Canyon Dam, and even contended that because the dam would create a wonderful trout fishery downstream, the club should urge the Bureau to construct elevators for public access. With the board on the verge of approving yet another Robinson compromise, David Brower played his last trump and asked Martin Litton (fig. 2), Sierra Club member, travel editor of *Sunset* magazine, and staunch Grand Canyon advocate, to make a presentation he had prepared beforehand. Litton rose and gave an impassioned argument in which he chastised the board for even considering the idea of standing by while the Bureau built dams in Grand Canyon. Litton referred to a detailed map and

Figure 2. Martin Litton of the Sierra Club. Litton initiated the Sierra Club letter writing campaign in 1963 that led to the loss of the Club's tax-deductible status; he also shamed the Sierra Club's leadership into supporting David Brower's antidam offensive. *Courtesy of the Bancroft Library, University of California, Berkeley.*

demonstrated how dams above and below the park would detrimentally affect the park itself, and he argued that all of Grand Canyon, whether it came under Park Service jurisdiction or not, was worth fighting for. As David Brower recalled later, Litton "devastated" Bestor Robinson's arguments, and when he finished Litton received a spontaneous round of applause from those in attendance. After an hour and a half of debate, board member Pauline Dyer moved that the club should oppose all further dams and diversions in Grand Canyon, and that it should advocate in favor of the enlargement of Grand Canyon National Park. The board approved. Now, because its leadership had taken steps to protect itself from the IRS should its wilderness advocacy prove too strident, the Sierra Club was ready to fight against the Grand Canyon dams without fearing the loss of its tax-deductible status.[22]

At the beginning of June 1963 all interested parties, whether for or against the dams, anxiously awaited the Supreme Court's decision in the fifth act of the continuing *Arizona v California* drama. For more than forty years the dispute between the two states had raged, beginning with Arizona's refusal to ratify the Compact of 1922, through the construction of Boulder Dam, the dismissal of three Arizona lawsuits on technicalities in 1931, 1934, and 1936 by the Supreme Court, and the defeat of Carl Hayden's two CAP bills in the House of Representatives in 1950 and 1951. Arizona filed its fifth suit against California on 13 August 1952, and the litigation filled forty-three volumes, lasted eleven years, and outlived the original special master, George I. Haight, who died on 30 September 1955.[23] The Court appointed Simon H. Rifkind to continue the proceedings and on 28 August 1958, the trial before the master ended. Rifkind issued his preliminary opinion in 1960,[24] and although it favored Arizona, the ruling did not bind the Court. Now it remained for the nation's highest tribunal, headed by Earl Warren, the ex-governor of California, to render its momentous decision and resolve this long-standing dispute.[25]

Although numerous issues divided the two states, the status of the Gila River was probably the most controversial and certainly had the most bearing with regard to the CAP. California contended that the Gila's flow should be deducted from Arizona's Colorado River entitlement because it was a tributary. Arizona countered, arguing that since the Gila's watershed lay almost entirely within the state, it was completely independent of the Colorado and, therefore, its annual flow should not be considered a part of Arizona's allotment. The difference represented by the Gila River amounted to about one million acre feet. Arizona feared that if the Supreme Court upheld California's position on the Gila River, it would reduce its allotment so drastically that in all likelihood, the CAP could never be built.[26]

The Supreme Court handed down its opinion on 3 June 1963. In a seven-to-one decision with Justice Warren abstaining, the Court held that in a year of average flow, California was entitled to 4.4 million acre feet, Arizona to 2.8 million, and Nevada to 300,000. Furthermore, it ruled that the flow of the Gila River was not a part of Arizona's entitlement, effectively granting the state an allotment of 3.8 million acre feet.[27] The decision constituted a monumental victory for the State of Arizona. Finally, pending congressional approval, construction of the CAP could begin. The next day Senators Carl Hayden and Barry Goldwater, and Representatives Morris Udall, John Rhodes, and George Senner introduced legislation to that effect in both houses of Congress.

Although Stewart Udall lobbied vigorously with Arizona's congressional delegation to try to convince them that a regional proposal constituted the best approach, Arizona's congressional delegation disregarded this advice and chose to follow Hayden's lead, in effect dividing Arizona's political influence when it should have been most united in the immediate aftermath of the Supreme Court decision. Arizona's political leaders were aware that water attorney Northcutt Ely, California's brilliant lower Colorado River strategist, intended to use his influence to reverse the Supreme Court decision through political action. CAP task force member J. A. Riggins expressed the frustration many Arizonans felt in a biting piece of satire about Ely's role in the Arizona-California controversy:

"The law of the West," my lawyer said, "is Prior Appropriation."
And on this point we'll stand or fall in the High Court of the Nation.
For ten long years we tried our case and never did give in—
Just kept on using water which belonged to you and him.
The day we lost, my lawyer spoke—sans fear or trepidation.
"What you have lost in Court today, regain!—by legislation!" . . .[28]

This was exactly what Udall's regional proposal was designed to avoid; the usurpation of the legal process by legislative obstruction, while the introduction of basic CAP legislation, in Udall's measured opinion, only guaranteed more of the same. Why, then, did Arizona's water leaders, Udall's own brother included, take such a course of action?

The answer lies in the reverence in which Carl Hayden was held by Arizona's CAP proponents, the public at large, and in Hayden's own perceptions of the proper congressional strategy. Why should Hayden, whose own legislative experience dated back to 1912, defer to a former representative with only six years of legislative experience, when he, as the Senate's ranking member in terms of seniority, had built political coalitions that had fostered the passage of dozens of reclamation bills, including many of great benefit to the states of California and Colorado, for nearly a quarter century? As chairman of the powerful Senate Appropriations Committee, Carl Hayden was well acquainted with the practical side of politics, and the influence he held, yet Hayden seldom used his position to force others to bend to his will.

Hayden believed that the major obstacle to the passage of the CAP had been removed now that the Supreme Court had adjudicated the water rights of the lower Colorado River Basin. "Ordinary principles of fair play are bound to operate to our advantage," Senator Hayden wrote to the rest of the Arizona delegation shortly before the Supreme Court decision. Carl Hayden expected that his colleagues in both the House and Senate, many of whom he had aided in obtaining benefits for their home districts, would now help him realize his lifelong dream for Arizona.[29]

Hayden feared also that a bill radically different from his previous legislation, such as a regional project along the lines suggested by Stewart Udall, would require more in-depth studies by the Bureau of Reclamation, resulting in additional lengthy delays. The senator also believed that if the CAP was tied to a basin account along with Hoover and Parker Dams, it would give the opponents of a high dam at Bridge Canyon ammunition to demonstrate that the CAP was feasible with a low dam and power revenues from Hoover. Finally, Hayden discerned that Congress was in a fiscally conservative mood in the summer of 1963 and that it would be reluctant to pass a multibillion-dollar regional proposal; hence, the senator believed that to tie the CAP in with a more ambitious plan would jeopardize the CAP unnecessarily.[30] Hayden, calling upon his fifty-one years of congressional experience, convinced the Arizona delegation of the practicality of his approach and consequently gained their support of a reintroduction of the CAP proposal of 1950–1951, which included a high dam at Bridge Canyon with no mention of a dam in Marble Canyon.

Undaunted, Stewart Udall continued to try to convince Hayden to throw his support behind the regional approach. Citing practical reasons of his own, Udall appealed to Hayden's bitter memories of past CAP failures, writing the senator that he had consulted several congressmen in "strategic" positions on the House Interior Committee who not only backed the regional proposal but argued that the old CAP legislation would create such controversy in the House that it would probably go down to defeat despite the respect in which Hayden was held in both houses of Congress. Cognizant of Hayden's great political influence and the important role the senator had played in Arizona's quest for the CAP, Udall pleaded with Hayden to "give the regional approach a chance," arguing that if Hayden pushed for CAP hearings in 1963, it would undercut his own negotiations with California Governor Edmund "Pat" Brown and Senator Thomas Kuchel. Udall contended that only by tying the CAP to the larger proposal would California's congressional representatives be induced to support it and that to strive for a separate CAP authorization would be "disastrous."[31] But the secretary failed to convince the senator of the efficacy of his plan, and Hayden obtained Senate approval to convene CAP hearings in the fall of 1963.

Udall now came under attack from Arizona Republicans, who invoked the secretary's recent trip to the Soviet Union and his subsequent positive comments about hydroelectric developments inside the USSR as evidence that he desired to "socialize" power production in the United States. On 21 July Arizona Republican Party Chairman Keith Brown accused Udall of being "a hatchet man for the New Frontier [who is] doing everything in his power to block Arizona from obtaining its long-fought-for goal." Brown invoked New Deal imagery which played well before the conservative Arizona electorate, calling Udall's regional proposal an "international Colorado Valley Authority," an obvious slap at the Tennessee Valley Authority, a New Deal legacy Senator Goldwater loathed. Brown also accused Udall of stalling the CAP to placate California to assure that the state's forty electoral votes would go to Kennedy in the 1964 presidential election.[32]

Indeed, despite the vituperative Republican rhetoric, it appears as though Udall was doing exactly that. California supported Richard Nixon in 1960, and Kennedy's advisors viewed its electoral bloc as pivotal because, in the light of JFK's razor-thin margin of victory in 1960, they sought to obtain a mandate for JFK in 1964. In addition, Arizona Senator Barry Goldwater was already being mentioned as a possible presidential candidate in 1963; in the event that he won the nomination, it would be highly unlikely that Arizona would vote to keep Kennedy—and Udall—in office.[33] Ironically, Udall, who believed that the best chance of obtaining the CAP for Arizona in any form was to gain California's support, was now forced into the position of having to oppose Senator Hayden of his own state and party because Udall feared the effect that Hayden's CAP strategy would have on the California electorate and ultimately upon his own ability to use the power of his office to influence the congressional debate.

With Hayden and Udall at loggerheads, Arizona's CAP offensive remained divided as conservationists now began to initiate a campaign in opposition to the proposed Grand Canyon dams. David Brower wrote Udall in late June 1963 attempting to open a dialogue about Grand Canyon and expressed concerns environmentalists held about the Hayden proposals, the regional plan, and the APA attempt to build Marble Canyon Dam. Brower believed that the APA proposal constituted the greatest threat to the Canyon because most of the gorge lay outside of the national park and monument, and it thus fell under the jurisdiction of the FPC pursuant to the Federal Power Act of 1935. Brower pointed out that the commission existed for the sole purpose of promoting water development and that it did so without considering the environmental impact of these projects. In light of the Glen Canyon debacle, Brower found it appalling that the FPC was empowered to authorize water projects in unprotected reaches of the Canyon without having to obtain congressional approval, so long as the projects did not infringe upon the national park or monument.

In an attempt to bring aesthetic arguments into the policymaking process, Brower urged Udall to try to persuade President Kennedy to use his authority under the Antiquities Act of 1906 to enlarge Grand Canyon National Monument so that it encompassed all of the Canyon from Lee's Ferry to the Grand Wash Cliffs, 277 miles downstream. Then, with the entire canyon removed from the jurisdiction of the FPC, proponents of water development and conservationists could air their respective views before Congress. Brower sent Udall a copy of *The Place No One Knew*, with its persuasive pictorial and philosophical arguments, and he also cited some quantitative evidence of his own, a USGS report compiled by hydrologist Luna Leopold in 1958 that concluded that Glen Canyon Dam constituted an unnecessary development on the already overextended Colorado River. Arguing that the American people did not have a chance to voice an opinion about Glen Canyon Dam, Brower contended that it was Udall's duty as the chief custodian of the public lands to ensure that the people were not denied this opportunity in the case of Grand Canyon.[34]

Evidently, Brower was unaware that Udall also opposed the APA action, and that the secretary had taken action to suspend the FPC's jurisdiction over the dam sites. Udall brushed aside Brower's arguments and the Interior Department moved forward with its plans for a regional development. In early July the Interior Department circulated a preliminary draft of what it called "The Lower Colorado River Project," which included a high dam at Bridge Canyon, and in early August the final draft of the project was ready for release. Udall stumped the western states trying to gain support for the regional proposal and, in doing so, he incurred the ire of Senator Barry Goldwater, who, together with Hayden, had cosponsored the CAP bill introduced in June.

Udall carefully avoided attacking Hayden, but on 22 August 1963, the secretary struck back at his antagonists during a town hall meeting in Los Angeles, calling Goldwater a "bitterender" who sought to "reactivate the competition among western states for water rather than work toward a regional solution." While Goldwater's office declined to comment, Eugene Pulliam, the publisher of the *Arizona Republic*, declared that "Udall's grandiose scheme is...nothing except a grab for personal power."[35] Despite this opposition within his own state, Stewart Udall released the regional proposal his departmental task force had formulated on 26 August 1963, one day before the CAP Senate hearings were scheduled to begin. Udall called this massive regional scheme the Pacific Southwest Water Plan (PSWP), and anticipated bringing it before Congress in early 1964.[36]

Udall patterned the PSWP after the Colorado River Storage Project, as Chairman Aspinall had suggested back in November of 1962, but on a much larger scale. In addition to the CAP, it also included projects in California, Nevada, Utah, and New Mexico. Recognizing that the Colorado River Compact of 1922 was based on a grossly overestimated flow of 17.5 million acre feet annually, this scheme called for development in two phases. The construction of these water projects within several western states would commence first, followed by water augmentation of the Colorado Basin from northern California rivers and desalinization plants up to a total of 7.5 million acre feet per year.[37]

The importation of this much water would necessitate the construction of aqueducts with huge lifting capacities to transport the water over mountain ranges, and require an immense amount of power to drive the pumps and produce enough capital to build the projects. To finance the plan, enormous "cash register dams," solely for the generation of hydroelectric power twenty-four hours a day, were planned for many of the West's great rivers. Consequently, the PSWP included dams at the Bridge and Marble Canyon sites to help pay for the project, which, according to initial estimates, would cost a staggering $4 billion and take thirty years to build. Phase one alone, including Bridge and Marble Canyon Dams, would cost $1.9 billion. Udall released the proposal to the five governors of the states affected by the plan, as required by the Flood Control Act of 1944, for their comments and suggestions. Although the draft the governors received included a high dam at Bridge Canyon, Udall refrained from endorsing it publicly, stating only that he supported the general concept of regional water development. Consequently Udall was able to obtain favorable publicity for the PSWP from the *New York Times*, even though John Oakes, a Sierra Club member and the paper's chief editor, opposed a high Bridge Canyon Dam.[38]

In the summer of 1963, various agencies within the Interior Department submitted their respective positions to the PSWP task force, including the National Park Service, which voiced opposition to the high dam. Preliminary versions of the Park Service statement also included a strong protest against the MCKC project; however, the final statement does not include this opposition, presumably because the draft of the PSWP released publicly on 26 August did not include the MCKC project. But in July, Merrill Beal, park naturalist at Grand Canyon, began compiling data for Udall's "crash study" about the detrimental effects that a high Bridge Canyon Dam and the MCKC project would have upon the park, and Park Service Director Wirth reiterated the opposition of his agency toward both projects in August, shortly before Udall released the proposal.[39]

For Udall, who was seeking to generate every possible kilowatt to fund his massive scheme, the MCKC project must have looked enticing. The Bureau estimated in 1961 that the project would be capable of generating 2.53 million kilowatts per year, almost twice the estimated capacity of a high Bridge Canyon Dam.[40] The proposal also promised a massive infusion of funds into the basin development fund that Udall hoped would entice California into supporting the CAP. Though it is impossible to determine with exact certainty the point in time when Udall decided against the MCKC project, the evidence suggests that as late as August 1963 the secretary contemplated including it in his regional water plan and discarded it only after considering the public outcry the proposal would generate, or the political impossibility of passing it.

Park Service officials faced this latest threat to Grand Canyon at a time of great uncertainty, when both the Interior Department and Carl Hayden promoted various plans for the construction of hydroelectric dams, as well as the MCKC project. Hayden wielded tremendous power over the Service because as chairman of the Senate Appropriations Committee he controlled the flow of funds to the agency. Thus, the Park Service could not actively oppose Hayden on Bridge Canyon Dam without inviting fiscal retribution. Though some Service officials at the superintendent and regional director levels opposed invasions of the national monument, they apparently were unable to convince Director Wirth to risk the consequences of combating both Hayden and the interior secretary.[41] Cognizant of the momentum and political pressure behind proposals to build Bridge Canyon Dam, Director Wirth focused upon limiting the height of the dam to keep the reservoir confined to the monument, and he favored shifting the boundary of the monument eastward to the high-water line of the proposed reservoir.

The Sierra Club and National Parks Association reacted to the PSWP with dismay. Both organizations devoted large sections of the October issues of their respective publications to the plan, condemning it in the strongest terms. Two articles in *National Parks Magazine* mourned the continuing destruction of the Colorado's canyons and argued that this process could only be arrested by "concerted and determined action." Though evidently its leaders desired a public reaction, the NPA did not suggest or endorse specific action for its members to take, and the Association confined its efforts to educating the readership of its magazine so that they could "decide for themselves" what to do.[42] By limiting itself to an educational role, the NPA, with attorney Anthony Smith as its president, stayed in compliance with the IRS lobbying regulations affirmed by the Supreme Court in *Harriss*.

The Sierra Club also published articles in the *Sierra Club Bulletin*, and in marked contrast to the NPA, the club took a confrontational stance and urged that its 22,000 members write their political representatives. In a strongly worded essay, Martin Litton attacked the dams by accusing the Bureau of manipulating its figures to make the dams appear economically feasible, and he also argued that it was ludicrous to partition Grand Canyon into separate pieces. Echoing the arguments Newton Drury had advanced thirteen years previously, Litton contended that just because the dams were planned for outside of the National Park did not mean that they would not injure the canyon, for how could one flood one part without damaging the whole? Acknowledging that currently the club faced threats on several fronts, Litton argued that the club did not have the luxury of picking and choosing its battles. Writing with a sense of urgency, he articulated dramatically the position and tactics that the Sierra Club would take in its fight to save Grand Canyon for the duration of the struggle:

> The men in government who might be induced to oppose the dams and who once did appear resigned to the loss of the canyon. But are we resigned? Shall we fail to go into battle because it is hard to win? . . . Could not 22,000 Sierra Club members, without strain, turn out 22,000 letters a day for a week? . . . There has never been a Congress, a President, a Secretary of the Interior, a governor or a newspaper editor who would not sit up and take notice of that kind of mail. . . . three letters each . . . and more to follow . . . could assure the Canyon's interim survival and rescue the opportunity for reason to prevail.[43]

At the conclusion of Litton's article, the magazine listed the addresses of Interior Secretary Udall, senators, representatives and the president of the

United States. By urging that its members write to their political representatives, the Sierra Club had now chosen to engage in "substantial lobbying" activity as defined by the Supreme Court. How tolerant the IRS would remain of the club's expanded attempts to influence legislation remained to be seen.

The proponents of Hayden's CAP bill also reacted negatively to Udall's introduction of the PSWP, because they believed that the regional plan would only confuse the Congress. Hayden set hearings on the bill for 27–28 August, and again for 1–2 October. Real progress on the Hayden CAP proposal could not be made until the Interior Department issued a new CAP report, and despite Senator Hayden's admonitions, Secretary Udall refused to issue a CAP report separate from the PSWP. As a result, Hayden's bill stalled, and tensions began to rise between Udall and members of Arizona's congressional delegation who viewed the secretary as being obstructionist. Without the Interior Department report, Rich Johnson argued, the "meaningless" Senate hearings were held only because Hayden's "Senatorial friends" would not deny Arizona's senior senator his desire to hold them.[44]

Officials within the state of California also began to question Udall's proposal. The planned diversion of water from the northern part of the state to the Colorado Basin so angered representatives from that region that Governor Pat Brown told the secretary that he could no longer support the PSWP without drastic modifications. Udall commissioned Undersecretary James Carr, a Californian, to rewrite the proposal to obtain the support of his native state, a move that in turn angered Senator Hayden, who feared even more delays. Hayden, unbeknownst to Udall, was also engaged in secret negotiations with Governor Brown and California Senator Thomas Kuchel, who had intimated that he might compromise on the CAP if the legislation was amended to grant California's 4.4 million acre feet of water priority over all other water interests in the lower Colorado. Hayden also was angry with officials of the APA who had somehow managed to convince the mercurial Goldwater to make statements supporting a state-funded project even though Goldwater had cosponsored Hayden's bill.[45]

With Arizona's water interests at each other's throats in the autumn of 1963, Interior Chairman Wayne Aspinall entered the fray. Aspinall, tired of the bickering, reiterated that he favored a regional water plan for the Southwest modeled on the CRSP, and that if the various state factions would cooperate with the interior secretary and present the House Interior Committee with such a plan, "it will receive the earliest possible consideration by the Congress." Then Aspinall declared that his committee would refuse to act on any CAP legislation unless unity existed within Arizona's political delegation and between the seven basin states. Furthermore, he emphasized that all parties must support a regional development. Aspinall's pronouncement, though seemingly harsh, laid the groundwork for future cooperation among the basin states, as all water interests realized that Aspinall's approval was indispensable to the House passage of any CAP or regional proposal.[46]

In November of 1963, supporters and opponents of dams in Grand Canyon could look back at a year of mixed successes and failures. Environmentalists viewed Hayden's CAP proposals and Udall's PSWP, and the momentum building behind them, with trepidation. Though perhaps encouraged by his pro-environmental rhetoric, many preservationists also viewed Udall cynically because they believed that the secretary could have taken action to prevent the tragic loss of Glen Canyon and the threat the rising waters of Lake Powell would soon pose to Rainbow Bridge. As new threats to Grand Canyon emerged, conservation organizations had begun to lay the groundwork for opposition campaigns; the National Parks Association and the Sierra Club both publicized the latest dam proposals, while the Sierra Club had gone further and initiated a public letter-writing campaign designed to influence CAP legislation, clearly crossing the line of permissible activity defined by the Supreme Court in the *Harriss* decision of 1954. The Sierra Club leadership now believed that only through participation in the policymaking process could environmentalists gain the legal protection necessary to preserve wilderness areas. Hence, these environmentalists now prepared for their first national campaign since the Echo Park controversy, having made a pragmatic decision to attempt to sway public opinion despite the known risk of an IRS revocation.

Proponents of the CAP could take encouragement from the landmark Supreme Court decision in *Arizona v California*, which finally awarded Arizona the water rights its advocates had long claimed. One faction, led by Senator Carl Hayden, believed that the barrier that had prevented the passage of the CAP in 1950–1951 had been removed, and they had introduced new CAP legislation in the summer of 1963. Hayden had also grown exasperated enough with the APA that he had introduced a bill to remove the lower Colorado River from the jurisdiction of the FPC to eliminate this potential obstacle to a federally constructed project. Hayden and his supporters believed that finally the CAP was within their grasp.

Stewart Udall's regional water plan, though it received mixed reviews, promised at least the potential for compromise between Arizona and the other basin states, particularly California. Though northern California objected strongly to the idea of a diversion of its water to the Colorado Basin, California Governor Brown had endorsed the regional proposal as a concept, albeit with some alterations. It now appeared that California's representatives might be induced to support the CAP in some form, a possibility that had previously never existed.

Udall could also be heartened by the fact that Wayne Aspinall, the cantankerous Interior Committee chairman, also endorsed the regional plan and sent a strong signal to the squabbling factions that they need only cooperate and he would throw his support behind the measure. In this era of seemingly limitless scientific advancement, the secretary had also carved out a niche for his department in the area of desalinization, and he served a president who was not only also enamored of big technology, but one who assigned the highest priority to desalinization, a major component of Udall's regional plan. Though Kennedy did not endorse the PSWP publicly and did not plan to until after he had secured California's electoral support in 1964, the president had given Udall his tacit approval of the project in the summer of 1963.[47] Udall looked forward to bringing the proposal before Congress in early 1964, and to gaining the president's public backing after the election. Major obstacles lay ahead but Udall believed that through negotiation with the basin states, technological advancements, and the support of the popular young president that Congress would approve the basin plan and resolve the water problems plaguing the Pacific Southwest. But an assassin's bullet ended Udall's hopes of public presidential support in late November of 1963.

The Battle is Joined

Nature lovers are a powerful, and almost unassailably virtuous voice in American affairs. Arizona had better watch out for them. They can influence many votes in Congress.

—Ben Cole, *Arizona Republic*, 29 December 1963

On 22 November 1963 Stewart Udall and five other members of President Kennedy's cabinet were aboard an Air Force jet en route to Japan to make preparations for a presidential visit scheduled tentatively for the following spring. High above the Pacific Udall learned the dreadful news that Kennedy had been slain in Dallas, Texas. Shocked into stunned silence, the secretary stared out at the ocean, and as the plane reversed course and headed back to Washington, D.C., he attempted to capture his thoughts and feelings about the president whom he had served for almost three years, and the man who—even as Udall wrote—was gathering the reins of presidential power. To Udall, Kennedy had been a "modern president," blessed with a keen intellect that "could catch up and deal with the most complex problems of the age," a president who had endorsed technological advances such as desalinization, nuclear power, and Udall's philosophy of resource conservation. As he fought to understand the day's events, the secretary conjectured that LBJ would fail if he did not carry on "the President's Civil Rights program," unconsciously expressing his own struggle to comprehend the transition of power that had already taken place. Turning his thoughts to the new chief executive, Udall wrote of Johnson's "ruthless[ness] with people" and numbered among his strengths his "skill as a politician," and "Johnson's roots in rural America."[1] Perhaps even now, Udall pondered whether Johnson, raised in the Texas hill country and so intimately acquainted with the struggles of farmers trying to scratch a living out of an arid environment, would embrace the Pacific Southwest Water Plan, designed to aid agricultural interests in the American Southwest.

Lyndon Johnson was more than just an ordinary politician; he was, in Udall's estimation, "easily the best Senate leader of the age," because of his ability to manipulate the legislative process and forge coalitions to obtain his objectives. To a great extent, Johnson's political career had been built upon his support of reclamation projects, first in Texas, and later the West. Indeed, as a senator, Johnson had backed the Central Arizona Project and Bridge Canyon Dam strongly when the Senate debated the proposal in 1950 and 1951, twice voting in favor of the project. As a result, LBJ forged ties with Arizona politicians such as Carl Hayden and former Senate Majority Leader Ernest McFarland, now a justice of the Arizona Supreme Court.[2] Given the new president's relationship with these and other western politicians, and his previous endorsement of the CAP, Udall as well as the proponents of a bare-bones CAP, had reason to be optimistic about obtaining President Johnson's support.

Stewart Udall also had reason to worry, for he now served the very man whom he had opposed during the Democratic primary race of 1960, and LBJ was not likely to forget Udall's efforts to relegate him to the vice presidency. But Johnson also posed a potential threat to the PSWP and CAP because of his own sense of political pragmatism and need for acceptance. According to historian Robert Caro, a leading Johnson biographer, LBJ's latent insecurities drove him to great lengths to gain the affection of people, even as he ascended to the heights of power. LBJ also proved adept at attracting support from conservatives and liberal Democrats alike because he masked his true feelings about controversial issues. Consequently, as a young congressman, Johnson gained and maintained favor with President Franklin Roosevelt, while only a few years later, he disassociated himself from the New Deal during his campaign for the Senate in 1948. Though Caro's analysis ends that same year,[3] the enigmatic Johnson continued to appeal to both sides of the political spectrum throughout his twelve years in the Senate. Because he had become president by default, Johnson looked to the 1964 presidential election with even greater anticipation than had Kennedy because it offered LBJ the chance to be elected on his own terms and legitimize his presidency by gaining a mandate from the electorate. As badly as Udall wanted presidential approval of the PSWP and Hayden desired it for the CAP, with eleven months to go until the presidential race, Johnson was too politically astute to risk antagonizing a state that controlled an Electoral College voting bloc the size of California's. LBJ viewed California's support as essential to his own place in history; consequently, though Udall and Hayden would try to obtain presidential support for their water projects throughout 1964, they would make these efforts in vain.

Udall made his first appeal for the PSWP to President Johnson on 27 November, two days after the majestic funeral procession for the late President Kennedy, laying out the priorities his office intended to pursue during the following year in a memo to Bill Moyers, now a member of Johnson's staff. The secretary emphasized the importance of his regional plan to the Southwest, and he also urged LBJ to authorize a dramatic increase in the saline-water conversion program. Udall also recommended that the president read *The Quiet Crisis*, especially the chapter about the resource policies of Theodore and Franklin Roosevelt, to gain "inspiration," and insights into his own philosophy of resource conservation.[4]

As Udall struggled with the transition from Kennedy to Johnson, he also came under increasing fire from Carl Hayden and proponents of the CAP because he continued to withhold a separate CAP report. However, Udall believed California Governor Pat Brown would view a separate report as a breach of faith, and he had gone to great lengths to assure Brown that the project would benefit California. The governor had responded by taking a great political risk, endorsing Udall's regional concept even though it included the CAP as a component. Hayden and Arizona Governor Paul Fannin accused Udall of favoring California and demanded that he give Arizona an "equal opportunity" to put its share of the Colorado River to beneficial use. In an attempt to limit the potential fallout, Udall dispatched Commissioner Floyd Dominy, whom Hayden respected, to Arizona to try to persuade state leaders that a regional plan promised the best approach to the Southwest's water problems.[5]

Dominy spoke to water leaders in Tucson on 11 December, and he stressed that even though he believed Arizona's politicians were justified in seeking the CAP in light of the June 1963 Supreme Court decision, state leaders needed to consider the overall situation in the Pacific Southwest before pressing forward. The current water crisis in the region had been caused by explosive population growth, and there simply was not enough water in the Colorado River to go around. Only through massive imports into the basin from northern California and the desalinization of seawater through the use of "mammoth nuclear power plants along the West coast" could future water supplies be assured. Dominy, framing his argument in the context of political practicality, pointed out that Wayne Aspinall desired a regional plan, the success of such a plan rested largely upon building up a development fund, and, therefore, it would be foolhardy to "partially utilize" the Bridge Canyon dam site by constructing a low dam. Invoking the imagery of the vanished Hohokam civilization, the commissioner closed by saying that "additional water must come to the State before the faucets in Tucson and other cities dribble dust." Though he was later to deny vehemently that he had ever supported either the PSWP or nuclear desalinization of seawater, Floyd Dominy advocated enthusiastically in favor of both in this and in other public addresses, although privately he may have felt differently.[6]

Just where this additional water was to come from, however, had not yet been determined, for northern California resistance to importation from the region had caused Brown to cool to the regional plan. But if water could not be imported from northern California, then what other options were available? Desalinization, though it appeared promising, still was several years away from becoming a reality, and the technological breakthrough to make it competitive with other water sources had not yet occurred, with no guarantee that it ever would, despite the optimism of leading scientists and the interior secretary. Consequently, in December of 1963 Udall's staff began to advocate quietly in favor of a diversion from the Pacific Northwest as a possible solution. Assistant Commissioner of Reclamation Bill Palmer specified that the importation should come from the Columbia River, which annually discharged 140 million acre feet into the Pacific Ocean, a "waste" of water equivalent to ten times the flow of the Colorado in an average year.[7] However, even to discuss this alternative risked incurring the wrath of Senator Henry Jackson from the state of Washington, whose influence as chairman of the Senate Interior Committee was almost as great as that of Hayden. An angry Jackson had the power to stop the PSWP or any other reclamation proposal in its tracks if he chose to do so. Still, the possibility of a Pacific Northwest diversion had now been raised and it would be up to the interior secretary to determine how, when, or whether the subject should be broached with Jackson.

Udall circulated a revised PSWP proposal to the western governors and other interested parties on 26 December 1963, and despite Hayden's "vigorous protests," he released it to the press on 15 February 1964. The proposal did not include the CAP as a severable project, and Carl Hayden continued to voice his objections to it. However, the plan changed the northern California importation proposal to a "feasibility study," an attempt to delay the portion of the plan most objectionable to the State of California. The secretary slashed almost one billion dollars worth of projects from the previous incarnation of the plan, which now had an estimated cost of $3.1 billion. The proposal included the Coconino Dam on the Little Colorado River, even though it would create a reservoir encroaching upon Wupatkai National Monument, and it also called for the construction of an additional silt-retention dam in the spectacular canyon of the Paria River, just downstream from Lee's Ferry. The savings were largely attributable to a redesign of the Bridge Canyon Dam, and the PSWP no longer included desalinization plants, making California's support more dependent than ever upon the augmentation of the Colorado River. Although the plan did not include any provision for the importation of water from a specific source, thereby avoiding Jackson's ire, the final draft included a potentially explosive issue: a high Bridge Canyon Dam.[8]

During the 1955 House Interior Committee Hearings on the Colorado River Storage Project, Stewart Udall sat across the table from David Brower and predicted that someday the two of them would face off over Bridge Canyon Dam. However, after the conservationists had succeeded in wielding enough muscle to have the Echo Park dams deleted from the legislation, Udall realized that the conservationists constituted a potent new political force. For the rest of the 1950s and well into 1962, Udall cautioned Arizona water interests against insisting upon the construction of a high Bridge Canyon Dam to avoid antagonizing these environmentalists. Udall's appeals convinced Senator Hayden to block the APA license in 1963 so that he could hold Marble Canyon Dam in reserve, in case the conservationist organizations mounted a viable threat to a high Bridge Canyon Dam.

However, Udall learned another lesson from his years in Congress as well; that the sheer power of the California delegation constituted an almost insurmountable obstacle to the CAP. Consequently, Udall premised the PSWP upon obtaining California's backing and incurred the wrath of Carl Hayden and other prominent Arizona water advocates in the process. Before arriving at his decision, the secretary considered carefully the positions of the different agencies within his department that had split over the high dam issue. Floyd Dominy made a powerful argument favoring a high Bridge Canyon Dam, stating that it promised the greatest potential for revenue generation to build the development fund, the key inducement for California's support. The National Park Service issued its report in which it opposed a high dam but accepted the inevitability of a dam that would create a reservoir in the national monument. Udall himself admitted in August of 1963 that a high dam would "impair park values." Assistant Secretary for Public Lands John Carver also made powerful arguments against the high dam, pointing out that the dam would precipitate such an outpouring of protest from conservationists that it would "threaten the success of the entire proposal." Voicing his concerns in unequivocal language, Carver wrote Ken Holum, the assistant secretary of Water and Power, on 6 January 1964:

> Inundation of a portion of one of the world's natural wonders ought to be contemplated only if absolutely necessary, as where the safety of the nation is faced with a clear and present danger. The Pacific Southwest region needs water and power. Whether this need amounts to such a crisis is, in my opinion, the issue framed for the department. If the lower structure at Bridge Canyon means a brake on the growth of the region, that is a price that must be weighed in the balance.[9]

The same day, Carver wrote the secretary, and urged Udall to consider the political ramifications of endorsing the high dam. Noting that the conservationists were still angry over Dinosaur and Rainbow Bridge, Carver argued that the conservationists would "mount the most vigorous and concerted campaign since Hetch Hetchy." As though environmentalist opposition were not enough, the assistant secretary also pointed out that the PSWP neglected to consider the position of the Native American tribes that would be affected by the proposal: sixty thousand acres of Hualapai and Navajo Reservation land would be flooded, and this did not include the Havasupai, who stood to lose a mile of the spectacular canyon they had lived in for hundreds of years. The south abutment of Bridge Canyon Dam and the east abutment of Marble Canyon Dam would have been located on Hualapai and Navajo land respectively (see map 4). Carver argued in practical terms, putting the aesthetic and

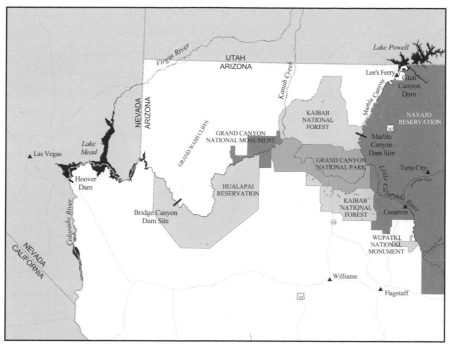

Map 4. Grand Canyon National Park and Monument and their relationship to the Hualapai and Navajo Reservations. Note the location of the Bridge and Marble Canyon dam sites. *(Map created by Gary Christopherson and Peter Johnson, Center for Applied Spatial Analysis, University of Arizona.)*

conservation factors aside; he believed that the secretary risked defeat if conservationists and Indians united against the dams, opposition that probably would not arise if Bridge Canyon Dam were just one hundred feet lower.[10]

National Park Service personnel also spoke out against the high dam. John S. McLaughlin, the superintendent of Grand Canyon National Park, blasted the proposed high dam in a December 1963 letter to the new Park Service director, George B. Hartzog Jr. McLaughlin lamented the loss of igneous geological features that would be inundated by Bridge Canyon reservoir: "to cover up a large part of this evidence of the Canyon's fiery past will obscure the primary interpretive story at Grand Canyon National Monument. Such volcanic activity did not occur in the park proper—if it is not preserved at Grand Canyon National Monument, it will not be preserved at all!" A few weeks later, McLaughlin wrote Hartzog again, citing evidence from an article written by Dr. Harold Myers, dean of the College of Agriculture at the University of

Arizona, who concluded that the PSWP would also be feasible with a low dam.[11]

Hartzog in turn, queried Interior Secretary Udall, asking for clarification as to whether a high dam was going to be included in the revised PSWP. The director also reminded the secretary that under the reclamation provision in the 1919 act, invasive projects could only be authorized "when consistent with the primary purposes of the park—that is, to not impair the scenic beauty." Hartzog argued further that during the 1930s, Park Service and Reclamation Bureau personnel discussed the Bridge Canyon project, and that all parties had only agreed to the construction of a low dam that would back water through the monument.[12] Though Udall did not respond immediately, the author of the Grand Canyon National Park Establishment Act did.

Carl Hayden, citing Park Service literature that endorsed the recreational values a high dam would create, wrote Hartzog on 19 February 1963 demanding a clarification of the agency's position. The next day, several newspapers published articles outlining the dispute, and soon afterward Park Superintendent McLaughlin issued orders to his staff at Grand Canyon that his and their official response would be "no comment" if reporters asked for an opinion. The final word on the Park Service's position was given by Assistant Secretary Carver who wrote the senator assuring him that the Interior Department favored the high dam and that: "The National Park Service, having discharged its responsibilities in advising the Secretary [of the Interior] as it saw fit, is now bound to the departmental position approved by the Secretary. I have every confidence that all of its actions will be in strict conformity with this decision." This correspondence with Hayden was distributed throughout the Park Service, eventually finding its way to McLaughlin and his staff. The secretary had now adopted the high Bridge Canyon Dam as official policy, and the Park Service director, having made his case, was now obligated to support Udall's decision as a matter of bureaucratic propriety. Never again, for the duration of the struggle, would the National Park Service oppose the high dam publicly.[13]

Leading preservationists, appalled at Director Hartzog's seeming acceptance of a Bureau reservoir in Grand Canyon National Park and Monument, quickly criticized Hartzog for failing to take a stronger stand. Relations between the Park Service and conservationists, which had been warm during Newton Drury's tenure and had grown tepid during Conrad Wirth's administration, largely because of his pro-development policies such as Mission 66 and the Tioga Road in Yosemite, degenerated further under Hartzog. Frosty exchanges permeated communications between Hartzog and David Brower, who developed what can only be described as a mutual dislike for one another. Brower, in a 1978 interview, gave this assessment of Hartzog: "He was always a hale and hearty man. He had a powerful handshake. He'd look you in the eye—and forget about wilderness." Hartzog, for his part also had strong feelings about Brower, stating later that "you were just a no good son of a bitch if you didn't agree with everything he said." Hartzog prided himself on his ability to compromise and work with people such as Dominy, whom others found difficult, and he realized that he was not the same caliber of preservationist as Drury. However, Drury was not a practical politician, and Director Hartzog believed that the PSWP required a pragmatic approach. Hartzog appreciated Udall's situation, and he recognized that the PSWP was going to include a dam at Bridge Canyon; he opposed the high dam as stridently as he believed it prudent to do so, but retreated because he did not desire to endanger other Park Service programs by being intransigent.[14]

Udall's attempts to find a politically practical solution placed him instead upon the horns of a difficult dilemma. If he favored the low dam, he would most certainly be faced with opposition from California, and possibly from Aspinall, who by now had become enamored of the possibility of water importation. If he chose the high-dam option, he was likely to be opposed by conservationists still smarting over the Rainbow Bridge and Glen Canyon fiascos, possibly united with Native Americans during a time of increasing public sensitivity to civil rights concerns. Director Hartzog did not envy Udall's position, and he recalled later that it was the "most painful decision that [he] ever witnessed the Secretary having to make."[15]

Having to decide upon the high dam as a matter of policy forced Udall to interpret the language in the establishment act and decide just what constituted an "interference" with the scenic beauty of the park. Clearly, in 1919 Senator Hayden believed that reservoirs and even dams within the park would not violate this provision, and in 1964 the senator still held the same position. Judging by the congressional and public support of the Hetch Hetchy reservoir despite John Muir's campaign against it, one would conclude a significant majority of politicians and the public agreed with Hayden in 1919. But by 1964, these perceptions had changed. Not even the Bureau of Reclamation proposed to construct dams within the park proper, and its intrusive MCKC project, although scorned by environmentalists and the Park Service, was actually an attempt to utilize efficiently the hydroelectric potential of the river's fall within the park boundaries without scarring the park with dams.[16]

The objections of conservationist organizations to the high dam had only surfaced recently, and many were still undecided; boating and fishing enthusiasts, for example, might welcome more desert reservoirs in the Colorado canyons. Even the Park Service, though it opposed the high dam, stated in its appendix to the PSWP that recreational benefits would accrue to the region, among them improved fishing and boating in a spectacular, "fjord-like setting," a relatively positive assessment.[17] Though many environmentalists use the word "conservationist" as a pejorative today, in 1964 the term as it was used commonly, was overarching enough to include disciples of Gifford Pinchot, such as Stewart Udall, as well as preservationists like David Brower and Anthony Smith.

In the spring of 1964, Udall realized he could no longer avoid making a decision, and he believed that a vast gulf existed between what the reclamation provision permitted and what the American public would accept. A narrow reservoir that raised the water level along thirteen miles of the park boundary in the most remote section of the park seemed a small price to pay when compared to the benefits that would accrue to the Pacific Southwest from the revenue generated from the dam. Ultimately, Udall chose the pragmatic route in both the court of public opinion and the political arena, and he believed most people would not view the small intrusion as damaging to the scenic beauty of Grand Canyon National Park. Politically, Udall was convinced that the support of California and Aspinall were indispensable if the project was to gain approval by the House, and that this support would overcome the potential opposition of conservationists and Native Americans. The secretary made his decision on the basis of that political reality—the final version of the Pacific Southwest Water Plan would include a high Bridge Canyon Dam, and he would now throw the weight of his department behind it to ensure the continued backing of California and Aspinall (fig. 3).

Conservationists felt betrayed by Udall's decision and intensified their opposition efforts against both dams. David Brower believed that it might be possible to attack the PSWP on legal grounds and asked Robert Jasperson of the Conservation Law Society to analyze this portion of the Grand Canyon

Figure 3. Interior Secretary Stewart Udall, second from right, unveils the massive Pacific Southwest Water Plan in January 1964. *Standing with Udall are from right to left:* Senator Carl Hayden, Udall, Representative Morris Udall of Arizona and Arizona Governor Sam Goddard. *Courtesy of Special Collections, The University of Arizona Library.*

National Park Act in the light of subsequent statutes: "Whenever consistent with the primary purpose of said park, the Secretary of the Interior is authorized to permit the utilization of areas therein which may be necessary for the development and maintenance of a government reclamation project." Jasperson based his analysis upon what he believed were the two most vulnerable sections of the provision: how courts had defined "necessary" park invasions for reclamation, and what Congress had meant by "consistent with the primary purposes" of the park. Jasperson found that even though the National Park Act of 1916 stipulated the primary purpose of the parks as meaning to leave them "unimpaired for the enjoyment of future generations," it did not appear as though Congress intended to conflate the term "unimpaired" with the term "untouched." Citing numerous park establishment acts that included similar reclamation provisions, and a 1935 opinion rendered by the Unit-

ed States attorney general, Jasperson concluded that the preservationists' argument—that the amended Federal Power Act of 1921 had superseded the reclamation provision—was invalid because Congress conferred "specific
authority" upon the secretary in the act of 1919—authority that was not
expressly overturned by the 1921 statute. Furthermore, he argued, even
though one federal court had distinguished between reclamation and
hydroprojects, the Bureau's policy of linking revenues from hydroelectric dams
such as those included in the PSWP, to irrigation diversions, made an attack
upon the high Bridge Canyon Dam based upon the contention that it was
not "necessary for reclamation," highly problematic.[18] Jasperson concluded
that prospects for mounting a successful legal challenge to the high dam
appeared remote at best.

Environmentalists began to formulate other strategies of opposition and
communicated with each other about coordinating their efforts. In addition
to the Sierra Club and the National Parks Association, the Western Federation
of Outdoor Clubs, composed of thirty-five thousand members of mostly small
western conservation organizations, adopted a resolution against the PSWP at
its Labor Day conference in 1963.[19] Now, at the March 1964 annual meeting
of the National Wildlife Federation (NWF), an organization with a total
membership of more than two million people, representatives of the Izaak
Walton League scheduled a special conclave to discuss the Grand Canyon situation. Leaders from prominent conservation associations attended, and Stewart Udall sent Henry Caulfield of the Interior Department's Resource Planning
Staff to try and convince these environmentalists how important the high
Bridge Canyon Dam was to gaining congressional approval of the PSWP. After
Caulfield's presentation, David Brower and Tony Smith stood up and rebutted
his statements, both leaders saying that their organizations would continue
their opposition. Smith also stated that the NPA had employed an expert in
resource management to formulate a plan based upon alternative energy
sources, and that study concluded that steam plants and atomic power constituted viable options. This PSWP alternative, Smith revealed, was scheduled for publication in a forthcoming issue of *National Parks Magazine*.[20]

Conservation organizations that favored the Grand Canyon dams also
used the National Wildlife Federation meeting as a forum to present a pro-dam
view. The Arizona Game and Fish Department (AZGF) launched a campaign extolling the recreational benefits that would result from the PSWP,

including the planned construction of fifty small reservoirs in Arizona alone, during its latter phases. The State of Arizona financed the Game and Fish Department offensive, designed to rebut the position taken by proponents of preservation at the NWF conference. The AZGF, supported by two Arizona conservation organizations, the Arizona Game Protective Association and the Arizona Council of Conservationists, proposed a series of "aerial safaris" over the sites of the proposed dams for the leaders of the national conservation organizations, to demonstrate that the high dam would not have a detrimental effect upon Grand Canyon National Park and Monument. Demand for the flights proved so overwhelming that Reclamation officials loaned the AZGF the Bureau's own airplane in addition to the plane the AZGF had chartered. AZGF officials tried to convince Governor Fannin that by emphasizing the recreational aspects of the PSWP it might well be possible to pose an effective counterargument to the preservationist opposition, one that might gain support among fish-and-wildlife-oriented organizations.[21]

The National Wildlife Federation constituted the largest conservation organization in the world in 1964, and its member organizations represented many different conservation viewpoints. Even more encouraging, from a pro-dam perspective, the NWF president, Thomas Kimball, had previously held posts in the state game and fish departments of both Arizona and Colorado and would probably be sympathetic to arguments based upon increased recreational benefits for hunters and fishers. By targeting the NWF, the AZGF, Interior Department, and other recreational enthusiasts hoped to prevent the National Wildlife Federation from joining with the Sierra Club, Izaak Walton League, and National Parks Association against the Grand Canyon dams as it had during the Echo Park controversy. If this strategy succeeded, it would isolate these smaller antidam organizations by portraying them as extremist in nature and suggest to both Congress and the public that their leaders did not speak for all conservationists. Indeed, the Sierra Club, the Izaak Walton League, the Wilderness Society, and the National Parks Association combined totaled only about 140,000 members, 50,000 of whom belonged to the Izaak Walton League, which itself was an advocate of sportfishing.[22] Thus, the supporters of the PSWP initiated a potentially devastating counterstrategy against the antidam organizations in the first quarter of 1964; by attempting to divide the conservationists themselves, proponents of the PSWP hoped to appeal to segments of the population that believed in balancing development and preservation who might be offended at the attempts of the antidam organizations to appropriate the term "conservationist" for their own use.

Proponents of the Grand Canyon dams pursued their objectives in the political arena in addition to rebutting the rhetoric of the preservationists. On 9 April 1964 Stewart Udall appeared before Senator Jackson's Interior Committee to give the Interior Department position during the latest round of CAP hearings on the Hayden-Goldwater CAP bill. Udall argued in favor of the regional plan and was subjected to intense questioning by Carl Hayden, who had recently accepted a position as a junior member of the committee to aid the CAP legislation. During the course of the hearings, Hayden congratulated Udall for proposing the regional approach, although he made it clear that he still sought the construction of the CAP first. However, the senator also endorsed the idea of a basin account along the lines of the PSWP development fund for the first time, one of the major points of disagreement between Udall and Hayden that had kept them from joining forces in the aftermath of the 1963 Supreme Court decision.[23]

Udall also described his dilemma in deciding between a high and low Bridge Canyon Dam to the committee, and in doing so, he echoed David Brower's arguments of the previous summer, in which Brower had urged Udall to allow Congress to decide the issue. Udall stated that although he favored the high dam for its revenue potential, and believed that the encroachment upon the park to be "peripheral," ultimately Congress must "balance scenic values against critical water needs." In framing his argument for the high dam, Udall argued that Congress had previously anticipated its construction by inserting the reclamation provision into the national park establishment act, and that the Park Service personnel who helped write President Hoover's December 1932 executive order proclaiming Grand Canyon National Monument, had acquiesced to the construction of either "a high or a low dam" that would, at the very least, create a reservoir in the national monument. To support this contention, Udall cited the letter from Park Service Director Horace Albright to Reclamation Commissioner Dr. Elwood Mead in which Albright assented to the construction of Bridge Canyon Dam in January of 1933.[24]

However, it appears as though the secretary used this evidence out of context, for if one examines the documentary record, it becomes clear that Albright and Mead only agreed upon a structure that would encroach upon the monument—a low dam. That a low dam would not affect the park was a common understanding among dam advocates and opponents alike since the first CAP debates of the late 1940s, and this meaning was reaffirmed within the language of the PSWP itself. Although Udall's assertion that the Park Service had agreed to the construction of a high dam was incorrect, it nevertheless had the potential to sway congressional opinion. Director Albright recognized this in his January 1933 letter when he stated that the secretary's approval of the Bridge Canyon project would carry with it the weight of both the Park Service and the Reclamation Bureau. Shortly thereafter, Albright took a definitive position against the high dam the following February when he wrote that the Park Service did not intend to "interfere with the Reclamation Service's work on the Colorado River *west* of Grand Canyon National Park" (Emphasis mine). At no time did he agree to the invasion of the park, and the increased invasion of the monument, that a high dam would cause.[25]

Subsequent memoranda written during the late 1930s reveal that even Bureau officials refrained from seeking a dam that would encroach upon the park, a position the agency did not repudiate until it included a high dam in the CAP report of 1944. The secretary did not inform the committee that the Park Service had long opposed a high dam, yet a reading of the testimony suggests that Udall invoked the Albright-Mead correspondence in an attempt to show that the Park Service approved of the construction of a dam of either height. When the correspondence between Mead and Albright is read in its entirety, it is clear that Director Albright and Commissioner Mead only agreed upon a low dam that would invade the monument, and never discussed the possibility of constructing a high dam.[26] The committee adjourned after two days of testimony and planned to debate whether to report the bill to the floor in the summer of 1964.

The secretary had also forwarded the PSWP to the Bureau of the Budget in January of 1964. The Budget Bureau completed its analysis by April, and the news was not promising from Udall's perspective. Budget Director Elmer Staats reported that the Department of the Army objected to the importation studies because the rivers of northern California lay within the purview of the Army Corps of Engineers, which had already obtained congressional authorization to study the potential utilization of these watersheds. Staats was even more concerned about a provision Udall had included at the behest of California, which guaranteed that the consumer cost of future water imports into the Colorado River would not exceed the cost of water already available in the river, the difference to be subsidized by the federal government. Staats also voiced concerns that the drafters of the PSWP had not adequately studied alternative proposals to the high Bridge Canyon Dam as a means to avoid conflict with preservationists. But the most difficult question the Budget Bureau raised was that of necessity. Noting that future lower-basin water shortfalls would be caused by the construction of new projects in the upper basin, particularly in Colorado, Director Staats questioned the desirability of expanding irrigated agriculture in the upper basin at a time when the nation produced annual agricultural surpluses of 8–9 percent, and he recommended that the Interior Department "take the lead" in creating a task force to study the problem.[27]

Staats's pronouncement constituted a bombshell of the highest magnitude for CAP proponents, for to question the efficacy of Colorado's irrigated agriculture would not only assure the undying enmity of Chairman Aspinall, but would open the CAP to the same type of criticism. Udall and other western politicians attempted to steer clear of the Budget Bureau's recommendation, and they appealed to President Johnson to help break the bill loose, but during this election year, LBJ refused adamantly. Carl Hayden made a personal appeal to the president, but even that was not enough to get Johnson to endorse the bill. Stewart Udall later reflected that he believed Johnson viewed the Pacific Southwest water controversy as a "sticky tar baby out there that Udall was struggling with," and that LBJ hoped that the situation would not harm him politically.[28]

When the Senate Interior Committee reconvened in the summer of 1964, its members debated three amendments to Hayden's bill that would prove crucial to the next four years of debate over the CAP in any form. Senator Hayden now approved the secretary's idea of establishing a development account and inserted it into the legislation without opposition. In addition, Carl Hayden and California Senator Thomas Kuchel had been negotiating behind the scenes about prioritizing the water rights among the lower-basin states. Kuchel had taken a proposal, first advanced by water attorney Northcutt Ely in 1961, that California would support the CAP only if its own 4.4 million acre feet per year allotment was granted priority. Hayden balked initially, but the secret negotiations continued and by the summer of 1964 they had entered a critical phase, for Hayden now seemed amenable to a California guarantee in some form. Utah Senator Frank Moss proposed an amendment assigning first priority to California's 4.4 million allocation for twenty-five years, after which enough water would be imported into the basin to make the priority unnecessary. Hayden and California Governor Brown accepted the provision and the committee voted to include the amendment, the only dissent coming from Kuchel, who sought a guarantee in perpetuity.[29] The California guarantee, as it later came to be called, would resurface during the months and years of negotiations ahead.

Senator Henry Jackson also inserted an amendment into the bill limiting the water augmentation studies to potential water sources in California, putting all parties on notice as to his stance on a possible diversion from the Pacific Northwest. Even though the Hayden bill and the PSWP did not broach the subject of a diversion from the Columbia or Snake Rivers, Jackson suspected that Bureau personnel were considering the idea. At Jackson's prodding, the Senate Interior Committee approved the amendment and, on 31 July reported the bill, now called the Lower Colorado River Basin Project Act, favorably to the floor. California Governor Brown immediately withdrew his support for the measure in the wake of Jackson's amendment.[30]

Hayden understood that without the support of the president, the bill could not run the gauntlet of a Senate floor debate in the brief time remaining before the 1964 elections, and so Hayden advised Arizona water leaders to look ahead to 1965, when, he felt, real progress could be made.[31] From the interior secretary's perspective, the 1964 congressional session yielded mixed results. Perhaps most important, Udall had convinced Senator Hayden to add some regional elements to his CAP measure, including the vital development fund, creating the possibility of a future alliance. Hayden aside, Udall realized that after a year and a half of negotiations, his attempt to implement a regional water plan had become entangled in the morass of presidential politics and continued bickering among the various water interests of the lower basin. Despite some encouraging progress, Udall knew Chairman Aspinall's grand accord had not yet materialized, and that all congressional debate over the CAP and the PSWP would remain at a standstill until Congress reconvened in 1965.

The National Parks Association published its study of alternatives to the PSWP in April of 1964. Stephen Raushenbush, an expert in natural resources management, predicated his study upon the assumption that alternative energy sources such as hydrogen fusion would soon be available, according to many leading scientists. "It [fusion] is expected to separate out the salts and minerals in a flash, producing vast amounts of completely fresh water and energy at the same time, both at very low costs indeed," Raushenbush wrote optimistically. He also proposed that in the event scientists could not perfect fusion, the fossil fuel resources of the Four Corners region or atomic fission plants should be utilized instead. Manipulating the PSWP figures, Raushenbush argued the proposal was feasible without the Bridge Canyon Dam, that Marble Canyon Dam alone could provide enough pumping power, and by altering the scale and order of the construction of the projects included within the plan, a development fund could still be created.[32]

Anthony Smith also wrote, in his introduction to Raushenbush's proposal, that Bridge Canyon Dam must be stopped because it would open the way to either the construction of dams in the park itself, or the MCKC project. Smith, as he had done previously, argued that the controversy would evoke a great reaction from the American public. However, nowhere did he exhort people to write their congressional representatives or take any action to precipitate this reaction. Carefully tiptoeing close to but not across the IRS line of permissible behavior, Smith emphasized that the NPA existed "strictly for educational and scientific" purposes, and that the proposed alternatives were simply in the furtherance of those objectives.[33] By enlisting an expert to formulate alternatives to Bridge Canyon Dam, the NPA became the first conservation organization to propose an alternative plan based upon quantifiable data. However, the NPA refused to join the Sierra Club in trying to foster a public outcry against Bridge Canyon Dam, and it limited its defense of the canyon to that portion already within the jurisdiction of the National Park Service. Indeed, Marble Canyon Dam, upstream of the park and monument, would constitute the major source of power generation for the Raushenbush proposal until other sources of electricity could be brought on line.

As other organizations debated strategy, the Sierra Club began to enlarge its role in enlisting public support for the fight against the Grand Canyon dams. In February David Brower created a special "Grand Canyon Task Force" to coordinate the Sierra Club's efforts, and he also proposed that the club publish a new exhibit book similar to *The Place No One Knew* to be used in the campaign. The task force consisted of conservationists such as hydrologist Luna Leopold, who began to funnel technical data secretly from the USGS for Brower and others to use against the Bureau. The planned book moved forward as well. All during the spring and summer of 1964, writer Francois Leydet, Sierra Club board member Martin Litton, and others rafted, hiked, and camped in Grand Canyon, taking photos and gathering information for the Sierra Club's latest publication, while Brower and his associates prepared to engage the dam proponents in what Brower accurately forecast would be the major environmental battle of the sixties, "one requiring that all conservationists keep themselves informed and militant."[34]

In early November the book was completed, and the club released it under the title *Time and the River Flowing*. Its format was similar to that of *The Place No One Knew*, and it featured stunning photos of Grand Canyon, including some rare color work by famed black-and-white photographer Ansel Adams. Brower wrote the foreword, and he argued that with alternative energy sources such as atomic power and fossil fuel available, it was not necessary for the Bureau to create reservoirs that would increase salinity through evaporation and decrease the total amount of water available for downstream uses. With these energy sources just over the horizon, why destroy a significant stretch of the free-flowing Colorado in Grand Canyon? The club intended *Time and the River Flowing* to be a tool to sway public opinion while the issue was still in doubt rather than a pictorial record of what would be lost. In addition to this book, Brower's Grand Canyon Task Force also began to develop traveling photo exhibits and a movie about Grand Canyon, budgeted enough copies of *Time and the River Flowing* for every member of Congress, and dusted off a film entitled *Two Yosemites* that Howard Zahniser had used effectively during the Echo Park campaign.[35] *Two Yosemites* offered striking footage of Hetch Hetchy before and after the construction of the dam, and the effects reservoir fluctuations had upon the landscape, an effective pictorial rebuttal of the Bureau's claim that a reservoir would enhance the beauty of the Canyon.

One member of the Sierra Club Grand Canyon Task Force, a tenacious physics professor at Colorado College, Dr. Richard Bradley, decided to take on Floyd Dominy himself. Bradley hailed from a large family of western river and outdoor enthusiasts who played an important role during the Echo Park controversy. His father, Harold Bradley, who became president of the Sierra Club in the late 1950s, took the family on rafting trips down the Green River and filmed his sons as they shot the rapids. In so doing, Bradley exploded the myth advanced by the Bureau that river running was a hazardous undertaking, and his film helped publicize the sport for a generation of Americans taking to the outdoors in the postwar period. Richard and his brother David had also testified in opposition to the Echo Park dams during the CRSP hearings, attacking the Bureau on both technical and aesthetic grounds.[36]

Richard Bradley's involvement in the Grand Canyon campaign started innocuously enough when he delivered a lecture in opposition to the PSWP during a campus guest speaker series at Colorado College in early September of 1964. In his speech, Bradley told the story of the triumph at Echo Park, the loss of Glen Canyon, and concluded with a discussion of the dams now proposed for Grand Canyon. The speech condemned the Bureau's Grand Canyon proposal as an exercise in self-perpetuation that was totally unnecessary in the light of alternative energy sources, including thermal and nuclear power, that could generate electricity less expensively than the proposed dams. Professor Bradley urged his audience to break this cycle, and he blasted the Interior Department's policy of imposing its will upon its subagencies, declaring that as with Echo Park and Glen Canyon, "once again we find the Park Service pathetically silent, unable to speak in its own defense."[37]

The *Denver Post* picked up the story, and soon Bradley received a letter from none other than Commissioner Dominy himself, in which Dominy not only countered his arguments, but disparaged him personally, accusing Bradley of "hoodwink[ing]" his audience. Dominy's letter also received play in the *Post*, and Bradley became embroiled in a letter exchange with the pugnacious commissioner. Bradley soon received another reply from Dominy that emphasized the necessity of hydropower for peaking purposes without refuting Bradley's contention that other forms of energy currently available were cheaper to produce. Acting on confidential advice from hydrologist Luna Leopold, Bradley then wrote to Representative John Saylor of Pennsylvania, a strong conservation advocate, about the possibility of forcing the Bureau to do cost comparisons between hydro and other forms of energy.[38]

The Sierra Club printed Bradley's lecture in the December issue of the *Sierra Club Bulletin*. Bradley also wrote an article for the December issue of the Wilderness Society Publication, *Living Wilderness*, in which he questioned the dams' necessity by quoting a provision within the PSWP itself, which stated that the power produced by Bridge and Marble Canyon Dams would "provide only a small increment of the projected future demand of the area.... The major portion of the future electrical energy demand of the area in the

Pacific Southwest will be generated by thermo-electric plants....Reserves of fossil fuels are more than adequate to meet foreseeable power needs." After citing this language Bradley then questioned why, with the availability of feasible alternative energy sources, the Interior Department insisted upon desecrating an area of such scenic grandeur to produce a relatively small amount of power? The Interior Department's own office of Science and Technology estimated that within ten years nuclear power plants would be able to produce electricity for about 40 percent the cost of hydropower, while Senator Clinton Anderson of New Mexico argued that coal-fired steam plants in the Four Corners region could produce power for two-thirds the cost of additional hydropower immediately. Bradley called for an extensive letter-writing campaign of "one million letters to congressmen," stating that only an "aroused public" can save the Canyon from destruction.[39] By publishing Bradley's article, the Wilderness Society had now joined with the Sierra Club in trying to foster a national outcry against the dams and became the second national conservation organization to challenge the IRS regulations against influencing legislation.

There were, however, few regulations preventing legislators themselves from attempting to influence other members of Congress. In November, the Arizona congressional delegation and the Central Arizona Project Association (CAPA) held a carefully orchestrated series of "field" hearings and social functions for members of the House Interior and Insular Affairs Committee, the primary purpose of which was to "impress the Committee," in the words of Arizona representative John Rhodes. Interior Committee staff member Sidney McFarland stipulated that no Californians would be allowed to testify and that adverse witnesses would be limited to water interests from within the state of Arizona who felt they had been left out of the plan. No conservationists were invited. Meals and lodging were provided at Phoenix's finest restaurants and hotels with a minimal charge to the committee members, while CAPA footed the rest of the bill, in order to give them "the full Arizona red-carpet treatment." After excursions that included opportunities for the committee members' wives to go shopping in Scottsdale, the grand finale consisted of an aerial tour of Lake Powell and the Bridge and Marble Canyon Dam sites, followed by a stop in Florence, where members viewed land that had gone out of cultivation owing to a depletion of groundwater.[40]

As Arizona water interests sought to sway the House Interior Committee, the Interior Department, just as it had during the Echo Park controversy, tried to influence public opinion with publications of its own. In late 1964 it issued a pamphlet entitled, *Bridge and Marble Canyon Dams and Their Relation to Grand Canyon National Park and Monument*, which attempted to justify the inundation of almost half of the unregulated Colorado through the canyon, including Lava Falls, its most spectacular whitewater. Referring to river running, it stated that "Below Kanab Creek, this recreational opportunity would be replaced by the usual reservoir boating type of experience." As for the dams themselves, the pamphlet articulated the department's position as favoring the regional and national economic opportunities the dams would create over the "impact on the scenic grandeur of the Grand Canyon."[41] Floyd Dominy, a skilled photographer, was also in the process of creating a publication along the lines of the Sierra Club books that he planned to release in early 1965.

Unbeknownst to Richard Bradley, Anthony Smith, and possibly even Luna Leopold, Interior Secretary Udall had charged the assistant secretary for Water and Power, Kenneth Holum, with the task of studying comparisons between hydropower and alternative energy and water sources. An April report from the department's science advisor, John C. Calhoun Jr., suggested that the technology for large-scale nuclear desalinization plants had advanced to the point that it might soon be feasible to construct facilities that could produce power and fresh water at rates competitive with water importation and hydropower plants. As a result Holum created a task force to initiate in-depth studies of desalinization that included Reclamation Commissioner Floyd Dominy and personnel from the Atomic Energy Commission. New Budget Bureau director Kermit Gordon, whose agency had stymied the PSWP over this very issue in April, directed Holum to initiate economic studies to determine whether desalinization might constitute the most economical water source for the Pacific Southwest.[42]

In December, with the preliminary studies complete, Holum wrote Stewart Udall and told him that the task force had completed a cost comparison of desalinization and the importation of fifteen million acre feet of water from the Columbia River, and had concluded that desalting constituted the cheapest method by which to augment the water supply of the Colorado. Holum's figures are indicative of the faith that Interior personnel had in technological solutions, optimism that had been reinforced by pronouncements from the scientific community; they also reveal that the Bureau of Reclamation had conducted studies of importations from the Columbia River without consulting Senator Jackson. Holum wrote Jackson to assure the Washington solon that the Interior Department was "plan[ning] no project," a move designed to soothe Jackson's fears that the Southwest sought to steal some of his constituents' water. Whether it had this effect is a matter for debate, but it certainly put Jackson on notice that stronger measures than a mere amendment to the CAP bill would have to be taken if he hoped to stop studies of water augmentation from the Columbia River.[43]

Despite Holum's attempt to reassure Jackson, there is strong evidence to suggest that the Bureau's studies of a Pacific Northwest importation were much more than just a hypothetical alternative to desalinization. In early December, Secretary Udall flew to Los Angeles for a series of confidential meetings to discuss the PSWP with California politicians and water officials in order to bolster California support, which had waned following Senator Jackson's amendment to Carl Hayden's 1964 CAP bill. During a meeting with Governor Brown, California officials rebuffed Udall's suggestion that water could be salvaged by phreatophyte control and lining canals with concrete but expressed continued enthusiasm for a regional plan that provided for the importation of water from outside the Colorado basin.[44]

Udall then met with representatives of the Metropolitan Water District of Southern California (MWD), as well as Otis Chandler, publisher of the *Los Angeles Times*. Joe Jensen of the MWD argued optimistically that "only the question of accepting a substitute for the twenty-five year guarantee of 4.4 million acre feet separates Arizona and California." Knowing that sufficient basin augmentation would render the 4.4 million guarantee relatively meaningless, Udall had brought Commissioner Dominy along to discuss a plan that the Bureau of Reclamation had been studying secretly since mid-November—the importation of 10–15 million acre feet of water from the Columbia River, a proposal that would "cost billions of dollars" in Udall's estimation. California congressman Chet Holifeld stated that California must be protected by the authorization of "the entire project," and that support would only be forthcoming if the importation feature was supported by a feasibility-grade study, certified by the interior secretary. Udall reemphasized that this Columbia River water would be made available "at the present price of Colorado River water," the difference to be subsidized by the "first power revenues" generated by

Bridge and Marble Canyon dams. Senator Jackson's probable opposition was noted, and Udall replied that he hoped to entice Henry Jackson with the offer of a "stepped up reclamation program" for the state of Washington to coun-teract the scheduled closure of several important federal installations there.[45] Udall left California convinced that he was close to working out a compro-mise to gain California's support—and it appeared that he had, provided he could persuade Senator Jackson to go along.

During 1964 the advocates of dams in Grand Canyon as well as their opponents formulated and implemented the strategies that they would follow for the length of the campaign. The preservationists abandoned legal chal-lenges except, perhaps, for rhetorical purposes, and began to focus instead upon questioning the figures that the Bureau used to justify the projects; they also instigated public appeals and suggested alternative means of power gen-eration reliant upon either existing coal deposits or technological solutions that appeared to be just over the horizon. With membership in most conser-vation organizations growing and public environmental awareness increasing as a result of the recent passage of the Wilderness Bill and the publication of Rachel Carson's *Silent Spring*, in 1962, leading environmental advocates believed that the prospects for precipitating a public outcry against the dams looked promising in December of 1964.

The dam proponents could also point to some gains as well. Although the CAP bill appeared stymied by the Bureau of the Budget and had not received President Johnson's endorsement, Carl Hayden and Stewart Udall had joined forces and the senator was now convinced that the best chance for the CAP lay in a regional solution. Technological solutions to many of the Southwest's water problems now appeared to be within reach, and agencies within the Inte-rior Department worked frantically to attain them.

Finally, and perhaps most important of all, California and Arizona appeared, at last, to be on the brink of the agreement that Stewart Udall had worked so long to obtain, raising the possibility that the roadblock the House of Representatives had posed to the CAP for almost two decades might be overcome. However, this agreement rested upon future water importation; now all eyes turned toward the enormous water resources of the Pacific North-west. Although Henry Jackson, chairman of the Senate Interior Committee, had objected previously to proposals to divert water from the Columbia River, the interior secretary believed that Jackson would change his mind when presented with a proposal that promised economic benefits for his own con-stituents. Surely, Udall believed, with the Columbia River discharging an average of 140 million acre-feet each year into the Pacific Ocean, he could persuade Jackson and other politicians from the states of Washington and Oregon to grant one tenth of that amount to their thirsty neighbors to the south.

4

"Grand Canyon,
Armageddon"

[T]he most sublime truth is that one need not actually
see it physically, or hear it or touch it or grasp it to know
its fundamental value.

—Thomas Dustin, Izaak Walton League,
in a letter to David Brower, 1965

A s the decade of the 1960s reached its halfway mark, the United States
of America was a nation in turmoil. Social anxieties, long repressed as
a result of cold war ideology, McCarthy-era paranoia, and America's
latent racism, had by 1965 emerged to the forefront of American political and
social thought. In the aftermath of the 1954 Supreme Court decision in *Brown
v Board of Education*, African Americans, inspired by the nonviolent example of
Martin Luther King Jr., claimed their rights of citizenship, and in August of
1963, Americans of all races descended upon the capital itself, where, on the
steps of the Lincoln Memorial, Dr. King called upon all Americans to put their
hatreds aside and accept one another as human beings untarnished by the artificial barriers of skin color and archaic prejudices. President John Kennedy
called for a nation where the rights and privileges of citizenship would accrue
to people of all colors, and after his death, Lyndon Johnson continued JFK's
program and pushed for the passage of landmark civil rights legislation in Congress. The issue of civil rights burned brightly in January of 1965 and served
as a catalyst for other social impulses that would also transform America during the rest of the decade.

The concern over civil rights precipitated anxieties over civil liberties such as freedom of speech and expression. In the autumn of 1964, a student radical who had participated in the "Freedom Summer" of 1964, Mario Savio, and others who had marched in local civil rights demonstrations, protested what they perceived to be arbitrary limits upon the free speech rights of students at the University of California at Berkeley. The situation smoldered for two months, finally igniting into a mass protest that resulted in a student takeover of the campus administration offices and hundreds of arrests, including that of Terry Sumner, a close friend of the Brower family. Other student groups followed suit around the country, beginning in January of 1965, protesting a wide range of issues related to free speech and expression. Student protests also precipitated another movement in the spring of 1965, one that would come to dominate the rest of the decade and create the gravest divisions within American society since the Civil War: the antiwar movement.[1]

Citizens who demonstrated against American military involvement in Vietnam would soon have civil liberties concerns of their own, as the government began cracking down on the protests. The antiwar movement would, in turn, fuel public concerns about First Amendment rights for the rest of the decade, culminating in the landmark Supreme Court holdings in *Brandenburg v Ohio*, in 1969, in which the Court upheld the rights of individuals to engage in speech and expression, which, though perhaps repugnant to the majority of Americans, were protected by the First Amendment so long as the speech or conduct did not have a likely chance of inciting lawless behavior; and in *New York Times v United States* (1971), which upheld the right of the *New York Times* to publish excerpts from the Pentagon Papers.[2]

By 1965, important publications such as Stewart Udall's *The Quiet Crisis*, Udall's own public involvement in outdoor activities, the passage of the Wilderness Bill, and Lady Bird Johnson's beautification campaign had also increased public awareness of environmental issues. Arguably the most important event was the publication of Rachel Carson's *Silent Spring*, in which the soft-spoken marine biologist warned of the hazards of pesticide and herbicide usage, consequences that, because of humanity's position at the top of the food chain, were inescapable. Carson's book, as well as efforts to counter her arguments made by the chemical industry and scientific community, brought the message home to millions of people that these environmental concerns affected them personally. Individuals who did not care if a slick-rock wilderness in a remote part of Utah became a part of the National Park System became quite concerned when contaminated food and water endangered their own health.[3]

As 1965 began, the American public wrestled with issues that it had only recently begun to confront, issues in political, social, legal, and environmental philosophy that would change, perhaps irreversibly, how many people viewed their government and its institutions, as well as their corporate society. Americans looked to science and technology as offering solutions for many of these concerns, and by 1965 both proponents and opponents of dams in Grand Canyon had appealed to public support on the basis of scientific solutions. The Grand Canyon dam controversy reached its apogee during this turbulent period, and one must remain aware of the broader social currents of the times in order to place the struggle over Grand Canyon into its proper social and political context. The social issues of the mid 1960s would play an important role in deciding both the outcome of the debate and the lasting impressions it would leave on American society.

Stewart Udall conceived of the Pacific Southwest Water Plan (PSWP) as a technological solution to political and environmental constraints. In 1963, Udall introduced it as a radical attempt to break the political deadlock in the House of Representatives, which, he believed, had thwarted Arizona's previous efforts to construct the Central Arizona Project (CAP) since the late 1940s. Now, one and a half years after the Supreme Court of the United States had adjudicated the water rights of the lower basin, Udall appeared to be on the brink of success, for despite the battering he had taken in the Arizona press and accusations of favoring California leveled by Carl Hayden, Governor Fannin, and other Arizona water officials, Udall returned to Washington in late December of 1964 with something that no one else had ever accomplished: a commitment of support for the CAP from California's water leaders. Ebullient about the chances of obtaining congressional passage of the regional proposal, and perhaps about his own place in history, Udall, along with Commissioner Dominy, each began to publicize that the water crisis of the Southwest was on the brink of being solved. In December of 1964, both officials stated publicly that the importation of water from the Columbia River would provide enough water to ensure that future projects would not create shortages in the lower Colorado River Basin. Udall's staff cautioned him to refrain from speaking about the Columbia diversion, fearing that it would antagonize the powerful chairman of the Senate Interior Committee, Henry Jackson, a prophecy borne out when Jackson returned to Congress in January of 1965, irritated over Udall's designs upon the water resources of the Pacific Northwest.[4]

Despite Jackson's uneasiness over the possibility of water importation from the Columbia River, the Arizona-California negotiations began to bear fruit when Congress reconvened in early January. On 6 January 1965 Senators Hayden of Arizona and Kuchel of California each introduced new CAP bills in the Senate. Additionally, Representative Craig Hosmer of California, an outspoken opponent of the CAP since his election to Congress in the early 1950s, introduced a bill identical to Kuchel's in the House on 11 January. Rich Johnson, of the Central Arizona Project Association, wrote: "The unbelievable had happened. There were California bills before the Congress which proposed authorization of the Central Arizona Project after more than 20 years of uncompromising opposition in the Congress and the Court." Differences remained between the Hayden and Kuchel proposals, most notably, Kuchel's inclusion of a provision granting California's 4.4 million acre feet priority over Arizona's CAP interest in perpetuity—the California guarantee—while in deference to Jackson, neither bill mentioned the Pacific Northwest as a possible source for water importation.[5]

The Hayden and Kuchel bills included aspects of Udall's PSWP, and both bills were regional in concept. Hayden and Kuchel continued to negotiate, and on 1 February 1965 Hayden agreed to give California priority, with one condition—that the bill must first pass the House of Representatives, forcing California's congressional delegation to support the CAP, something it had never done. Kuchel agreed and incorporated the compromise into his bill, which he amended on 8 February 1965. That same day, thirty-five of California's congressmen introduced identical bills calling for the construction of a "Lower Colorado River Basin Project" in the House, clearing the way for the arduous process of congressional debate.[6] Wayne Aspinall's insistence upon cooperation had paid handsome dividends to the water and power interests; it finally appeared that some significant progress could be made. Stewart Udall's Pacific Southwest Water Plan had metamorphosed into a project that had gained the support of California, attaining, finally, his objective for proposing a regional plan.

While these political maneuvers were occurring, the Interior Department moved to counter the Sierra Club's exhibit book series with a pictorial effort of its own, and in early 1965 it released a slick twenty-eight page publication, photographed and written mostly by Reclamation Commissioner Floyd Dominy (fig. 4), entitled *Lake Powell: Jewel of the Colorado*. Though perhaps not at the level of the Sierra Club exhibit series, *Lake Powell: Jewel of the Colorado* compared favorably with magazines such as *Arizona Highways* in terms of photographic quality. Dominy and his associates captured with their cameras the reservoir in its setting of spectacular red and orange sandstone cliffs, and these pictures underscored the argument advanced by proponents of recreation that in some instances, it was possible to improve upon nature. Dominy also composed brief verses as captions, suggestive of the Sierra Club publications, and these pieces of poetry have entered the lore of environmental history as some of the most reviled writing ever set down, from an environmentalist's perspective. Personifying the Colorado River, Dominy penned:

> To the sea my waters wasted
> While the lands cried out for moisture
> Now Man [sic] controls me
> Stores me, regulates my flow.

Though *Lake Powell: Jewel of the Colorado* was mostly a celebration of Lake Powell, the commissioner turned his thoughts from Glen to Grand Canyon in the last two pages of the magazine, and he stated clearly the purpose for Bridge and Marble Canyon Dams: "These dams are cash registers. They will ring up sales of electric power produced by Colorado River water." He then advocated the superiority of hydroelectric energy over other potential alternatives sources because of its usefulness as peaking power, and he also argued that the dams would have little effect upon Grand Canyon National Park and Monument.[7]

Though repugnant to environmentalists, this publication constituted an effective counterargument for the Interior Department, which was beginning to receive mail from concerned citizens opposed to the dams. *Lake Powell: Jewel of the Colorado* presented the reservoir as a paradise for people who loved outdoor recreation, set in the incomparable scenery of what remained of Glen Canyon. Millions of Americans, enjoying the prosperity of the early 1960s, engaged in boating, water skiing, and fishing during their spare time, and visitor totals at Lake Powell had increased exponentially since Bureau personnel closed the gates of Glen Canyon Dam in the winter of 1963.[8] This publication promised more of the same recreational opportunities in Grand Canyon, in

Figure 4. Floyd Dominy, commissioner of the Bureau of Reclamation, dam builder extrordinaire and archnemesis of environmentalists opposed to the Grand Canyon dams. *Courtesy of the American Heritage Center, University of Wyoming.*

what Interior Department officials described as a "fiord-like" setting, an expression that originated within the National Park Service during the 1950s.[9] The Interior Department distributed copies of Lake Powell: Jewel of the Colorado, to members of Congress and prominent newspaper editors, and the Central Arizona Project Association also began to distribute it in Arizona.

Perhaps the best articulation of the Interior Department argument in favor of the recreational benefits created by the Bureau's dams is captured in this short verse Floyd Dominy wrote for the inside front cover of Lake Powell: Jewel of the Colorado:

> Dear God
> Did you cast down 200 miles of canyon and mark:
> 'for poets only?'
> Multitudes hunger for a lake in the sun.

In this and other pronouncements, Dominy and other advocates of the CAP hoped to portray environmentalists who sought to preserve Grand Canyon as elitist, selfish people who wanted to lock up the West's public lands for themselves. These arguments of elitism would increase as the year wore on, as Bureau officials cited official Park Service figures showing that only a few hundred people had ever seen the reach of the lower canyon that Bridge Canyon Reservoir would make accessible—people who either possessed the money to pay for an expensive rafting trip or were blessed with the physical stamina to hike to this remote area. By contrast, Glen Canyon Dam had created a recreational paradise enjoyed by millions and a water highway that ordinary Americans could travel and view the wonders of the canyon country of the Colorado Plateau, including Rainbow Bridge. The CAP dams would open up previously inaccessible portions of Grand Canyon to millions more. Interior Department officials and other proponents of the CAP would direct charges of elitism at preservationists for the remainder of the controversy, forcing environmentalists like David Brower (fig. 5) and Richard Bradley to adopt arguments designed to appeal to a mass audience.

The Sierra Club and other environmental groups arranged for their leaders to speak to local conservation organizations across the nation, along with local chapters of women's clubs and garden clubs. Opponents of the dams also circulated traveling exhibits of canyon photos and Time and the River Flowing, which had received a favorable review in the New York Times. Indeed,

Figure 5. David Brower, executive director of the Sierra Club, contemplates mud deposits at the headwaters of Lake Mead. The Sierra Club argued that the Bridge/Hualapai and Marble Canyon dams would create similar destruction upstream. *Courtesy of the Bancroft Library, University of California, Berkeley.*

the antidam efforts of the preservationists had begun to receive favorable coverage in the *Times*, largely through the efforts of John Oakes, its chief editor and a Sierra Club board member. In spring of 1965 other national publications began to carry occasional coverage of the controversy from a perspective favorable to the preservationists; Richard Bradley managed to convince the editors of *Life Magazine* to print an antidam editorial, and *Fortune Magazine* also carried a brief essay about the controversy. The leaders of seven major conservation organizations, including the Wilderness Society, Sierra Club, and Audubon Society, were so pleased by the "fair and factual" nature of the *Fortune* article that they ordered over ninety thousand reprints and sent them to their members and other interested parties. However, as promising as these developments were, the *Life* and *Fortune* articles were only a page or two in length, not long enough, preservationists believed, to state effectively the arguments against the dams.[10]

With the exception of the short *Life* and *Fortune* pieces, and occasional articles in the *New York Times*, the conservationists had not succeeded in obtaining national exposure. Environmental leaders such as Richard Bradley, who had written an article published in *Living Wilderness*, became alarmed that so few people seemed to know that the latest Colorado River dams were planned for Grand Canyon. Bradley believed that the proponents of the dams had intentionally omitted the words "Grand Canyon" from publicity favoring the CAP in an attempt to preclude people from associating it with possible intrusions into Grand Canyon. Indeed, the Central Arizona Project Association sponsored a symposium at Arizona State University in the summer of 1964 called "Project Rescue" and released a publication derived from this conclave devoted entirely to the CAP without once mentioning Grand Canyon, even though it contained a large map of the affected area. Likewise, none of the bills brought before the House in the spring of 1965 mentioned the words "Grand Canyon." To Richard Bradley and other opponents of the dams these and other omissions were evidence of "political skullduggery," and they believed that only through national publicity would the American people understand what was at stake. In an attempt to present the threats to Grand Canyon to the American public, Richard Bradley and his brother David began corresponding with the editors of *Atlantic Monthly*, a magazine with millions of subscribers throughout the United States, hoping that they could convince them to publish an in-depth discussion of the controversy.[11]

In the spring of 1965, the Sierra Club printed another exhortation written by Brower in the February issue of the *Sierra Club Bulletin*. The article outlined the strategy of the Grand Canyon Task Force, reemphasized the technical and aesthetic arguments against the dams, and concluded with a plea for members to join the campaign to protect Grand Canyon. One person who responded was Alan Carlin, an economist with the RAND Corporation, a Southern California think tank, with a doctorate in economics from the Massachusetts Institute of Technology. Carlin informed Brower that he specialized in irrigation project analysis and knew of studies that RAND engineers had conducted in 1958 showing that the cost-benefit analysis formula the Bureau had used to gain congressional approval of its projects for decades was invalid. Brower needed this type of expertise to combat the Bureau experts who would testify before the House and Senate Interior Committees, and he asked Carlin for his help. Carlin became the first of three experts holding degrees from MIT on whom the antidam advocates would rely to rebut the technical arguments put forth by those in support of the projects. The other two were Lawrence Moss, a nuclear engineer, and Jeffrey Ingram, a mathematician, and together with Carlin, they made up what Brower would later call his "MIT trio."[12]

While environmentalists scrambled to mount their antidam campaign, the interior secretary engaged in an ongoing struggle with the Bureau of the Budget. In November of 1964 Budget Bureau Director Elmer Staats met with Udall's assistant secretary for Water and Power, Ken Holum, to discuss Budget's continuing uneasiness about the Pacific Southwest Water Plan, including the high Bridge Canyon Dam. Staats urged the Interior Department to formulate a compromise proposal to "protect national park values," but Interior personnel refused. In late spring the Budget Bureau issued its formal report upon the Lower Colorado River Basin Project bill now being advanced by representatives from Arizona and California, and it recommended the deferral of Bridge Canyon Dam for later consideration by a national water commission of distinguished citizens.

Carl Hayden was reportedly "jubilant" over the recommendation, for even though it removed the greatest source of power production from the proposal, the Budget Bureau had cleared the way for congressional consideration of the rest of the project. Despite opposition from some Arizona water leaders, the "old fox" Hayden, as he was sometimes called in the Phoenix newspapers, had obtained Senate passage of a bill in 1964 placing a moratorium upon construction at the Marble Canyon site, holding it in reserve just in case problems arose with Bridge Canyon Dam. Now the Budget Bureau's action made the venerable Arizona Senator appear prophetic, and Arizona newspapers castigated those who had opposed him, especially officials of the Arizona Power Authority. The release of the report also demonstrated that President Johnson had at least approved of the project in principal, support that would be indispensable in the event of congressional passage of the bill. However, the Budget Bureau report also demonstrates that the president desired to avoid potential controversy over Bridge Canyon Dam.[13]

Having gained the backing of the Bureau of the Budget, Arizona's congressional team had reason to be cautiously optimistic in June of 1965 about the chances of obtaining passage of the CAP in some form. The interior secretary, who had accepted Budget's report, shared this optimism and urged Chairman Aspinall to convene hearings at the earliest possible date. John Rhodes of Arizona reluctantly assented to the deletion of the Bridge Canyon Dam but argued that it should remain in the bill for "strategic reasons," presumably to keep California's support and as a negotiating tool to use against preservationist arguments. Even Floyd Dominy resigned himself privately to the idea that the Bridge Canyon Dam might have to be reduced in height owing to the conservationists' opposition to it. Because the measure before Congress had been hammered together as a result of trying negotiations between Arizona and California, Rhodes viewed the deletion of Bridge Canyon Dam as a threat to the project, for without Bridge Canyon Dam—the major source of revenue for the basin account—the incentive used to gain California's crucial support had now been removed. Consequently, the congressional delegations for both Arizona and California pressed Interior Committee Chairman Aspinall for hearings on the bill as it was originally submitted—with a high Bridge Canyon Dam, defying the Budget Bureau's recommendation.[14]

In July of 1965, with action on the CAP legislation imminent in the Congress, Senator Jackson made an adroit maneuver to limit the ability of agencies of the executive branch from initiating feasibility-grade studies of water diversions. Jackson had stated publicly his opposition to a Columbia River diversion since the Senate hearings the previous year, and in the summer of 1965, he had not changed his mind. Stewart Udall and Floyd Dominy viewed the Columbia River as the solution to future water shortages in the Colorado Basin, and Jackson feared that the Interior Department would drum up so much local support that it could present the diversion as a fait accompli to Congress, whose members would risk political repercussions if they failed to approve it. Without mentioning the Columbia River by name, Jackson tacked his proposal onto a minor reclamation bill granting the Bureau the authority to develop the recreational potential of its reservoirs. Despite pressure from the National Reclamation Association and Interior Department officials, Lyndon Johnson signed the bill, leaving Floyd Dominy so frustrated that he refused to discuss it afterward.[15] Prior to the enactment of Jackson's provision, the Bureau only needed to gain the routine approval of the interior secretary to initiate a feasibility-grade study of the diversion. Now the Bureau was required to obtain congressional approval, and thus, proponents of the CAP would be faced with a most difficult situation should an indispensable source of political support such as California insist upon a feasibility study of a Columbia diversion if the equally indispensable Jackson remained opposed.

In August, Chairman Aspinall acquired a sudden case of cold feet, and he delayed the initiation of hearings in the House Interior Committee. Aspinall hired an engineering firm to analyze the effect that the CAP would have upon the water supply of the upper basin and, to his dismay, these experts reported that the CAP would create water deficits upstream. John Rhodes and Morris Udall pointed to Bureau of Reclamation studies that concluded just the opposite—that water available for upper-basin usage would increase as lower-basin reservoirs filled—but the chairman, concerned with his constituents' future water supply, balked. California water attorney Northcutt Ely, viewed suspiciously by Arizona water leaders because of his long role in combating the CAP, suggested a compromise meeting in August 1965. Representatives of the seven Colorado basin states met and, at Ely's urging, agreed to seek a water-importation feasibility study as a part of any lower-basin project, hoping they could bring so much political pressure to bear upon Henry Jackson that he would be forced to go along. After the seven states reached this accord, Chairman Aspinall finally agreed to schedule hearings before the House Subcommittee on Irrigation and Reclamation, the first formal House hearings on the CAP since 1951.[16]

The proponents of dams in Grand Canyon came to the 1965 House hearings armed with studies of how the project would allow the states of the lower basin to continue the economic growth they had enjoyed since the end of World War II. Floyd Dominy prepared numerous charts and graphs demonstrating how the project would sustain the agricultural economy of Arizona, and he emphasized that the project would not bring any new land into cultivation. Dominy argued further that the proposal would create great opportunities for recreation and new habitat for fish and wildlife. Then, as the astonished committee members listened, Dominy revealed that he had photographed personally the entire length of Grand Canyon from Lee's Ferry to Lake Mead from a helicopter. The commissioner produced two sets of pictures, the originals and, opposite them, duplicates onto which he had airbrushed the proposed reservoirs to demonstrate that they would have no detrimental effect upon the Canyon. Now, Dominy believed, every member of the Interior Committee could see just how little the effect of raising the water level a few hundred feet in a canyon a mile deep would actually have. As if these photographs were not convincing enough, the commissioner ordered his personnel to build a large scale-model of the entire Grand Canyon several yards in length that included removable plastic inlays of the proposed dams and reservoirs, and he "plugged the hall with it," just outside the hearing room so that congressmen and witnesses alike could gain a perspective of how minimal an impact the dams and reservoirs would actually have upon the Canyon.[17]

Representative Thomas Foley of Washington grilled Stewart Udall about the water importation provision, at one point asking the secretary three times whether he sought to take water from the Columbia River. Udall ducked the questions as best he could but finally admitted to seeking a study only so that other means of augmentation could be compared with a Columbia diversion. Foley then asked the secretary whether the CAP was feasible without augmentation and Udall answered that it was, despite Dominy's data that showed that, without augmentation, the CAP would merely delay the inevitable destruction of Arizona's agricultural economy. With Foley on the offensive, Representatives Craig Hosmer of California and Morris Udall of Arizona entered the debate and argued that for one state or region to hoard its resources was not only selfish but contrary to President Johnson's vision of the Great Society, an argument that rescued the interior secretary.[18]

The preservationists showed up in force; no less than twenty-five witnesses, representing various preservationist organizations including the Sierra Club, Wilderness Society, Izaak Walton League, National Parks Association, and Audubon Society, testified before the subcommittee. However, a surprise awaited them when they arrived in Washington. Chairman Aspinall had scheduled two days of opposition testimony commencing on Monday, 30 August, but when the morning session commenced, Aspinall called former Arizona senator Barry Goldwater to testify instead, and he did so, making a strong argument in favor of the dams. As a result, Goldwater received much of the coverage that preservationists hoped to garner for themselves. Most of the members of the press left the room after Goldwater completed his testimony, and some annoyed conservationists reflected that this situation appeared to be a prearranged attempt on the part of the pro-dam forces to steal their publicity.[19]

When preservationists finally took the stand, most of the witnesses stressed that they understood Arizona's need for water and that their objections lay, not with the concept of the CAP, just with the method used to generate power for the proposal. Why, argued Charles Callison of the Audubon Society, was it necessary to desecrate Grand Canyon with hydroelectric dams and power plants when thermal plants, using the plentiful fossil fuel available in the Four Corners region, could generate the power at an even lower cost? Why, protested Anthony Wayne Smith of the National Parks Association, scar one of the world's great natural wonders with dams and reservoirs when the Interior Department's own Office of Science and Technology predicted that atomic power would soon sell for less than hydropower? Smith also invoked the president's rhetoric, arguing that a "truly Great Society," would preserve the entire stretch of the Grand Canyon from Glen Canyon Dam to Lake Mead.[20]

Though David Brower made impassioned arguments, many conservationists agreed that Anthony Wayne Smith of the NPA was the most formidable antidam witness as he presented the Raushenbush proposal as an alternative, and rebutted strident objections from Representative Craig Hosmer of California. Preservationists also introduced an economic analysis of the project conducted by Alan Carlin of the RAND corporation, in which he demolished the Bureau of Reclamation's economic justification for Marble Canyon Dam by using projections of the future cost of nuclear energy as an alternative power source. Many other conservationists testified, including Madelyn Leopold, the seventeen-year-old daughter of USGS hydrologist Luna Leopold and granddaughter of naturalist Aldo Leopold, and Bruce Knight of the Wasatch Mountain Club. Knight's testimony, coming after several hours of heated debate over alternative energy sources, evoked a rather humorous exchange with Representative Morris Udall of Arizona. Frustrated after hearing Knight repeat the now familiar argument that nuclear energy would soon replace hydroelectric power, Udall pounced, expecting to embarrass Knight by revealing both his lack of expertise on the topic and the fact that he was parroting the standard preservationist argument. Udall asked Knight several leading questions setting him up for what he thought would be an easy rebuttal, and then he asked the witness what, if any, credentials he had that would qualify him to speak on the promise of nuclear power. Knight responded, "I am a nuclear physicist." "That," a furiously backpedaling Udall exclaimed to Chairman Aspinall, "is all I have."[21]

Morris Udall was far more effective when he attacked *Time and the River Flowing*, which, Brower testified, represented a photographic record of what the dams actually threatened. Udall produced a detailed analysis of the book, and hammered home the point that in his opinion, *Time and the River Flowing* misrepresented the effect that Bridge and Marble Canyon Dams would have upon Grand Canyon. Critiquing the book photograph by photograph, Udall concluded that of the seventy-nine pictures of Grand Canyon presented, only twelve showed scenes that would be inundated by the proposed lakes, while another ten were of scenes that "would be altered to some degree." Furthermore, six of *these* pictures were of areas that would be affected by Marble Canyon Dam, which was "completely outside Grand Canyon," meaning, Grand Canyon National Park. Forty-five of the photos were of rock formations, flora, and fauna far removed from the areas that would be flooded. Udall prepared overlays of the twelve photos that would be affected, in order to show just how minimal the effect upon the canyon would be.[22]

Brower responded, arguing that the book intended to present the canyon as a complete "geological entity," that could not be divided into separate parts. To injure one part with a dam and reservoir, he contended, would injure the canyon in its entirety. The river, though altered by Glen Canyon Dam to some degree, still flowed and constituted the single most important element of Grand Canyon. To replace the free-flowing river with slack-water reservoirs would effectively ruin the major interpretive aspect that people came to see, a living river still in the process of creating the greatest geological spectacle in the world.[23]

Several of the committee members, along with Commissioner Dominy, leveled charges of elitism at the preservationists, and at the Sierra Club in particular. Calling the club's position "the height of exclusion," Craig Hosmer stated that he could not understand why Congress should heed the wishes of a few people who did not "have sense to stay out of the river" and keep the "vast majority of the American people" out, people such as his own family who would enjoy a boating experience in Grand Canyon. Morris Udall agreed, lamenting that only 900 people had braved the rapids of the Colorado in all of recorded history, and he asked the rhetorical question, "how many cabdrivers, carpenters, and bricklayers, and ordinary God-fearing taxpaying citizens are members of the Sierra Club?"[24] Sounding the theme of elitism again and again, pro-dam advocates on the Interior Committee argued that Bridge and Marble Canyon Dams would create new recreational opportunities for all Americans, an argument they believed would resonate with Congress as well as the American public.

The dam proponents also arranged for George Rocha, chief and chairman of the Hualapai Tribe to testify in favor of the dams along with tribal counsel Royal Marks. The Hualapai had negotiated a lucrative contract with the State of Arizona in 1960 when the APA was exploring the possibility of building Bridge Canyon Dam as a state project. Rocha argued that although the tribe favored the construction of the dam because of the economic benefits that would accrue to his people, the present CAP proposals contained no provision for compensating the tribe for the 20,132 acres of Reservation land the project would require. Citing the contract of 1960, Rocha contended that the federal government should at least match what the APA had agreed to pay, and in addition he revealed that the tribe would demand money up front to avoid problems like those encountered by the Sioux and Seneca tribes when they sought compensation from Congress after losing parts of their Reservations to reservoirs. Addressing the Budget Bureau's recommendation that Bridge Canyon Dam should be deferred, Rocha and Marks each testified that the tribe would seek a license from the Federal Power Commission to build the dam as a tribal project in the event that Congress upheld the deferral, and they insisted that the dam should be renamed "Hualapai" no matter who constructed it. If the tribe developed the site, Marks argued, it proposed to build a low dam in accordance with FPC guidelines; hence, the dam would be constructed so that it would not back water into the national park or monument.[25]

The hearings before the House Irrigation and Reclamation Subcommittee ended on 1 September 1965. Both sides had scored heavily, and both spent the next few weeks assessing the strengths and weaknesses of their own arguments as well as those of their opponents. Pro-dam advocates such as John Rhodes and Morris Udall, though clearly impressed by the expert testimony presented by the preservationists, had rebutted their arguments effectively and appeared more troubled by signs that the fragile agreement between the seven states of the Colorado Basin might be unraveling. While Arizona and California maintained a tenuous truce, representatives from the upper-basin states began voicing concerns about the unlikely prospects of gaining the approval of the Pacific Northwest for the study of importation from the Columbia River. Without additional water, politicians from the upper basin feared that their region's allotment would be endangered if the CAP were built. However, the hearings satisfied Congressman Aspinall, because now all the respective positions of both the basin states and the preservationists were out in the open. Aspinall announced that he intended to push for passage of the proposal in the spring of 1966, provided that the seven-state agreement held.[26]

Proponents of the CAP raised three important issues during the hearings of 1965. First, they portrayed the preservationists as selfish elitists who wanted to keep the American public out of the lower reaches of Grand Canyon, creating an argument with the potential for considerable mass appeal. Second, Representative Hosmer queried Charles Callison of the Audubon Society about his association's lobbying activities and asked him specifically whether the Society had attempted to generate a national letter-writing campaign in violation of the 1946 Lobbying Act. Callison denied the charge. Morris Udall also questioned David Brower about the purpose of the Sierra Club's publication *Time and the River Flowing* and argued that it was a part of a campaign to influence legislation. Brower responded, stating that the book was intended to be used as an educational tool, and it was the right of the Sierra Club to petition Congress. Thus, by early September of 1965 conservationists were now aware that political supporters of the CAP were questioning their opposition tactics in the light of the provisions of the Lobbying Act of 1946, looking for possible violations of the IRS code.[27]

Third, Hualapai Chief Rocha testified that the federal government had neglected to include the tribe as a part of the policymaking process, even though the construction of the Bridge Canyon project would involve a taking of more than 20,000 acres of his people's land. In 1965, public sensitivity to issues of race relations was particularly high as a result of the Civil Rights movement; to have the chief of the Hualapai Tribe testify during a public hearing that Congress and the Interior Department had virtually ignored the rights of the Native Americans the project was most likely to affect was a potentially devastating development. A related issue of concern to CAP advocates was that tribal attorney Royal Marks also articulated a position that might appeal to many preservationists who had not accepted the Sierra Club's stand against all development within the Canyon. If the tribe sought to build the dam on its own, Grand Canyon National Park and Monument would be completely out of danger.[28]

Morris Udall, John Rhodes, and other CAP proponents embarked hurriedly upon a program of damage control. Udall was angry particularly at Marks, who, Udall believed, had "bragged" to the committee that the Hualapai could construct the dam on their own. But the wily Udall also saw in the Hualapai testimony a potential solution that might save the high Bridge Canyon Dam and the political alliance between Arizona and California that depended upon it. Udall believed that the Native American position could be used to gain a public windfall for the CAP and that it might be possible to paint the Sierra Club and other CAP opponents as anti-Indian during a time of heightened public sensitivity to racial issues.[29]

The opponents of the Grand Canyon dams had also learned some lessons from the hearings in autumn of 1965. First, and perhaps most frustrating, the letter-writing campaigns initiated by several of the conservation organizations had succeeded in generating a great deal of mail to Congress and the Interior Department. However, it also appeared as though the Interior Committee members viewed the letter writers as though they were the victims of a misinformation campaign conducted by the environmentalists. Clearly, these politicians believed, the public would agree that the preservation of over one hundred miles of free flowing river, combined with the two reservoirs and their recreation potential, constituted a reasonable compromise. Consequently, the Interior Committee kept track of the volume of mail but only considered it as an "imponderable."[30]

It also appeared to some environmentalists that the machinations of the congressional system constituted an almost impenetrable barrier. Richard Lamm of the Colorado Open Space Coordinating Council, Sierra Club mem-

ber, and future governor of Colorado met with the Colorado congressional delegation, including Chairman Aspinall, and came away convinced that the issue
was much more complex than he had realized initially. Although the issues
of the preservation of the Canyon and upholding the integrity of the national
park system were of paramount importance to conservationists, Lamm
observed that these considerations were of secondary concern to politicians, a
veritable "flea on the elephant," to members of the Interior Committee.[31]

Instead, most of the political players from the western states were concerned with the Gordian knot of political intrigue that surrounded the legislation. Arizona, they argued, was now in a powerful bargaining position because
of its influence in the House and Senate, and western politicians who opposed
the CAP risked having the powerful Hayden using his influence to block their
own reclamation projects. Most alarming to Lamm, however, was that politicians considered reclamation to be such a time-honored political formula for
power development that it appeared as though the Bureau's cost-benefit justification of its projects was virtually unassailable because it at least created the
illusion that hydroprojects were not a direct federal subsidy. Even though
conservationists had demonstrated that thermal steam plants could generate
power cheaper than hydroelectric dams, for Congress even to suggest the
idea of federal thermal plants risked renewing the bitter debate over public-
private power that had raged for thirty years, a controversy that had only
recently abated. Politicians believed that federally owned steam plants would
be viewed as "creeping socialism," by the western electorate, even though
federal hydropower projects had long been sought by these same people as a
means to spur development and economic growth. Members of the Colorado
delegation confided to Lamm that although thermal plants appeared to be the
best economic alternative, politically it was impractical to suggest them; they
believed federally owned steam plants could never gain congressional approval
because of the political risks. Lamm stated succinctly the situation conservationists hoping to preserve Grand Canyon faced: "despite the fact that there are
more economic, more practical solutions, they are not enough at this point to
overcome the tendency to allow these matters to flow in the accepted orthodox
political channels." Richard Lamm observed that many of the major political
players in this drama were willing to dismiss the environmentalists' major
argument—that the construction of dams in Grand Canyon would create a
precedent that would endanger the rest of the National Park System—in

favor of political pragmatism, and he communicated these concerns to Brower and other preservationist leaders.[32]

Preservationists also confronted accusations by Morris Udall, Floyd Dominy, and others that they were deliberately trying to mislead the American people into believing that the dams would inundate a substantial portion of Grand Canyon National Park and create a lake that people could see from the popular tourist overlooks located on the South Rim. In his analysis of *Time and the River Flowing*, Morris Udall charged that the club intended for the reader to infer that the canyon would be filled with water from rim to rim, a charge that Brower vehemently denied. But in rebutting these charges of misrepresentation, preservationists failed to see that the dam proponents themselves were guilty of misleading both the public and members of the Interior Committee. During the hearings, Mo Udall and Dominy referred to the Albright-Mead correspondence of 1933, and they used it to assert that the Park Service had agreed to a high Bridge Canyon Dam years before.[33] As has been discussed previously, Horace Albright acceded only to the construction of a low dam that would flood the monument.

However, the misuse of the Albright correspondence did not escape the notice of Park Service Director George Hartzog, who, in intraservice memoranda, had voiced his concern about Dominy's misuse of this exchange of letters since 1964. Hartzog asked his subordinates to confirm Dominy's misrepresentation of the Park Service position during the 1965 hearings, but no evidence exists to suggest that he took action to stop it. The director also refused to allow Service personnel to speak out against Bridge Canyon Dam, despite Interior Secretary Udall's acceptance of the Budget Bureau's recommendation that Bridge Canyon Dam be deferred. Although Director Conrad Wirth voiced actively his opposition to the dams planned for Echo Park when Interior Secretary McKay reversed the approval of his predecessor during the mid 1950s, Hartzog, in the case of Grand Canyon, took disciplinary action against a Park Service employee who was caught handing out literature opposing Bridge Canyon Dam in October of 1965.[34] Hartzog's actions added further stress to his already strained relationship with conservation organizations whose leaders felt that Service employees should now be free to express their opposition should they feel so inclined.

Slowly, as a result of the efforts of many concerned individuals and organizations, the preservationists' campaign gained momentum after the Interior

Committee hearings of 1965. Although leaders from the major organizations carried on the most publicized aspects of the effort—testifying before Congress, and producing literature for distribution—the campaign also began to accelerate at the grassroots level among the ordinary membership. Concerned citizens and influential environmentalists alike had been writing letters to Congress since Udall first proposed the Pacific Southwest Water Plan in August of 1963,[35] and the volume of letters began to increase noticeably during the summer of 1965. A great preponderance of these letters came from professionals such as businesspeople, college professors, doctors, and lawyers. Many of these individuals wrote the Sierra Club and asked what they could do to help, or explained what they had already done. For example, Frank Griffin, an insurance consultant from Chicago, wrote Brower offering to help pay for the distribution of *Time and the River Flowing* to all members of Congress, and he also informed Brower that he and his wife had written to all one hundred senators and desired reprints of articles from the *Sierra Club Bulletin* to distribute to friends and neighbors.[36] Many such letters can be found in the Sierra Club files.

An analysis of a representative sample of this correspondence reveals that although the ordinary membership of environmental organizations was participating in the fight to save Grand Canyon and had responded to the articles and pleas for support, the letter-writing campaign had not moved far beyond the aggregate membership of these organizations, for few letters arrived without their authors' claiming an affiliation with an environmental group. Although some conservationists looked to the Sierra Club to provide leadership, others agitated for the creation of a national "save the Grand Canyon" organization to coordinate the effort. When queried about this possibility, David Brower responded that he believed that all the conservation organizations needed to do was to continue their present efforts and communicate with one another more closely. By now Brower was immersed in speaking engagements and only rarely appeared at Sierra Club headquarters, and the Sierra Club had hired two full-time staff members to keep up with his schedule and answer his mail.[37] Clearly Brower believed that with the Sierra Club having taken the lead to generate public awareness—risking its tax-deductible status in the process—and having formed its own "Grand Canyon Task Force," another organization was unnecessary. If it was possible to stop the Grand Canyon dams, it would be Richard Bradley's "aroused public" rather than a bureaucracy created by environmentalists that would do it.

Indeed, people interested in participating in the fight to save Grand Canyon had begun to create organizations of their own. One good example of this type of grassroots activity was the Colorado Open Space Coordinating Council, a group begun by Eugene and Ruth Weiner of Denver. Starting with a nucleus of fifty people in March of 1965, including Professors Richard and William Bradley, and Richard Lamm, this organization was created solely to oppose the Grand Canyon dams. By September of 1965, the group had increased to approximately two hundred members, distributed eight thousand "fact sheets," countless bumper stickers and buttons, and contacted 350 conservation organizations. By December the group had scheduled public debates between CAP proponents and prominent preservationists and booked Sierra Club's Glen Canyon movie for showings all over the state of Colorado.[38]

In addition to his activities with the Colorado Open Space Coordinating Council, Richard Bradley continued his own efforts to combat the Grand Canyon dams. Bradley pressed his campaign to interest the editors of *Atlantic Monthly* in publishing an article from the preservationist perspective during the last half of 1965, and he also attempted to enlist distinguished environmental author Wallace Stegner in the fight, but Stegner begged off, citing his demanding teaching and research responsibilities at Stanford University. In addition, Devereux Butcher, former executive secretary of the National Parks Association and a longtime conservationist, persuaded John Vosburgh, the editor of *Audubon Magazine*, to ask Bradley whether he would be willing to write an article for a forthcoming issue. Vosburgh made it clear to Bradley that he was free to write a no-holds-barred excoriation of the proposed Grand Canyon dams. "We are interested in a hard hitting piece exposing the bold and thoughtless plan which would ruin much of the Grand Canyon if the Marble Gorge and Bridge Canyon dams should be constructed," Vosburgh wrote. "Much of the public is unaware of this scheme of the Bureau of Reclamation."[39] Although *Audubon* was not a magazine with the national circulation Bradley had hoped for, he nonetheless prepared an article that Vosburgh scheduled for publication in early spring of 1966. More importantly, this signaled that the Audubon Society, the oldest and one of the most respected conservation organizations in the world, had now leapt into the controversy with both feet.

Proponents of the Grand Canyon dams also intensified their publicity efforts after the 1965 hearings, and in September, representatives from the

Central Arizona Project Association, the Metropolitan Water District of Los Angeles, and several large lobbying groups, including the American Public Power Association, met in Washington, D.C., to discuss strategy. A consensus was reached that the next few months might prove decisive in the struggle for the Lower Colorado River Basin Project, and that a committee headquartered in Washington, D.C., should be formed to lead the effort. These officials agreed that the primary purpose of creating this centralized strategy was to combat the "preservationists' opposition" to the Grand Canyon dams. A comprehensive plan of attack was drawn up, and delegates were assigned tasks such as contacting the national media, influential industrial lobbyists, and key members of Congress. Literature counteracting the preservationists' arguments was also proposed, and a special emphasis was to be placed upon developing "favorable relationships" with the states of the Pacific Northwest.[40]

Morris Udall was optimistic following the hearings and looked forward to their resumption in 1966. Udall believed that negotiations with Jackson, Foley, and other politicians from the region would eventually bear fruit because, in his opinion, the testimony at the recently concluded hearings had "shamed" politicians from the Pacific Northwest into admitting that they had a water surplus. Meanwhile, Floyd Dominy and Stewart Udall stumped the American West, trying to drum up public support for the project. The Bureau of Reclamation also produced a film entitled "Power for the Nation," narrated by actor Frederick March and accompanied by music from the Air Force Band, extolling the economic and recreational benefits of hydroelectric dams. Anthony Wayne Smith criticized the Bureau and the Interior Department for using public funds to generate this type of propaganda for public consumption, and he wrote the Board of Trustees of the National Parks Association asking them to formulate a strategy to combat it.[41]

By the winter of 1965, conservation leaders such as Smith, Bradley, and Brower realized that the pro-dam propaganda must be countered in the mass media in order to generate the public response they believed would merit congressional attention, the third incarnation of the preservationists' strategy since the Grand Canyon dam controversy began in 1963. When Stewart Udall first introduced the Pacific Southwest Water Plan, environmentalists attempted to create a legal argument against the dams based upon the reclamation provision in the Park Establishment Act of 1919 and the Federal Power Acts of

1920, 1921, and 1935. However, the dubious nature of these arguments soon became apparent, and preservationists had largely abandoned them by 1965. Consequently, witnesses testifying against the dams during the 1965 hearings attacked the proposals with technologically viable alternatives and strong rhetorical arguments emphasizing that if Congress approved the construction of dams that would create invasions of Grand Canyon National Park and Monument, it would set a precedent, allowing development in the rest of the national park system.

In the post–Hetch Hetchy era, the argument of precedent originated with Park Service Director Newton Drury, when he used it to defend Grand Canyon National Park against the high Bridge Canyon Dam and the destructive Marble Canyon–Kanab Creek Project during the CAP debates of the 1940s. Congress failed to enact legislation approving either of these proposals; however, conservation organizations adopted Drury's strategy and used it to defend Dinosaur National Monument during the Echo Park controversy.

Historian Mark Harvey writes that the conservationists' triumph in the Echo Park controversy overturned the Hetch Hetchy verdict, and these environmentalists believed Congress had established a new principle: that the lands held by the National Park Service could no longer be violated for development. Now conservationists believed they had a legal argument, sanctioned by Congress, with which to resist other intrusive proposals. Ironically, when the rising waters of Lake Powell threatened Rainbow Bridge National Monument a few years later, environmentalists found themselves in the position of having to urge Congress and the Interior Department to force the Bureau to deface the spectacular canyon country of Southern Utah with roads and barrier dams to uphold the sanctity of the national park system and maintain the validity of their legal strategy. Congressmen Stewart Udall and Wayne Aspinall opposed the construction of dams and the damage they would cause, and when Udall became interior secretary in 1960, he came under intense pressure from environmental groups urging him to uphold the provision in the 1956 Colorado River Storage Project act that guaranteed the monument's protection. Ultimately, many congressmen were not convinced that the intrusion of a small sliver of water into Rainbow Bridge National Monument constituted a precedent that would endanger the national park system. Senator Frank Moss of Utah argued that a lake beneath the Bridge would "add greatly to its scenic lure," while Wayne Aspinall and Commissioner Floyd Dominy favored the intrusion because they believed it would enable millions to see the arch rather than just a privileged few.[42]

Environmentalists fighting to preserve Grand Canyon in 1965 had no choice but to rely upon the precedent argument established during the Echo Park controversy, once the weakness of their initial legal arguments had been revealed, because although weakened by the Rainbow Bridge fiasco, the precedent argument still constituted their strongest weapon. However, many of the same contentions used to defeat the environmentalists' "sanctity" argument in the Rainbow Bridge controversy reappeared during the House Interior Committee hearings of 1965. Congressmen argued that a lake would improve the scenery of the Canyon, open it up to public access, and that the environmentalists who sought to prevent construction of such a "water highway" were selfish—the antithesis of President Johnson's Great Society. More than anything else, the congressional hearings of 1965 demonstrated to environmentalists that mere arguments of precedent were not enough to stop congressional approval of the projects, for these arguments by themselves were not powerful enough to dissuade Congress from continuing to view reclamation hydropower as a politically pragmatic means to perpetuate economic growth in the western United States.

With proponents of dams in Grand Canyon couching their arguments in the rhetoric of President Johnson's Great Society and hammering home the theme that opponents of the dams were a selfish group of people who sought to reserve vast stretches of Grand Canyon for their own use, leading preservationists realized in the winter of 1965 that they needed a new strategy that would transcend mere legal arguments and gain widespread public appeal. Though in Grand Canyon environmentalists had perhaps the world's greatest symbol of natural grandeur, and despite numerous articles in conservation magazines, traveling photo exhibits, and the stunning book *Time and the River Flowing*, they had not communicated successfully the impending threats to Grand Canyon beyond the membership of their own organizations. So far Richard Bradley's efforts to gain publicity in the national media had yielded mixed results. While he had not been able to convince the editors of *Atlantic Monthly* to publish his article, they had put him in touch with *Life Magazine*, which agreed to print a short antidam editorial. *Harper's* also published a short satirical piece, criticizing Stewart Udall for endorsing "piddling enterprises" such as Glen Canyon, Marble Canyon, and Bridge Canyon Dams and called instead for a dam "one mile high" across the entire canyon. However, when Bradley attempted to publish a more conventional article in *Harper's*, Bernard DeVoto's former employer turned him down. And though the *New York Times* carried regular articles about the controversy, *Time* had featured an article on conservation in late September of 1965, just after the House hearings, and failed to mention the growing threats to Grand Canyon. Some environmentalists suspected that the Bureau had somehow applied pressure behind the scenes to influence the editors of *Time* to avoid publicizing the controversy.[43] Although David Brower was unable to discern whether these allegations were accurate, soon conservationists would see just how far the Bureau and other proponents of the CAP would go to prevent environmentalists from publicizing the threats to Grand Canyon. Unless something dramatic occurred, it appeared as though Morris Udall, John Rhodes, Carl Hayden, Stewart Udall, and other proponents of the Lower Colorado River Basin Project had finally made the political deals necessary and gained enough momentum to break the bill free in the House during the upcoming congressional session. Thus, leading environmentalists like David Brower and Richard Bradley believed if they were to have any chance of saving Grand Canyon in 1966, that it was imperative to gain access to the national media in order to inform the American people of the threats looming over their greatest scenic wonder while there was still time to act.

C/\nyon in the Bn1/\nce

Far from ruining the canyon, these dams will insure that no serious and damaging incursions will occur in the future. The job will be done, and it will be done right.

—Morris Udall, in a speech,
"Flooding the Grand Canyon," June 1966

As the year 1966 dawned, environmentalists and supporters of the Grand Canyon dams and the Central Arizona Project remained locked in the struggle to gain a consensus in Congress and in the court of public opinion. Morris Udall, John Rhodes, Carl Hayden, Stewart Udall, and the other dam proponents waited impatiently for Wayne Aspinall to reconvene the hearings on the Lower Colorado River Basin Project, hoping the compromises that the seven states of the Colorado Basin so painstakingly negotiated during the previous two years would endure long enough for the bill to reach the floor of the House for a vote. Although dozens of people were working on obtaining passage of the Central Arizona Project bill, by January of 1966 Morris Udall had emerged as the quarterback of the effort. Mo Udall, the "one eyed Mormon,"[1] as he laughingly referred to himself, had taken his brother's congressional seat in 1960 upon Stewart's appointment as interior secretary, and after winning reelection twice, he now held Arizona's only seat on the vital House Interior Committee. Morris Udall found himself caught in the same conundrum as his brother: generally a supporter of conservation, Mo, in the case of the CAP, found himself opposing conservationists with

whom he was usually allied, all the while fighting a personal struggle to reconcile his obligations to his Arizona constituency and his desire to develop
Arizona's water resources with his own environmentalist sympathies. Possessed of a dry and sarcastic wit, Morris Udall also, by 1966, was known among
his colleagues as a politician of keen intellect with a tireless work ethic, a man
who was not above playing hardball politics when the situation demanded it.

Opposition from the Pacific Northwest still threatened the Central Arizona Project bill. However, Morris Udall believed that through tactful negotiations and Carl Hayden's influence Senator Jackson could be persuaded to
approve of at least a feasibility-grade study of the importation of water from the
Columbia River.[2] The promise of water augmentation was what held the fragile seven-state coalition together, and though Udall was optimistic about his
prospects of success with Jackson, he was also aware that if he failed, the
upper-basin states as well as California would withdraw their support. Udall
knew he could do little about the position held by politicians from the Pacific
Northwest at the beginning of the year; the real negotiations, he believed,
would occur while the bill was under consideration, probably during the joint
House/Senate conference committee meetings after passage, which he anticipated would occur in the summer of 1966. But in order for these political deals
to be made, the bill first had to be passed by the House and Senate. Udall
realized that if the conservationists grew strong enough to prevent the passage of a high Bridge Canyon Dam, it would doom the proposal because California's representatives and Wayne Aspinall all believed that without the high
dam, the development fund would take a great deal longer to accrue enough
revenue to build water importation works—too long in their view, given the
imminence of the Southwest's water crisis.

Proponents of the CAP now moved to strengthen their position against
the environmentalists, and they launched a preemptive strike to prevent the
alliance of conservationists and the Hualapai Tribe over the construction of a
low dam at Bridge Canyon. During the autumn 1965 hearings, tribal attorney Royal Marks had testified that the tribe desired to build Bridge Canyon
Dam itself with the approval of the Federal Power Commission. Since the
FPC did not have the authority to approve the construction of a dam that
would flood national monument or park lands, the tribal project would, by law,
have to be a low dam.[3] Arizona water advocates viewed this testimony as
adversarial, and it became a matter of utmost priority to garner Indian back-

ing for the project because it would both remove a potential obstacle to passage and provide "public relations value." Fearing that the removal of threats to the park and monument would appease some of the conservation organizations, Arizona Representatives Morris Udall, John Rhodes, and George Senner wrote a joint letter to the Hualapai Tribe asking for its "specific demands."[4]

The Hualapai Tribe began voicing its concerns about a federally constructed Bridge Canyon Project almost as soon as the Arizona delegation introduced CAP legislation in the wake of the favorable Supreme Court ruling in June of 1963. Royal Marks, whose law firm had represented the tribe since 1948, expressed his concern to John Rhodes that the legislation contained no provision for compensating the tribe in the event that the Bureau of Reclamation built the dam. Specifically, Marks expressed dismay that the Arizona delegation would introduce federal legislation that made no mention of Indian interests only three years after the Hualapai had entered into the lucrative contract with the State of Arizona for use of the dam site. Rhodes pled ignorance and said that he had taken Senator Hayden's word that the legislation introduced in 1963 was "identical" with that submitted in 1950, which did in fact, guarantee compensation. Marks's cocounsel, Arthur Lazarus, made similar inquiries of Interior Secretary Udall in October of 1963, but despite these inquiries, both the interior secretary and the Arizona congressional delegation failed to take any action until after the House hearings of autumn 1965.[5]

By fall of 1965, the "Indian problem,"[6] as some Arizonans had begun to call it, could no longer be ignored in the face of the explosive civil rights issues involved. The surprise threat from the Hualapai threw the Arizona delegation into a panic, and Mo Udall asked the Bureau of Reclamation to assess the impact that the Hualapai contract of 1960 would have upon the development fund. The Bureau's analysis revealed the stunning and inescapable fact that the annual payments the agreement called for would reduce the development fund by over $65 million by 2025 and almost $93 million by 2047. Attorneys for the Hualapai Nation confirmed that the tribe expected, at the minimum, for the Interior Department to compensate it at the rate the Arizona Power Authority (APA) had agreed to back in 1960, when the authority was seeking to construct a low dam, and that their demands would probably increase because the Interior plan called for a high dam. The Hualapai also expected the purchase of power at the lowest market rate, the control of the revenue generated by tourists using the south shore of the reservoir, and the construction of a road to the reservoir for recreational purposes. Additionally, the tribe demanded that the Interior Department change the name of the dam from Bridge Canyon to "Hualapai."[7]

As if potential conflicts with the Hualapai Nation were not enough, the Arizona delegation also knew that the Navajo Tribe was interested in a substantial portion of revenue from Marble Canyon Dam. However, because the tribe had failed to convince the FPC during the APA proceedings that it had a legitimate claim to the dam site in the early 1960s, Arizona politicians concluded that the Navajo Nation did not constitute a serious threat and focused their efforts on getting the Hualapai on board.[8]

Morris Udall and John Rhodes met with Marks in early January of 1966 to try to get the tribe to budge on some of its demands, but Marks was adamant, giving the Arizona representatives a thinly veiled take-it-or-leave-it response. Morris Udall wrote his brother shortly after this encounter, and Stewart issued an immediate directive to his staff to get moving on a solution. Mo Udall now found himself confronted with a most uncomfortable choice, for to give in to the Hualapai demands would result in a great depletion of the development fund—a proposition that not only was sure to anger the states hoping for water importation at the earliest possible date—but would also increase the importance of the high Bridge Canyon Dam even more, leaving little room for compromise. However, Udall also recognized that he had little alternative, because he believed the potential fallout that would result if the CAP proponents failed to placate the tribe constituted such a grave threat that it would imperil the entire project, or at least delay it indefinitely.[9]

Virtually everyone concerned with the passage of the Central Arizona Project recognized the importance of avoiding a conflict with the Hualapai Tribe over the project. Spurred on by Secretary Udall to find a solution, Interior Department staff came to him with their recommendations. Harry Anderson, the assistant secretary for Public Land Management argued that the Department should agree to the Hualapai demands as a matter of "public policy" and "equity." He also contended that the Indians stood in danger of being "exploited nationally" by the conservationists if supporters of the CAP failed to gain their support. Les Alexander of the Arizona Interstate Stream Commission put the situation more bluntly in a conversation with Congressman John Rhodes: the price of giving in to the Hualapai demands must be the

tribe's affirmative support of the project. If this could be achieved, it presented the opportunity to turn the Hualapai desire to have Bridge Canyon/Huala-
pai Dam built "to our advantage against the so-called conservationists."
Alexander urged the hiring of a professional advertising agency to mount "a
professional type rebuttal" against the conservationists, arguing that "the
plight of the poor Hualapais would be one fine avenue for bringing national
pressure to bear for the construction of Bridge Canyon."[10] Clearly, Alexander, John Rhodes, and other Arizona water advocates believed it possible to
portray the preservationists as anti-Indian and gain a tremendous public windfall from people sympathetic to racial and civil rights issues.

Preservationists, unaware of the pro-dam lobby's attempts to gain the
backing of Native Americans, continued in January of 1966 to seek a national
forum in which to articulate their position. By late January of 1966 there
were two schools of thought among conservationists: those who believed in a
centralized, coordinated antidam campaign, such as Richard Lamm, and those,
including David Brower and Richard Bradley, who thought that a grassroots
type of action stood the best chance of success, feeling that if conservationists
gained access to the national media, their message would galvanize the public
into action. With hearings but a few short months away, preservationists had
acquired some powerful allies, including the *New York Times;* although it had
opposed only Bridge Canyon Dam in previous editorials, the *Times* now took
a stand against Marble Canyon Dam as well, even though it was upstream of
the park and monument. The editors of the *Times* published an editorial in January criticizing the potential destruction of Grand Canyon, and they questioned the necessity of hydroelectric dams, given current advances in thermal
and atomic energy.[11] Encouraged, but knowing time was growing short, Brower and Bradley continued their efforts to gain more media attention.

In January the defenders of Grand Canyon received the first break in their
efforts to gain access to the national media because the Audubon Society
came through on its promise to publish Richard Bradley's hard-hitting article
it had solicited the previous fall. Richard and his brother David had been
unsuccessful in gaining access to the widely circulated *Atlantic Magazine*
because, as Richard later put it, the editors "couldn't believe that Stewart Udall
would support such a dumb project." Bradley rewrote the manuscript and sent
it to *Audubon*. The article appeared in the January-February issue, an event that
was to have far-reaching consequences for the remainder of the campaign

against the Grand Canyon dams. The article, entitled "Ruin for the Grand Canyon," stressed many of the same themes that environmentalists had been sounding since 1963: alternative energy sources were available; the Kanab Creek tunnel still loomed as a potential threat; the dams would desecrate Grand Canyon; and other familiar arguments. Although written forcefully, the article reached only the relatively small membership of the Audubon Society, a total of about 48,500 people, not an audience of the size that Bradley and Brower sought.[12]

Alone, Bradley's article was no more significant than other essays published in environmental and scientific magazines that had circulated among a dedicated but limited number of specialized readers for the previous two years. However, the last week of January 1966 Bradley received a letter from Marjorie Nicholson of *Reader's Digest*, asking for permission to publish the article in an upcoming issue. Elated opponents of the Grand Canyon dams believed that they now stood on the brink of gaining the national exposure they had been seeking, for *Reader's Digest* had an estimated domestic circulation of 35 million readers, and 20 million more in foreign countries, twice that of *Life* or the *Saturday Evening Post*. An employee of the *Digest*, who was also a Sierra Club member, had informed David Brower previously that the magazine received seventy-eight thousand unsolicited manuscripts every six months, and an estimated one out of every four Americans read it. Gaining access to the most widely circulated publication in the world constituted a coup of stupendous proportions for the preservationists, one they believed could potentially swing the momentum of the campaign in their favor.[13]

These developments were not lost on Floyd Dominy, and the commissioner resolved to do everything in his power to stop the publication of Bradley's article. When *Reader's Digest* called Dominy to confirm some of Bradley's assertions, the commissioner responded with a point-by-point rebuttal of "known errors or misstatements," criticizing Bradley for: comparing the proposed Grand Canyon dams with Hetch Hetchy; "raising the ghost of the Kanab Creek diversion," which had been abandoned for "several decades"; and arguing that steam plants could produce peaking power. Dominy argued that the Park Service had approved the Bridge Canyon project, and he included a copy of Park Service Director Albright's 1933 letter to substantiate his contention.

Although it appears that both Bradley and Dominy made some erroneous assertions, the editors of the *Digest* accepted Bradley's contentions, and after doing some research of their own, they decided to publish the article in April of 1966. Bradley was cautiously optimistic. However, he feared that Interior Secretary Udall possessed the influence to "kill the article" by leaning on the *Digest*'s editorial staff, and he told Brower that he wouldn't believe he had succeeded until he had "seen [the article] in print."[14]

The Colorado Open Space Coordinating Council (COSCC) also continued its efforts in spring of 1966, scheduling a television debate between Floyd Dominy and Dr. Daniel Luten, Sierra Club treasurer and a geography professor at the University of California, Berkeley. Also pursuing means to gain national exposure, the council, along with the Rocky Mountain chapter of the Sierra Club and the Colorado Mountain Club, raised enough funding to take out a full-page ad in March in the *Denver Post*, with a circulation of 347,000 readers. The advertisement featured a stunning photo of the Colorado River from Toroweap Point, the highest sheer face in Grand Canyon, and it urged concerned citizens to write their congressional representatives, President Johnson, and, perhaps most importantly, television and radio stations, magazines, and newspapers. "Tell them it is your Grand Canyon," the article admonished, "and you want it left as it is," invoking the language of Teddy Roosevelt. The COSCC then began to raise money for advertisements it intended to take out in the *New York Times* and the *Christian Science Monitor*.[15]

The supporters of the Grand Canyon dams also won a substantial victory in March of 1966. The two-million-member National Wildlife Federation, the largest conservation organization in the world, had not taken an official position on the Lower Colorado Basin Project, despite the overtures that prominent conservationists opposed to the dams had made to its leadership. The second week of March, the New Mexico Wildlife and Conservation Association offered a resolution at the NWF annual convention calling for the national leadership to oppose the two dams proposed for the Colorado River because of their effect upon Grand Canyon National Park and the evaporation they would cause. However, Phil Clemons and Bill Winter, of the Arizona Game Protective Association, offered a counterresolution calling for a "balance between conservation and full development of the water and power resources" of the Colorado River. Winter and Clemons managed to persuade the executive committee of the National Wildlife Federation to table the New

Mexico resolution.[16] As a result, the largest conservation organization in the world remained officially neutral regarding the Grand Canyon dams.

Preparations for the publication of Bradley's article continued to move forward. The *Reader's Digest* sent out offprints of the essay in March, including one to Arizona Governor Sam Goddard, who suggested that the magazine send some of its staff to the Grand Canyon so that they could see what the uproar was all about. The editors agreed, and asked David Brower to mediate a symposium 30–31 March at the El Tovar Hotel on the south rim of the canyon to allow the preservationists to present their arguments to the national press. The magazine hired the J. Walter Thompson Company, a prominent New York public relations firm, to make the arrangements for the conference, and the firm chartered a plane for eighty members of the national media. Although *Reader's Digest* intended the event to be a celebration of the publication of Bradley's article and an opportunity for opponents of the dams to present their side without interference from supporters of the project, the representatives of the Thompson Company misunderstood, and asked Goddard to provide them with a list of project supporters that should be invited to attend. Unbeknownst to environmentalists, Morris Udall, California water attorney Northcutt Ely, and Barry Goldwater made plans to crash the meeting. Additionally, Floyd Dominy, though unable to attend, arranged for the Bureau to send several personnel and its large scale-model of the Canyon with the plastic inlays for the dams and reservoirs. All these arrangements were made without the consent or knowledge of the opponents of the dams, who believed that the program would include only conservationists.[17]

From the outset, the symposium degenerated into a veritable free-for-all. David Brower and MIT mathematician Jeff Ingram arrived the night of 29 March to assess the situation and make preliminary seating arrangements. Brower fired the preservationists' opening salvo, sending a telegram to Stewart Udall in which he accused him of "muzzling the National Park Service" by not allowing Park Service personnel to voice objections to the dams. Brower claimed that he had received a copy of an Interior Department memo, "leaked" to the Sierra Club by a Park Service employee outlining the official position of the agency and requesting that all recipients destroy it after reading it.[18]

At noon the next day Ingram and Brower left the hotel to take a short walk along the rim of the canyon, and when they returned, they discovered that

Figure 6. Morris Udall and Dr. Richard Bradley, of the Sierra Club, at the March 1966 Grand Canyon symposium sponsored by *Reader's Digest*. Udall is using one of the Bureau's plastic models of Grand Canyon—which almost led to a brawl between environmentalists and dam supporters—to illustrate his point. Richard Bradley's 1966 article in *Reader's Digest* constituted the first national publicity against the dams. *Courtesy of Special Collections, University of Arizona Library.*

Bureau personnel had arrived in the interim and set up the large scale-model (fig. 6), used during the August House hearings, in the middle of the El Tovar dining room where the meeting was to be held. A furious Brower demanded that the Bureau remove it, and he threatened to throw the model out himself—along with the Bureau personnel who had set it up—while Ingram, according to Northcutt Ely, threatened to "punch one of the Bureau people in the eye." Bureau personnel and representatives of the Thompson Company then placed a series of frantic phone calls to the upper echelons of the Interior Department, eventually reaching Interior Secretary Udall, who apparently ordered the Bureau personnel to keep the model where it was. Floyd Dominy remembers that order was restored and a brawl averted only by the timely arrival of the Grand Canyon National Park Police. A tenuous truce was agreed upon, and the Bureau's model stayed.[19] The near donnybrook of 30 March 1966 has entered the lore of the Bureau of Reclamation as "The Battle of El Tovar";[20] however, the real battle, the war of words, would begin later on that afternoon.

Although the *Reader's Digest* and Hilda Burns of the Thompson Company told Brower that the conference would be organized by the preservationists and that they could conduct it any way they chose, actual events soon outstripped all previous arrangements. Morris Udall, using his status as a congressman, obtained permission to ride the charter plane from New York, with the eastern press, and he used the transcontinental flight to lobby in favor of the dams. When the plane arrived, Udall discovered that although he, Ely, and other dam proponents would be allowed to mingle at a cocktail party that evening, they were excluded from participating in the evening panel discussion. When more pro-dam advocates and a contingent of the Arizona press, including the CBS affiliate from Phoenix arrived, Udall threatened to call his own press conference unless he and other CAP proponents were allowed to take part. Brower claimed later that Burns backed down in the face of this pressure. Udall and Ely were given an opportunity to speak that night, and the morning session was reconfigured to accommodate them and the anticipated attendance of Barry Goldwater. Brower relinquished his position as moderator to Dr. Stephen Spurr from the University of Michigan, a "neutral" observer, because as a "partisan" Brower believed he could not be unbiased toward the supporters of the dams.[21]

According to author and Sierra Club member George Steck, who was in attendance, Mo Udall so antagonized Brower that "David…cried right there on the podium," having been reduced to emotionalism rather than a technical rebuttal of the dams. Harold Bradley, father of Richard and a veteran of the Echo Park fight recalled that "[Morris] Udall made an ass of himself," by being so aggressive. The verbal skirmishes continued throughout the evening and catcalls and boos from the largely antidam audience rained down upon Udall and Ely when they tried to speak. When Udall commented that neither dam would create a reservoir visible from any point on the rim to which one could drive, several environmentalists shouted "Toroweap," forcing Udall to retract his statement. Ely, in an attempt to demonstrate the extremist position of the environmentalists before the press, asked the audience how many of them would like to see Glen Canyon Dam torn out, and was met with thunderous applause.[22] The first day ended with the conservationists in retreat, feeling they had been "steamrollered"[23] by the strong-armed tactics of Udall and the rest of the pro-dam supporters.

Barry Goldwater arrived in time for the morning session, and while he admitted to not being "married to the Marble Canyon idea," he advocated strongly in favor of Bridge Canyon Dam. Goldwater also emphasized that the dam would bring tremendous economic benefits to the Hualapai Tribe, reiterating the argument that other Arizona lobbyists had articulated early in the spring. Goldwater's comment piqued the interest of Dr. Stephen Jett, a young professor of geography at the University of California at Davis without affiliation with any conservation organization, who had written his recent dissertation about the Navajo Tribe. Jett, posing as a member of the press, asked Goldwater whether the proposal would confer benefits upon the Navajo people. Goldwater replied that to the best of his knowledge, the Navajo Indians possessed no legal rights in the Marble Canyon site, and consequently, they had "not been consulted," a comment that struck Jett as "unjust" given that the east abutment of Marble Canyon Dam would have rested on Navajo land. Goldwater turned the morning session to the advantage of the dam supporters, and environmentalists complained later that Goldwater dominated the morning panel because the moderator was overawed by Goldwater's status as a former senator and presidential candidate. Indeed, a glance at the transcript reveals that Goldwater received almost 75 percent of the airtime during the morning session.[24]

The preservationists in the audience refrained from their disruptive tactics of the previous evening, while the antidam panel participants gave a good account of themselves in the time remaining. When Richard Bradley gave his presentation, the supporters of the dams failed to rebut his arguments about alternative energy sources on technical or economic grounds—Morris Udall only responding on rebuttal that reclamation policy prevented the Bureau from undertaking studies of alternatives such as thermal power plants.[25] The Sierra Club representatives even managed to show their poignant film, "Glen Canyon" during breaks in the presentation. However, when the session ended and members of the press boarded helicopters for overflights of the Canyon, most environmentalists felt that the pro-dam faction had upstaged them, one conceding that "Barry Goldwater is pretty hard to beat on his home ground."[26]

From all outward appearances, it looked as though Morris Udall, Barry

Goldwater, and the pro-dam lobby from Arizona had succeeded in co-opting the conference upon which the preservationists had placed such high hopes. But pro-dam advocates who thought they had distracted the media—and preservationists who believed the conference a disaster—failed to consider the powerful effect that the visual impact of the canyon overflights and the impassioned narrative of Sierra Club director Martin Litton produced. Standing at the dramatic Toroweap overlook on the north rim, Litton showed the press just what the dams would do—and there was no better place in the Canyon from which to make this argument—for Toroweap overlooks the world-famous Lava Falls, one of the most intense stretches of navigable white water in North America, with a drop of almost forty feet. Using the same arguments he had used to persuade the Sierra Club's board of directors to oppose the dams several years before, Martin Litton now used this spectacular setting to tell the national press about the importance of preserving the canyon as a whole, with the roar of Lava Falls thundering upward from thirty-five hundred feet below, a roar that would be silenced if Bridge Canyon/Hualapai Dam were built. Litton's presentation, made beyond the reach of the political prestige of Morris Udall or Barry Goldwater, managed to salvage at least part of the conference for the preservationists, and several members of the press corps who had supported the project previously, such as Bert Hanna of the *Denver Post*, commented that they now realized what the conservationists were fighting for.[27] So even as Richard Bradley, David Brower, Jeff Ingram, and others returned home believing that they had failed to take advantage of their opportunity, the Grand Canyon dam controversy now became front-page news across the country, and several prominent magazines began to consider publishing articles about it.

One supporter of the dams who understood how difficult it was to overcome the visual impact of Grand Canyon and the arguments of the preservationists was Morris Udall. Though pushing for the Central Arizona Project with all his political acumen, Udall believed that it was he and the pro-dam lobby that had been bested. Twenty years after the *Reader's Digest* conference, Udall wrote:

> The weakness of the arguments in favor of the dams was borne home to me the day I had to debate David Brower—as clever, tough, and tenacious an opponent as you could want—in front of a gaggle of national press at the worst possible venue: the *rim of the Grand Canyon*. [Empha-

sis his] This was a tough assignment—comparable to debating the merits of chastity in Hugh Hefner's hot tub in front of an audience of cen-
terfold models and me being on the side of abstinence.[28]

The *Reader's Digest* symposium and the publication of Richard Bradley's
article had a tremendous impact on the Grand Canyon dam controversy
because a significant portion of the American public that had been previously
unaware of the threat to Grand Canyon now knew about it through the
national media. Rich Johnson and Floyd Dominy have each stated that they
could not match the publicity advantage gained by the preservationists in the
spring of 1966. Although these claims appear at first to be ridiculous—after all
the Central Arizona Project Association ranked twenty-second in financial
reserves among Washington, D.C., registered lobbyists, and Dominy was commissioner of one of the most powerful government bureaus—the facts bear
out these arguments. For all his influence, Dominy had published exactly one
magazine-quality brochure, *Lake Powell: Jewel of the Colorado*, and managed to
distribute only 60,000 copies. Though Bureau and CAPA personnel tried to
match the preservationists speech for speech and distributed tens of thousands
of flyers, the Bureau was prevented by statute from mounting a counteroffensive. The Central Arizona Project Association tried nonetheless, and at John
Rhodes's suggestion, its directors considered mounting a national publicity
campaign of their own, but the firm they consulted, Hill and Knowlton,
responded that a campaign to counteract the *Reader's Digest* article and symposium would cost $250,000, a figure far beyond what the Association could
afford; even if such a campaign were launched, it was too late to counteract
the preservationists' publicity in time for the spring 1966 hearings. Thus, the
impetus to rebut the preservationists fell back upon Rich Johnson and other
members of the CAPA, who began to prepare their own in-house lobbying
strategy. The Central Arizona Project Association, with help from the *Arizona
Republic*, initiated a letter-writing campaign of its own, urging Arizonans to
write *Reader's Digest* voicing their displeasure about Bradley's article and the
Grand Canyon conference, and the magazine's editors soon received hundreds
of angry letters from dam supporters. Floyd Dominy and other Bureau personnel also continued their indefatigable efforts, giving speeches and handing
out literature across the West, including a presentation at the Los Angeles
"Sportshow," an outdoor recreation and boating convention that drew over
500,000 people in one weekend.[29] But the damage had already been done from

the CAPA perspective, for by early April 1966, the preservationists had gained the upper hand in attaining access to the mass media, and through it, had presented their side of the controversy to the American public.

Articles opposed to the dams soon appeared in the May issues of *Life* magazine, *Newsweek*, and *Outdoor Life*, precipitating an avalanche of mail to Congress, the interior secretary, and President Johnson. Other publications began to print satirical pieces about the proposed dams, and Floyd Dominy in particular. In a biting essay, *Biophilist*, a bimonthly newsletter published by a small group of preservationists in Denver, proposed to write a new national anthem entitled "America the Bureautiful," the first verse of which reads:

> Bureautiful for specious tries
> To obfuscate the plain
> And concretize falliciousness
> For departmental gain!
>
> America! America!
> Bow down to Dominy
> Poo-Bah who dreams to dam all streams
> From sea to shining sea.

Hilda Burns of the J. Walter Thompson company wrote Brower in early May, confirming what many conservationists were now beginning to suspect, that the conference had not been the debacle they had feared. "We're just delighted with the way this thing is turning," Burns wrote. "It's a completely different story now that the national people are making themselves heard."[30] As a result of this conference and the media attention it garnered, the public opposition that Martin Litton called for in 1963, the only force he believed could stop the dams in Grand Canyon, was at last becoming a reality.

Even as the conference was occurring at Grand Canyon, two thousand miles away, on 31 March 1966, Representatives John Saylor and John Dingell of Michigan introduced legislation calling for an expansion of Grand Canyon National Park. This bill, drafted by members of the Sierra Club, included the entire 277-mile length of Grand Canyon within the park and removed and vacated all reservations previously made by the Federal Power Commission (FPC) and the Bureau of Reclamation. The bill also proposed to redesignate parts of the Hualapai Reservation and Kaibab National Forest as a part of the enlarged park. As a result, the proposed legislation drew opposition from wildlife-oriented conservation organizations such as the Arizona

Game Protective Association because it sought to include most of the north Kaibab within the park boundaries, thus eliminating one of the prime deer-hunting areas in the nation.[31] Although destined for defeat, the bill represented the first attempt to obtain congressional approval of a proposal to bring all of Grand Canyon into the purview of the National Park Service, and it also publicized the divisions that still existed between conservation groups.

However, proponents of the Grand Canyon dams still held the upper hand in Congress, and Morris Udall, Wayne Aspinall, and other project supporters began to prepare for a renewal of House hearings before the Interior Committee. Aspinall initially scheduled the hearings for mid-April at the urging of CAP proponents in an attempt to ram the bill through the committee before the environmentalists' campaign was fully organized. However, the price Aspinall demanded for his support—the inclusion of five reclamation projects on the upper Colorado River in his home state of Colorado—created a delay because the Interior Department had not analyzed these proposals. John Rhodes and Morris Udall urged Aspinall to expedite the hearings, but he was forced to reschedule them for May because the Interior Department did not release the report until the middle of April. The report recommended only two projects for immediate construction and the deferral of the other three; although Aspinall did not receive everything he had asked for, he announced his intent to hold the hearings anyway. The Arizona representatives also pressed Roy Elson, aide to Senator Hayden, to convince the senator to initiate action in the upper chamber, but Elson intimated that Hayden would not move on the bill until the House had approved it.[32]

By the end of April a new threat to the passage of the Lower Colorado Basin Project bill had arisen—the State of New Mexico now demanded fifty thousand acre feet of water from the lower basin in exchange for its continued support of the project. Udall and Rhodes were bewildered by this latest threat, while Rich Johnson termed it "blackmail," but they could not ignore this demand because New Mexico Senator Clinton Anderson chaired the Senate Subcommittee on Irrigation and Reclamation. Not even Carl Hayden possessed enough power to overcome the objections of both Anderson and Henry Jackson, so Udall and Rhodes confronted this latest problem while an exasperated Aspinall bowed to mounting pressure and scheduled the hearings to commence on 9 May 1966. Seventy-three witnesses were slated to testify, and despite Morris Udall's attempts to exclude all antidam testimony,

Aspinall included fourteen dam opponents, most notably: Jeff Ingram, a mathematician; Alan Carlin, an economist from the RAND Corporation who had testified in 1965; and Laurence Moss, a nuclear engineer—all graduates of MIT who intended to offer new evidence to disprove the technical justification the Bureau had relied upon when formulating the proposal.[33]

Thomas Kimball of the National Wildlife Federation was also scheduled to appear as a witness, and despite the neutral position taken by the Federation in March, Kimball intended to testify against the dams and advocate the substitution of alternative power sources for the Central Arizona Project. In early May, it appeared as though the NWF and its two million members were about to weigh in against the Grand Canyon dams. However, Bill Winter of the Arizona Game Protective Association learned of Kimball's pending testimony, called him, and managed to convince the NWF executive secretary to cancel his scheduled appearance before the committee. Understating his victory, Winter wrote John Rhodes and said that the members of the AGPA believed that for Kimball to testify against the dams would have been "highly detrimental to the CAP." Winter believed that he could convince Kimball to oppose the proposed expansion of Grand Canyon National Park because of its inclusion of the Kaibab deer herd, a strategy he believed would prevent the NWF from ever becoming allied with the Sierra Club and other antidam organizations, and he told Rhodes that the Arizona group would continue its efforts to keep the NWF from adopting an official position against the dams.[34] Consequently, as the crucial hearings began in the House Interior Committee, preservationists seeking to keep dams out of Grand Canyon were still without the support of the largest conservation organization in the world.

Although Aspinall had planned for the hearings to last only three or four days, this soon proved unrealistic because of the number of witnesses. The proponents of the dams testified first. Floyd Dominy demonstrated his prowess before the committee again, offering exhaustive testimony to justify the projects on technical grounds, as well as to rebut the preservationists' arguments. Under questioning from Morris Udall, Dominy stated that although the project was theoretically "possible" without Bridge/Hualapai and Marble Canyon Dams, if these revenue producers were deleted from the proposal, irrigation water costs to Arizona farmers would have to be subsidized by the sale of power revenues, something that went against "longstanding reclamation policy." While Dominy's statement is accurate, it left the committee with the inference that this policy would be difficult to change. However, in gaining Southern California's support in December of 1964, Dominy himself, along with Stewart Udall, had promised California water interests that any water imported from the Columbia River would be sold at the prevailing rate for Colorado River water—the difference to be subsidized by the sale of power from Bridge and Marble Canyon Dams.[35]

Carl Hayden, now in his late eighties, did not testify, but his statement supporting a regional concept with the CAP as its centerpiece was read into the record. Arizona's congressmen Morris Udall, John Rhodes, and George Senner then presented a joint statement in support of the bill, and Stewart Udall also prepared a statement. An unexpected development occurred when Representative George Mahon from Texas appeared, demanding that his home state should benefit from the water augmentation scheme, and he proposed that any importation from the Columbia River should include 15 million acre feet for the West Texas Panhandle, adding to the fears of Senator Henry Jackson, Representative Thomas Foley, and other politicians from the Pacific Northwest.[36]

The most dramatic exchanges while pro-dam witnesses were on the stand took place between Assistant Secretary for Water and Power Kenneth Holum, speaking on behalf of the Interior Department, Representative Thomas Foley of Washington, and an "indignant" Wayne Aspinall, who was furious that the Budget Bureau had approved the construction of only two of his five projects. Aspinall questioned why the Interior Department was now insisting upon the formation of a National Water Commission to study interbasin transfers, which if created, would delay a Columbia diversion. Foley, alarmed by the intentions of the Pacific Southwest and the new pronouncements by Texas Representative Mahon, subjected Holum to a withering interrogation, forcing Holum to admit that the Interior Department had not determined that water importation from the Columbia River was the best approach to water augmentation. "Is there any reason why this Committee should direct a feasibility study . . . for importation," Foley asked, "rather than desalinization or weather modification or some other means of augmenting water?" "No sir," Holum replied.[37] Representative Foley's cross-examination of Kenneth Holum left little doubt that politicians from the Pacific Northwest had not been enticed by Interior Secretary Udall's offer of a stepped-up reclamation program. It soon became painfully clear that the powerful Jackson still stood in direct opposition to the CAP if it contained an import provision from the Columbia River, a problem that the testimony did little to resolve.

Preservationists from all over the United States came to Washington, D.C., to support the testimony in opposition to the dams. In contrast to the well-financed efforts of the Central Arizona Project Association and other pro-dam organizations from the Colorado Basin states, the conservationists' war room was in effect a microcosm of their nationwide grassroots effort, for despite their success in gaining access to the national media, their Grand Canyon campaign was still underfunded. The preservationists established their headquarters in a room at the Dupont Plaza Hotel, and volunteers came in to type up testimony and exhibits. David Brower remembers that people "pounded away on a couple of old typewriters," sleeping on the floor in the wee hours of the night. In response to Brower's invitation, Morris Udall came by even while the hearings were taking place to see the nerve center of the opposition effort. "He came in and saw this bunch of devoted people working hard to beat his dams," Brower recalled. "I think he was impressed by that."[38]

The dam opponents began to testify on 13 May, and from the moment they took the stand, it became apparent that Aspinall's decision to allow them to testify was not approved by all members of the committee. Craig Hosmer of California raised the most vociferous objections, starting even before Brower began his testimony, establishing a pattern of rude and discourteous behavior that would continue for the duration of the conservationists' appearances. Each time a witness attempted to testify, Hosmer objected on the grounds that the testimony was repetitious—though he never objected to hours of repetitive testimony from Dominy and other dam proponents—and Aspinall, or the acting chair, would be forced to overrule the objection. This happened time and time again, sometimes touching off testy exchanges between Hosmer and John Saylor of Pennsylvania, who opposed the dams. Aspinall, to his credit, conducted the hearings with fairness, granting the same courtesies to the preservationists as to advocates of the projects—as did Morris Udall. However, Chairman Aspinall could only control the procedural aspects of the hearings; he had little control over the committee members' treatment of witnesses, a fact that Craig Hosmer was to use to his advantage in his vituperative, often baseless attacks.[39]

Jeff Ingram was the first of the Sierra Club's technical experts to take the stand. Using the Bureau's own figures, Ingram demonstrated how the construction of Bridge/Hualapai and Marble Canyon Dams would actually reduce the amount of revenue that would accrue to the development fund until the year 2021, fifty-five years in the future. Ingram reasoned that since the dams were not needed to generate power for the Central Arizona Project specifically, but were only to generate power to sell at a profit to undetermined markets, the Arizona portion of the project could be powered by other means. The development fund was also to be augmented by power revenues from Hoover, Parker, and Davis Dams beginning in 1987; however, the tremendous capital outlay of 1.2 billion dollars needed to construct the two dams and their appurtenant structures would delay the realization of actual profit until 2021. If the revenue stream were projected out over seventy-five years, the profit generated by the dams plus the revenue from other hydroplants would still only amount to a return of 1.33 percent. However, if the dams were deleted, real profits from Hoover, Parker, and Davis could begin to accrue starting in 1987—without having to overcome the 1.2 billion dollar outlay. Thus, Ingram contended, revenues would begin to accumulate in the development fund thirty-four years earlier without the dams. Ingram also questioned the proposal arguing that without the "subsidy" from Hoover, Parker, and Davis Dams, Marble Canyon Dam would not be able to pay for itself, a violation of the Bureau's own policy, which stipulated that projects must break even and have a cost/benefit ratio of one to one. John Saylor confirmed, from separate documentation, that Ingram's figures matched those compiled by the Bureau "to the penny," and little if any rebuttal was offered by the rest of the committee.[40]

Dr. Alan Carlin and Dr. Laurence Moss testified next, and Carlin's 1966 economic analysis of the proposal was, if anything, even more devastating than his testimony of 1965. Carlin submitted a report written by himself and a colleague, Dr. William Hoehn, also of the RAND corporation, that used figures supplied by the Bureau, the Atomic Energy Commission, and Floyd Dominy in his 1965 testimony to demonstrate that nuclear power plants combined with pumped storage plants could generate more and cheaper power than the Grand Canyon dams, while adding a comparable amount to the development fund.[41] Craig Hosmer then launched a blistering attack upon Carlin, who found testifying to be difficult because he struggled to overcome a speech impediment. Hosmer interrupted him repeatedly, often with spurious and nonsensical remarks. For example, Carlin's report had been submitted to the Department of Defense for review in accordance with a contractual agreement with the RAND Corporation. When this came out in the testimony, Hosmer accused Carlin of making the inference that Defense Secretary McNamara was against the Grand Canyon dams. John Saylor leapt into the fray and restored a semblance of tranquility to the hearings, allowing Carlin to address unresolved issues, as well as to testify to his expertise in evaluating the economics of hydroprojects, something he had not yet had an opportunity to do.[42]

Next, Laurence Moss took the stand, and although his arguments paralleled those of Carlin, he contended that Carlin's figures actually gave the Bureau the benefit of the doubt in a number of instances, making the Grand Canyon dams look better than they actually were. Aspinall voiced the concern that despite the optimism surrounding the potential for nuclear power, it appeared as though its future was still uncertain. However, according to Moss, private utilities had ordered over 5700 megawatts of nuclear generating capacity in 1965, and during the first fifteen weeks of 1966 private utilities had ordered between 8815 and 12,315 megawatts of capacity, a definite sign that nuclear energy was now increasingly perceived as a viable alternative to hydropower. Moss then confirmed Ingram's arguments independently that the development fund would accrue revenue more quickly if neither dam were built.[43]

The Hualapai Nation was also represented at the hearings by Chief George Rocha (fig. 7), who testified earlier in the week. Wayne Aspinall had stressed the importance of having Rocha testify in late April when he told Mo Udall that he believed it would be a good strategic move to "have an Indian, preferably the Chief of the Hualapai tribe...to testify...in support of the bill." Aspinall intimated to Udall that he wanted to "put those who opposed Bridge Canyon Dam in the position of being anti-Indian," and he also suggested that the Hualapai do some lobbying, emphasizing that the dam would lift them out of poverty and ensure the success of their Reservation. Rocha indeed confirmed the CAP backers' hopes, testifying that the dam constituted the tribe's only hope for economic salvation and stressed that without it his people would continue to live in poverty.[44]

Preservationists anticipated the pro-dam lobby might try such a move, and so they attempted to enlist the aid of a prominent anthropologist, Cornell University Professor Henry Dobyns, a leading authority on the Hualapai Tribe who had done extensive archeological assessments and excavations in lower Grand Canyon. However, this move backfired and instead, Dobyns replied that

Figure 7. Arizona Representatives Morris Udall and John Rhodes, *far left*, enlist the aid of George Rocha, chief of the Hualapai Nation, to support Bridge Canyon Dam—tactically renamed Hualapai in 1966. *Courtesy of Special Collections, University of Arizona Library.*

he would not oppose the dams but that he in fact would be "very happy to testify...in favor" of Bridge Canyon Dam because it offered economic opportunity for the Hualapai Tribe, and would help them to become integrated into the "United States' body politic." Blasting the preservationists' campaign, Dobyns accused them of racial discrimination and of attempting to hold the Hualapai Tribe in "economic, social, and political subordination."[45]

Many supporters of the dams now believed Dobyns and the Hualapai Tribe were the perfect solution to the preservationists' antidam offensive. The Phoenix newspapers soon published Dobyns's remarks, and Morris Udall gleefully referenced Dobyns's letter to Weiner during a speech on the floor of the House of Representatives entitled, "The Conservation Plot That Failed," and inserted the letter itself into the *Congressional Record*. Dobyns himself testified before the House Committee on 13 May, and he admonished Brower and his "fellow liberals" for not seeing "the wisdom of the conservation of Indians as well as rocks and ducks."[46]

Preservationists, in turn, offered a counterargument. Dr. Stephen Jett, who had questioned Barry Goldwater about the potential benefits for the Navajo Nation at the Grand Canyon conference, also appeared. Although he met with David Brower and other leaders of the preservationists' effort prior to the hearings, Jett testified as a private individual because he believed, on the basis of his own doctoral research, that the "interests of the tribe should be represented." Though his testimony lacked the official blessing of the Navajo Tribal Council, it was only because the tribe had just learned of the hearings and did not have time to prepare a response. Jett assured the committee that he had the approval of the tribal chairman, who was very concerned about the proposed inundation of the scenic beauty of Marble Canyon, and inserted a detailed statement into the record that pointed out that the federal government had failed to consult with the tribe on the proposed legislation. Professor Jett argued that projections indicated that the demand for "scenic tourism" would increase exponentially over that for water-based recreation during the next four decades, and in anticipation of that, the tribe wished to develop tourist access to overlooks along the "Navajo Rim" of the gorge. Alternative sources of power would also create opportunity for the poverty-stricken Navajo people because the Reservation contained vast, undeveloped deposits of coal and uranium. Jett maneuvered so that he could testify after Dobyns, thus having a chance to rebut him, and he entered a statement demonstrating how the Hualapai Tribe would also benefit from scenic tourism if tribal parks were developed in lower Grand Canyon.[47]

Proponents of the Grand Canyon dams and preservationists alike had attempted to gain approval of the Native Americans in the region. However, the preservationists only had this opportunity because the CAP lobby failed to fully anticipate the potential impact Native American testimony would have in a larger social context. Between 1957 and 1962, proponents of a state-constructed Marble Canyon Dam had antagonized the 100,000 members of the Navajo Tribe by failing to include them as beneficiaries to the project. However, even with this evidence, Stewart Udall's Pacific Southwest Water Plan and its incarnations did not consider offering compensation to the Navajo Tribe. Yet, beginning in 1965, these same federal proposals included compensation for the Hualapai, a tribe with a total population of just over nine hundred people. As a result, the CAP lobby missed a tremendous opportunity in the spring of 1966 to gain the support of all Native Americans in the region.

Consequently, although CAP proponents had also gained the tacit approval of several other Arizona Native American groups, including the White Mountain Apache, San Carlos, and Pima Nations, and could argue truthfully that most Arizona tribes approved of the project, the preservationists could counter by pointing out that most Arizona *Indians* opposed it, because the Navajo Nation, the largest Indian group in the United States, far outnumbered the combined population of the rest of Arizona's Native American groups.

Despite failing to gain the approval of all the Native American groups in the region and the continuing concerns of the Pacific Northwest states, Wayne Aspinall concluded the hearings and announced that he would remand the proposal to the Subcommittee on Public Works to work out compromises in closed sessions and then pass the bill to the full Interior Committee. Both Marble and Bridge/Hualapai Dams remained in the bill despite the Budget Bureau's recommended deferral of the latter; and although the Interior Department had adopted the Budget Bureau's position, Secretary Udall believed privately that if Congress passed the bill with both dams in it, Carl Hayden's influence would prove decisive and the senator would be able to persuade President Johnson to sign it. These were heady times for CAP proponents, for not since 1950 had a proposal including the CAP come before the full Interior Committee, and Morris Udall and John Rhodes canvassed the members from both sides of the aisle to see where they stood. Rhodes and Udall also conducted polls of the Rules Committee—the last stop before a floor debate—and the House at large. The results were encouraging; despite the preservationists' offensive and the increasing volume of mail, it appeared as though these efforts were having little or no effect upon Congress. In late May at the conclusion of the open Reclamation Subcommittee hearings, Rhodes and Udall reported to members of the Arizona lobby that they believed they had the votes to gain passage of the bill in the Rules Committee and in the House as a whole, although Rhodes stated that the bill's chances would be greatly improved if its supporters could obtain the backing of the president.[48]

Opponents and advocates of the Grand Canyon dams now awaited the next stage of the controversy and steeled themselves for the floor debate that both sides believed was coming. With Chairman Aspinall behind the bill, and the Arizona-California alliance still intact, it appeared that the bill stood a good chance of gaining a favorable report from the full Interior Committee, a milestone in Arizona's struggle to obtain the CAP. Despite the preservationists' media offensive, the proponents of the dams appeared to have retained their hold on the Congress, and the only imminent danger to passage lurked in the form of the opposition from the Pacific Northwest. Morris Udall still believed that he could convince Thomas Foley and Henry Jackson, of Washington, to work out a solution acceptable to all parties, and though compromises made to gain political support had swelled the bill to a cumbersome size, these deals had forged a powerful political juggernaut that congressional opponents would find difficult if not impossible to overcome once the legislation made it to the House floor.

Supporters of the dams also continued their lobbying efforts to sway Congress and public opinion. Morris Udall and John Rhodes organized a series of luncheons the first week of June 1966 and invited all members of Congress to "have a steak on Arizona" and hear presentations by themselves and Barry Goldwater demonstrating why the dams constituted an indispensable element of the Lower Colorado Basin Project. They of course added that, contrary to the Sierra Club's "misrepresentations," the dams would not harm Grand Canyon National Park at all. The Bureau's large-scale model of Grand Canyon was once again pressed into service, and a detailed memorandum refuting the Carlin and Moss analyses extolling the cost savings of nuclear power was passed out at each meeting. The response was very favorable, and the action adroit, for by using their incumbency and celebrity status to their advantage, the personal touch offered by Rhodes, Udall, and Goldwater had a much greater effect upon members of Congress than letters from faceless constituents using language copied directly from the *Sierra Club Bulletin* or other conservation publications. Despite the preservationists' media blitz, Morris Udall's informal vote projections as well as his correspondence from his colleagues suggest that the preservationists' publicity campaign, while having a great effect upon public opinion, had not translated into congressional opposition.[49]

Arizona water lobbyists also planned a massive letter campaign to try to counteract the effect of the national publicity gained by the preservationists; however, their audience was not as widespread. Seeking to make up for its lack of mass appeal, the CAP task force selected its targets with care, aiming to sway individuals of great influence, or to associate the CAP with issues that would resonate with the American public. On 3 and 6 June the task force met and agreed to target corporate America through its registered Washington lobbyists. An examination of the lobbying plan reveals a veritable "who's who" of American business, with letters sent to dozens of lobbyists, including fifty major oil companies, General Electric, Goodyear, the Southern Pacific Railroad, and U.S. Steel.[50]

Morris Udall, Wayne Aspinall, and other CAP supporters also increased their efforts to paint environmentalists as racist with a stepped-up and somewhat devious public relations campaign. Arizona's CAP task force decided to send an avalanche of letters from the Hualapai chairman, and from other Arizona and Colorado tribes, to Congress, President Johnson, the National Council of Churches, Secretary Udall, and 12,000 "Indian friends," emphasizing that Hualapai Dam would enable them to cast off their bonds of poverty. A special letter "to be released to the press" was to be sent from Chief George Rocha to David Brower in a move designed to taint the Sierra Club Executive Director personally. However, Rocha was not entrusted with the actual writing of these letters; that task was delegated to Central Arizona Project Association President Rich Johnson. All the chief was asked to contribute was his signature, along with some Hualapai Tribal Council letterhead.[51]

Johnson, the high-powered Phoenix attorney and lobbyist, ghostwrote this excerpt, signed by Chief Rocha, as a plea for support from selected "Indian friends":

> My people have lived in isolation and poverty for so long that we have almost forgotten how to hope for a better way. The progress and prosperity of the nation have not touched our lives. Our world is the canyon country of the Colorado River in Arizona. There are no jobs for us. We have no businesses to run and no resources to sell, but now there is a new hope for us. I will tell you about it because we need your help to make the dreams of our people come true....[Hualapai Dam] will make jobs and businesses for us and we will not be a poor and forgotten people any longer.

Johnson also wrote similar letters that were signed by the chiefs of the San Carlos, Pima, and the White Mountain Apache Nations, while Felix Sparks of the Upper Colorado River Commission was recruited to write letters from the chiefs of the Southern Ute, and Ute Mountain Tribes.[52] This strategy conceived by the CAP lobby demonstrates that they understood the larger social context in which the controversy was taking place and that they believed that they could succeed in turning current civil rights concerns in their favor by portraying opponents of the dams as selfish elitists who not only desired to keep most ordinary Americans out of lower Grand Canyon, but who also sought to deny the rightful owners of the Hualapai Dam site the right to profit from their own resource. This strategy had real potential to negate the gains environmentalists had recently made in the court of public opinion.

Opponents of the Grand Canyon dams, unaware that they were about to be accused of being racist, also continued to make appeals to the American public, believing that the critical phase of the controversy was about to be fought.[53] Richard Bradley—who, since the publication of his *Reader's Digest* article, had received a steady stream of correspondence from people asking how they could help—refused to rest on his laurels, and he continued to correspond with the editors of *Atlantic* magazine to try to convince them to carry the story. However, the magazine continued to stall.[54] Meanwhile, at the grassroots level, two intrepid ninth graders, Jeff Mandell and Kenneth Light, from East Meadow, New York, began a club they called "the Grand Canyoneers," recruited seventy-five compatriots, and wrote letters to all members of the House and Senate, even managing to extract a token donation from U.S. Supreme Court Justice William O. Douglas.[55] The members of the Colorado Open Space Coordinating Council's Grand Canyon Task Force also continued scheduling debates, and by June they had purchased four Glen Canyon films from the Sierra Club and had shown them an estimated two hundred times, consulted with *Science* magazine about a proposed article, started branches in Baltimore and Detroit, and organized a three-day antidam "marathon" at the University of Colorado, during which members had shown movies and handed out literature. However, the COSCC also faced the harsh reality that they would not be able to afford placing an ad in the *New York Times* as they had planned because they simply could not afford the $10,000–$15,000 it would cost.[56]

The Sierra Club also faced financial hardship as a result of its book publishing and its simultaneous campaigns to preserve the North Cascades, portions of the Coastal Redwoods, and Grand Canyon. Although it had brought high-powered technical expertise to bear upon the proposal during the recent congressional hearings, in late May it seemed as though Congress had ignored this testimony and was proceeding to negotiate a compromise in accordance with existing reclamation policy. The critical debate in the House during which the battle might be won or lost was imminent, and preservationists needed to sustain the momentum of their stunning success in gaining access to *Reader's Digest*. Yet even as the hearings were taking place, David Brower was pursuing other means by which to bring the issue before the public in dramatic fashion, and was considering running ads in national newspapers, a tactic that had already, in December of 1965, raised public awareness of the Sierra Club's crusade to establish a Redwood National Park.[57]

Brower hired Freeman, Mander, and Gossage—an advertising firm out of San Francisco—to help plan strategy; however, Brower's conferences with Howard Gossage and Jerry Mander revealed sharp differences in philosophy over what approach they each believed stood the best chance of precipitating a public reaction. Brower, the amateur, desired a simple, clear message, one that would reiterate the arguments he and other conservationists had been disseminating for the past several years. However, Gossage and Mander believed that the ad should be more than just a recitation of facts and arguments; it must be "an event," something people would talk about. Otherwise, argued Gossage, "there's no point." Reviewing one of Mander's ideas, Brower reflected that it was "Madison Avenue, not Sierra Club." Ultimately, neither side could convince the other and so amateur and professionals remained divided over tactics. "I was a bit chicken," Brower recalled later, and he called *New York Times* editor John Oakes and convinced him to split the run, something that the paper had never done before, so that both approaches, conservative and aggressive, could be utilized. However, with legislation calling for the construction of dams in Grand Canyon on the threshold of approval in the Interior Committee, there was one issue that all parties agreed was of utmost importance: the release of the ad must be timed exactly to have its maximum effect upon public opinion.[58] And as events were soon to prove, the timing, in this instance, was perfect.

6

The Hinge of Fate

Next year for...Senator [Hayden] is always
problematical.

—O. M. Trask, Central Arizona Project Task Force,
letter, August 1967

Ever since the beginning of the Grand Canyon dam controversy in 1963, the proponents of Bridge and Marble Canyon Dams argued that they would create vast new recreational opportunities and open the lower canyon to millions of people. Attempting to manipulate public opinion, dam advocates such as Floyd Dominy, Craig Hosmer, Morris Udall, and Wayne Aspinall contended that the preservationists wanted to reserve the lower canyon for the relatively few people who possessed either the financial resources to take a float trip down the river or who had the physical stamina to explore this remote region on foot. Citing Lake Powell as an example of how reservoirs could improve the accessibility of nature, proponents of the Grand Canyon dams portrayed preservationists as a selfish minority, out of step with President Johnson's Great Society.

Accusations of elitism hit home with preservationists, who sought to distance themselves from ideas that they themselves had advocated only a short time before. Even David Brower had voted in favor of dams in Grand Canyon in 1949, and Sierra Club leaders such as Bestor Robinson and other longtime members still argued that recreational reservoirs constituted an appropriate use of national park lands. Indeed, the National Park Service had tried to accommodate reservoir construction during the 1930s until the tenure of Newton Drury, and even Drury, though steadfast in his defense of Grand Canyon National Park, wavered over whether reservoirs and national monuments were irreconcilable, in all probability because he believed that monuments would be more difficult to defend from encroachment.[1] Bestor Robinson's arguments in favor of recreation during the 1940s began appearing in Bureau of Reclamation and Interior Department publications during the 1960s, much to the chagrin of preservationists.[2]

According to historian Stephen Fox, public awareness of environmental issues increased tremendously in the twenty years after the conclusion of World War II, so that by the mid 1960s a revolution of sorts was occurring within the environmental movement itself. People were not only becoming increasingly concerned over threats to the national park system and wildlife, they also were worried about threats posed by pesticides, declining air and water quality, and other environmental issues that threatened their personal health and quality of life, a trend that is at least partially indicated by a steady rise in membership of conservation organizations. By 1969, a National Wildlife Federation poll showed that fewer people were concerned about the preservation of open spaces and, arguably, natural phenomena—what historian Alfred Runte calls "monumentalism"—than about contaminated air, water, food and other threats to the global ecosystem.[3] In 1966 these two strands of environmental thought permeated environmental discourse as the leaders of the movement sought to determine the direction in which the movement was headed, while environmentalists, having cast off the ideology of wise use, now confronted issues that threatened to make mere preservationism an anachronism as well.

Environmentalists trying to save Grand Canyon utilized these two approaches with varying degrees of success. In *Time and the River Flowing* the Sierra Club attempted to depict the Canyon as an ecosystem that should not be divided into parts because of the harm it would do to the whole. However, attempts to demonstrate that Grand Canyon was still an untouched ecosystem failed to resonate with the American public and, in any case, the argument is inaccurate. Drastic changes within the Colorado River system began to occur with the construction of Hoover and other dams during the first three decades of the twentieth century, while Glen Canyon Dam forever altered the ecosystem of Grand Canyon itself. Native fish such as the Colorado River squaw-fish, which reached a length of six feet and had annual runs reminiscent of the salmon and steelhead migrations of the Pacific Northwest, were virtually eradicated by 1940, their migratory patterns interrupted by impenetrable concrete barriers, while the removal of silt wrought havoc with their spawn-ing redds. In addition to the squawfish, humpback chubs also virtually disap-peared after the construction of the main-stem dams, while exotic species such as trout, stocked initially in Grand Canyon tributaries such as Bright Angel and Tapeats Creeks, flourished in the cold, clear tailwaters of these dams. The trout grew in size and population at such a rate that Lee's Ferry and Wil-low Beach, below Glen Canyon and Hoover Dams respectively, became world-renowned trout fisheries, and the prolific explosion of the main-stem trout population, in turn, created an artificial rookery for eagles and other birds of prey in Grand Canyon, drawn by the new supply of food.[4] Though Alfred Runte contends that preservationists abandoned ecological arguments in their defense of Grand Canyon because of lack of public understanding,[5] in all probability these arguments were never considered seriously because they would have been too easy to disprove.

Preservationists seeking to defend Grand Canyon appealed to the great mass of the American people, not with complex ecological arguments, but through a simple direct approach that turned the Bureau's argument of elit-ism on its head. Grand Canyon belonged to everyone, preservationists argued, and it was those who sought to deface it with dams who were selfish, not the people trying to save it. Grand Canyon encompassed the whole canyon, not just the hundred-mile section contained within the artificial boundaries of the national park and monument. While preservationists contended that the entire canyon should be preserved for future generations within an enlarged national park, and that there was still time to do it, proponents of the dams contended that Marble and Hualapai reservoirs would create new recreational opportunities in a spectacular, previously inaccessible setting. Thus, preser-vationists and developmental interests alike tried to portray the other side as selfish, and these two arguments crashed head on into each other in early June of 1966.

The Sierra Club placed full-page advertisements in the *New York Times* and other national newspapers on 9 June 1966, an event that altered the Grand Canyon dam controversy dramatically. The *Times* split the run, and David

Brower's relatively tame ad consisted of an "open letter" to Secretary Udall in which Brower reiterated many of the arguments that Jeff Ingram, Laurence Moss, and Alan Carlin advanced during the May hearings. The ad contained an appeal for people to write their congressmen, senators, Stewart Udall, and the president, and closed by asking the interior secretary to find [the Bureau] "something better to do." In contrast, the professional ad submitted by Jerry Mander and Howard Gossage was confrontational and eye-catching. "Now Only You Can Save Grand Canyon From Being Flooded...For Profit," the ad screamed in large, headline-sized text. A recitation of the arguments followed, including a statement implying that Stewart Udall had silenced other bureaus within the Interior Department such as the National Park Service. The ad also suggested that readers send contributions, and mail either separate letters or cut out and send the attached coupons, which had the names and addresses of key government officials already printed on them. Emphasizing that the Canyon belonged to all Americans, the ad closed with this admonition: "Remember, with all the complexities of Washington politics and the ins and outs of committees and procedures, there is only one simple incredible issue here: This time it's the Grand Canyon they want to flood. *The Grand Canyon.* [Emphasis theirs]"[6]

Supporters of the dams reacted angrily, claiming that the ads were misleading, and they accused the Sierra Club of trying to deceive the American public into believing that the dams would flood the entire canyon from rim to rim. Representative Morris Udall quickly counterattacked in an impassioned speech delivered on the floor of the House the same day the advertisements were released. Expressing "shock and indignation," Udall raged that the advertisements were "dishonest" and "inflammatory" and stated that "[he had] seldom, if ever seen a more distorted and flagrant hatchet job than this." In Udall's opinion, the ads were misleading and dishonest because they included a picture of a portion of Grand Canyon that lay outside the boundaries of the national park; hence, he felt that the Sierra Club's contention that Hualapai Dam would inundate part of Grand Canyon was simply untrue because he believed the American public viewed "Grand Canyon," and "Grand Canyon National Park," as one and the same.[7]

Were the Sierra Club advertisements misleading as Udall charged, or merely the product of the methodology of professional advertising? Brower himself wrote Udall shortly before the publication of the ads and emphasized that while in his view a lake five hundred feet deep would indeed flood out the Colorado River, for reclamationists to accuse him of trying to dupe the public into believing that the dams would flood the canyon from rim to rim was simply "preposterous." The ad Udall focused his most intense attacks upon was written by Mander and Gossage, which was designed to generate mass appeal, through an eye-catching headline. If one were to read only this portion of the ad, one might be left with the impression that Grand Canyon would indeed be flooded from rim to rim—and not just inside the park. However, the text of the ad states clearly that the canyon would only be flooded to a maximum depth of five hundred feet. Brower's ad, though it did not specify the actual depth of the reservoirs, included a large photo of the Bridge Canyon site taken by the Bureau of Reclamation itself, which had recently been published in a *Newsweek* article, upon which the Bureau had superimposed Hualapai Dam and Reservoir. The photo demonstrated clearly that the reservoir would occupy only the inner gorge of the canyon even at its deepest point and would not even inundate that completely. A smaller copy of this same photo was also included in the Mander/Gossage ad. So while the Sierra Club advertisements may have been sensational, and perhaps inflammatory from the perspective of a CAP supporter, to say that they were deliberately misleading is an accusation not supported by the evidence and is in fact refuted by the inclusion of the Bureau's own pictures.[8]

Indeed, in the same speech where Udall accused the Sierra Club of lying, he made at least two false assertions on the floor of the House himself: that former Park Service Director Albright approved of a high Bridge/Hualapai Dam; and that both dams were to be utilized as run-of-the-river projects when, as Floyd Dominy had exhaustively testified in congressional hearings, they were absolutely indispensable because of their ability to generate peaking power. Preservationists contended that if the dams were operated as peaking plants, reservoir fluctuations would scar the canyon walls owing to silt and mineral deposition as was the case at Hetch Hetchy. In addition, Udall, Rhodes, and other dam proponents continued to deny that the Bridge/Hualapai and Marble Canyon dam sites and reservoirs were in Grand Canyon, despite the assertions of professional geologists, a strategy clearly designed to keep the public from associating the CAP dams with Grand Canyon. The semantic gymnastics of these CAP proponents appear every bit as misleading as the Sierra Club's arguments that the dams would "flood" the canyon.[9]

Scarcely had the smoke cleared from Morris Udall's blast at the preservationists than another event, one that has entered the mythology of environmental history, occurred. On 10 June 1966, less than twenty-four hours after
the publication of the Sierra Club's advertisements, the Internal Revenue Service notified the club leadership that it was now under investigation for vio-
lating IRS regulations governing lobbying. Specifically, it was charged that the
club through its advertising had attempted to have a "substantial" influence on
the pending legislation, a direct violation of IRS statutes based upon the
Supreme Court's 1954 *Harriss* decision. As a result, the IRS stated that it could
no longer guarantee the tax-deductibility of contributions made to the club
while it investigated the club's lobbying activities. Sierra Club president Edgar
Wayburn remembered later "a small faceless man in a dark blue suit" hand-
delivered the IRS notice to the Sierra Club office in San Francisco, while Brower insisted at the time that it was delivered by a "federal marshal...for dramatic
effect."[10]

Although it has never been determined who precipitated the IRS action,
many prominent conservationists blamed Morris Udall for initiating the investigation. The popular account as related by many preservationists is that Mo
Udall was either having lunch or drinks at the Congressional Hotel bar in
Washington with Assistant IRS Commissioner Sheldon Cohen on 9 June
1966 when he showed Cohen the Sierra Club ad in the *Washington Post* and
said emphatically, "How the hell can the Sierra Club get away with this?"
David Brower and Sierra Club President Edgar Wayburn insisted that Udall
later admitted to them personally that he had not only initiated the IRS action,
but that he recognized it as a colossal blunder on his part because of the public reaction that followed.[11] Floyd Dominy also credited Mo Udall, "based on
some pretty good surmising," for "being smart enough" to think of this strategy and wished he had thought of it himself.[12]

However, Morris Udall denied vehemently the charges that he asked
Cohen to revoke the Sierra Club's tax status, an assertion that brings a ring-
ing defense from his brother Stewart, who blamed the "White House" for
ordering the investigation.[13] Regardless of who was ultimately responsible, and
despite Assistant Commissioner Cohen's assertions that the IRS was merely
trying to "administer the tax laws as they have been enacted by Congress," it
is indisputable that the Internal Revenue Service reacted to the Sierra Club
advertisements with unprecedented speed; and that speed, when combined

with the fact that the IRS applied its decree retroactively to include all contributions made after 9 June, appears to give the preservationists' assertions that they had been singled out a basis in fact.

Roy Elson, aide to Senator Hayden, rejected the notion that Hayden had anything to do with the IRS action, although he admitted in an interview that he had suggested it to Hayden but that "the Senator would have no part of it."[14] California Representative Craig Hosmer, perhaps the most antagonistic opponent conservationists faced, asked preservationist witnesses point-blank about the expenditures their organizations had incurred in trying to defeat the Grand Canyon dams on at least two separate and public occasions: the September hearings of 1965 and the May hearings of 1966, where Wayne Aspinall and Mo Udall joined him in this line of inquiry.[15] Sierra Club director William Siri believed that Mo Udall brought the ad to the attention of an IRS official without actually suggesting that the IRS investigate the club's tax status.[16] This version of events is supported by the documentary evidence: Mo Udall wrote Cohen on 10 June 1966, the day after the ads were placed, inquiring as to whether contributions to the Sierra Club elicited by the newspaper ads were tax-deductible; however, he did not ask for an investigation into the Sierra Club's activities in this letter.[17] Perhaps Cohen, prompted by Udall's letter, or perhaps after their alleged conversation at the Congressional Hotel, initiated the investigation himself. It is also possible that the suggestion was made over the telephone by Udall or someone else and that no record of it exists. However, the argument, as some preservationists have made it,[18] on the basis of hearsay evidence, that Morris Udall definitively initiated the investigation and intended to use the IRS revocation as a weapon to damage the Sierra Club, is not conclusively supported by the documentary record.

Although it is impossible to determine who initiated the investigation, clearly the possibility of IRS intervention had been discussed widely among CAP proponents for some time, and of course, the Sierra Club had created a tax-exempt foundation in 1960 in anticipation of this very event.[19] Although the Sierra Club and other conservation organizations were to play the role of the martyr effectively for the next few months, it is inconceivable that the IRS investigation came as much of a surprise to leading proponents and opponents of the dams alike. Possibly the most enduring mystery of the IRS revocation is not who ordered it, but rather, why it took so long for someone to do so, given the widely held hostility for the preservationists' position.

Historians have focused upon trying to determine who was responsible for ordering the IRS investigation; however, perhaps the more relevant question is: What effect did it have upon the controversy? Sierra Club historian Michael Cohen argues that the IRS action turned a conservation issue into a civil rights issue without elaborating far beyond this observation, other than to state that the "young American public...took the ferment of Berkeley to the national stage,"[20] an accurate but incomplete assessment. The Grand Canyon dam controversy was being fought on at least two levels: in the court of American public opinion, and in the political arena. The impact the IRS action had upon the controversy in the first case was nothing short of seismic, for now the issues transcended mere preservation and recreation. In June of 1966, with the nation already in a frenzy over civil rights, student protests, and growing opposition to American involvement in Vietnam, the IRS revocation constituted only the latest example of heavy-handed federal repression of civil liberties, particularly the rights of free speech and petition. When news of the IRS action became public knowledge, tens of thousands of people reacted, inundating Congress with angry letters. Estimates of the volume of mail vary, and the tabulations are scant, but California Senator Thomas Kuchel later recalled that it was "one of the largest letter writing campaigns I have ever seen."[21] Stewart Udall's staff counted over twenty thousand letters mailed just to the interior secretary,[22] while the papers of important political players contain tens of thousands more. How many letters came in to Washington as a result of the ads and IRS action is open to debate; Morris Udall described the mail as a "deluge,"[23] while some historians have put the figure at "millions," one citing an interview with a Bureau official who claimed that dump trucks were used to haul it to congressional offices.[24] Though difficult to obtain an exact figure, clearly a veritable avalanche of letters arrived at the offices of federal officials in the wake of the IRS revocation.

A representative sample of the letters contained within the Interior Department and Sierra Club archives and in the papers of the Wilderness Society, Mo and Stewart Udall, Carl Hayden, John Saylor, and John Rhodes demonstrates that a shift in focus occurred after the IRS revocation.[25] Prior to the IRS action, the letter writers generally claimed affiliation with one or more conservation organizations and wrote only of their concern for Grand Canyon. After 10 June 1966 people wrote Congress citing concerns with violations of free speech, petition, and due process, along with their concerns about Grand Canyon; many others wrote the Sierra Club, stating that they wanted to become members as an act of protest because they believed the IRS action threatened the fundamental rights that constituted the very foundations of the Republic itself.[26] Editorials appeared in newspapers across the nation criticizing both the proposed damming of Grand Canyon and federal interference with basic constitutional rights. Terms such as "police state" and "tyranny" appeared with regularity in correspondence and published newspaper editorials; the *New York Times* accused Secretary Udall of prohibiting free speech within his own department by "silencing" agencies that could be presumed to oppose the dams while at the same time allowing the Bureau of Reclamation to "lobby the public shamelessly and tirelessly with the public's own money."[27]

Whether Stewart Udall muzzled the National Park Service is a matter of debate. Udall responded to Brower's accusations by stating that once the Interior Department adopted a position as a matter of policy, it would inhibit his agency's ability to function if it were torn by dissension. However, Park Service Director George Hartzog censured a Park Service employee for distributing literature against Bridge Canyon Dam in October of 1965, six months *after* Udall adopted the Budget Bureau's recommendation that Bridge Canyon Dam be deferred.[28] Yet the interior secretary failed to communicate this policy shift to Park Service personnel for more than a year, and it was only after Brower's 30 March telegram from Grand Canyon that Udall informed park superintendents that their subordinates could oppose Bridge Canyon Dam.[29] Even after Udall's pronouncement, Yosemite National Park Superintendent John Davis, with Director Hartzog's subsequent approval, intervened to prevent a concessionaire from showing the Sierra Club's Glen Canyon film in June 1966 because the film opposed the Bureau's proposals for Grand Canyon, an incident that evoked accusations of censorship from Sierra Club officials.[30] Merrill Beal, Grand Canyon National Park naturalist during the controversy, contended that he was "instructed" to not oppose the programs of the Bureau of Reclamation, which favored Bridge Canyon Dam throughout the controversy.[31] Thus, it appears that Park Service personnel received an admonition to refrain from opposing Bridge Canyon Dam from the upper echelons of either the National Park Service or the Interior Department even after Secretary Udall had abandoned Bridge Canyon Dam in April of 1965.[32]

Though the Sierra Club leadership as early as 1960 had planned for the likely eventuality that the club's lobbying activities would result in an IRS action, they did not anticipate the enormity of the public reaction it precipitated. Brower stopped short of stating that he had planned his strategy in anticipation of a public windfall, only admitting that he felt "confident" that the public would react in such a fashion and that he "hoped that the IRS would be that stupid," that is, to attack the club for so stridently opposing the Grand Canyon dams.[33] It appears that although the Sierra Club leadership from Brower, Richard Leonard, and even Bestor Robinson agreed to challenge the free-speech restrictions of the Federal Lobbying Act should the Sierra Club's activities evoke a reaction from the IRS, they remained unaware of the larger social context in which this episode was playing out and thus did not realize the great potential for public sympathy should such a revocation occur. Evidently the club's leadership was not Machiavellian enough to try to antagonize the IRS into taking away its tax-deductible status in anticipation of a public windfall; Brower commented upon the serendipitous nature of the event by saying that "I was just lucky it worked out that way." However, in the wake of the 9 June advertisements, club leaders recognized immediately that larger social forces were at work and released several more ads during the congressional debate of the summer of 1966, each of which gave prominent space to the club's IRS travails.[34]

Ironically, it was the dam supporters who understood the social context of the times, and though unable to plug into public perceptions of federal interference with individual rights, they attempted to turn public concerns over racial issues to their advantage by portraying opponents of the dams as prejudiced against Native Americans. Rich Johnson's letters, signed by Hualapai Chief Rocha and other Native Americans, began arriving in the offices of congressmen, newspaper editors, and their other intended recipients at the beginning of July, and Arizona Representative George Senner read one aloud on the floor of the House and inserted it into the *Congressional Record*. Western newspapers began running articles arguing that the Hualapai Dam would confer great benefits upon the Hualapai Tribe, some printing passages "written" by Chief Rocha.[35]

In addition, Morris Udall, John Rhodes, Floyd Dominy, and other project advocates initiated a counterattack in the news media and scheduled television and radio appearances nationwide. Udall argued his case so convincingly that the editors of the *Washington Post* wrote in August that, contrary to the Sierra Club's assertions, "it is plain nonsense to speak of these proposed minor changes ruining the Grand Canyon."[36] When Mrs. E. P. Pierce, president of the General Federation of Women's Clubs, wrote an opposition letter to John Saylor, which the Pennsylvania representative entered into the *Congressional Record*, John Rhodes produced a letter and resolution favoring the dams from the president of the Arizona Women's Club.[37] The *Arizona Republic* and *Arizona Daily Star* encouraged their subscribers to write Congress, and the *Republic* claimed later that over seven thousand of its subscribers sent coupons to Congress, while an ephemeral organization, the Southwest Progress Committee, sponsored the production of a movie, "Grand Canyon, the Ever-Changing Giant," and scheduled it for television slots across the U.S.[38]

One Sierra Club member from Tucson alleged that the editor of the *Arizona Daily Star* went so far as to make threatening phone calls to local library officials and to the sisters of a Catholic hospital who had allowed him to use their buildings to show a Sierra Club film and make an antidam presentation.[39] Pro-dam newspapers, at the behest of the CAPA, also began to publicize that the Sierra Club had once supported the Grand Canyon dams itself.[40] This counteroffensive began to yield results, and less than one month after the Sierra Club advertisements of 9 June a steady stream of letters began trickling into congressional mailboxes whose authors wrote in favor of the dams. By mid-August, John Rhodes could write to a pro-dam constituent that many of his congressional colleagues were receiving as much mail in favor as opposed, while the *Arizona Republic* began to print letters from disgruntled Sierra Club members who disapproved of Brower's tactics.[41] Though the volume of pro-dam mail never came close to the deluge of the opposition, it was enough to let Congress know that there were two sides to the issue, and several congressmen communicated that they disliked the Sierra Club tactics and had received many letters in favor of the dams.[42]

Virtually forgotten by environmental historians, many of whom contend that the Sierra Club advertisements and the IRS revocation constituted the turning point at which the defeat of the dams became inevitable, is that the political process continued to move forward despite all the public protests and angry letters. The House Interior Committee kept working in the summer of 1966 and the political alliance among the basin states, forged by almost two years of heated negotiations and exasperating behind-the-scenes intrigue, remained intact, along with Hayden's formidable influence waiting in reserve in the Senate. Despite heated debates over the political deals already agreed upon, and numerous speeches delivered on the House floor by John Saylor and Michigan Representative John Dingell against the dams, the House Subcommittee on Public Works announced on 10 June that the bill would contain both dams, a payment of $16,398,000 to the Hualapai Tribe, and the formation of a water commission that would initiate a feasibility-grade study of water importation.[43]

The Lower Colorado River Basin Project now moved to the Subcommittee on Irrigation and Reclamation, chaired by Walter Rogers of Texas. Once there, representatives from the seven basin states blocked attempts by John Saylor to remove both dams, and by Thomas Foley, who tried to delete the feasibility study. At the conclusion of the debate the Subcommittee on 28 June voted 13–5 in favor of the proposal, with the dissents coming from Saylor and four politicians from the Pacific Northwest. With the Subcommittee hurdle cleared, the bill moved to the full House Interior Committee, the first time that the Central Arizona Project had come before the Interior Committee since the defeat of 1950. Carl Hayden, watching anxiously, looked forward to the coming floor debate, and he announced that despite Henry Jackson's opposition to the idea of importation from the Northwest, the Senate Interior Committee Chairman had promised to move on the bill immediately after House passage.[44]

On 13 July 1966 the Lower Colorado Basin Project was brought before the full House Interior Committee, and once again, the representatives from the Pacific Northwest attempted to amend the bill to delete the feasibility study. Saylor offered an amendment to delete both dams, and, as in the subcommittee, these attempts were defeated. However, after a week of tumultuous debate, Chairman Aspinall initiated action that threatened to unravel the fragile seven-state alliance. Aspinall, a stickler for legislative protocol who had a well-earned reputation for presenting bills that the Senate would find agreeable, was displeased with the stridency of the Pacific Northwest's objections. Believing that Senator Jackson would never allow such a feasibility provision to leave the Senate Interior Committee, Aspinall now proposed that the feasibility language be downgraded to a reconnaissance study, and he recommended the creation of a national water commission with jurisdiction over any proposal to import water into the Colorado Basin. California's representatives reacted angrily and threatened to walk out of the proceedings. Aspinall's suggestion, though a practical move, threatened to tear the seven-state agreement apart. Morris Udall, caught in an agonizing dilemma, voted in favor of the amendment, although he lamented the probable loss of California's support. On 21 July the House Interior Committee voted 20–9 to downgrade the importation analysis from a feasibility- to a reconnaissance-grade study.[45]

Frantic water officials from the seven basin states, faced with the prospect that years of painstaking negotiations would come to naught, met to try to work out a compromise solution; however, it looked as though the differences were now irreconcilable. It appeared as though one side would have to give, and the prospects for that seemed unlikely, especially now that Aspinall himself had intimated to some of his colleagues that he "had a deal in the Senate" based upon his proposal. California's support appeared irretrievably lost when Morris Udall, the future of the alliance and the Central Arizona Project hanging by a thread, proposed a solution to Aspinall that demonstrated his knowledge of the parliamentary system and his astute political instincts. Proposing to utilize a rare "motion to recommit," Udall's strategy involved some freewheeling semantics that would give Chairman Aspinall more flexibility to fight for the bill on the floor of the House, combined with creative usage of the rules for parliamentary procedure. Instead of calling for a feasibility study outright, Udall suggested that the bill be rewritten to include a reconnaissance study initially, with the promise that a feasibility study would follow immediately if the proposed national water commission determined that water importation was feasible. Udall brokered this agreement with Aspinall's blessing and regained California's backing without the knowledge of Saylor and Foley, who sought to keep the proposal bottled up in the committee.[46]

On 28 July 1966 the House Interior Committee met to vote on the Lower Colorado River Basin Project bill, John Saylor and Thomas Foley confident that the legislation would go down to defeat because of Aspinall's controversial amendment of the week before. Prior to the final vote, Craig Hosmer implementing Udall's strategy, moved to recommit the bill back to the Reclamation Subcommittee for alteration. The motion passed 20–10, and despite strenuous objections from Foley, Saylor, and Walter Rogers, the subcommittee chair, the bill was remanded back to the subcommittee, where the reconnaissance/feasibility language was added and approved. Aspinall then brought the altered bill back before the full committee, which was still obligated to vote on 28 July. After a bitterly contested session, during which an outraged Saylor accused the "selfish interests" from California and Arizona, as well as Chairman Aspinall, of "nefarious legislative shenanigans," the House Interior Committee voted 22–10 to report the bill favorably to the House floor.[47] Despite strong objections in the committee and another Sierra Club advertisement printed in the *New York Times* on 25 July,[48] now only the House Rules Committee, which included two congressmen from the state of California, stood between the Central Arizona Project and a House floor debate.

The Rules Committee is not typically a place where legislation is altered drastically; its function is to shape legislation so it conforms to the House rules of procedure for the upcoming floor debate. Consequently, Arizona's congressional representatives were euphoric after the favorable Interior Committee report, viewing the floor debate as a foregone conclusion. The bill included both dams, ignoring the Budget Bureau's recommendation that Bridge/Hualapai Dam should be deferred. While Representatives John Rhodes and Morris Udall congratulated each other, George Senner cried with joy. After years of waiting, it appeared that the CAP was close to becoming a reality. However, John Saylor, still seething about Mo Udall's tactics, angrily remarked: "If you think I'll offer any kind of a motion or anything else to get one drop of water for Arizona . . . after the way Arizona has acted in this, I'll see them in hell first."[49]

Morris Udall had polled the members of the Rules Committee in early May, to see whether the committee would object to releasing the bill to the floor in the event of a favorable Interior Committee report, and the fifteen members overwhelmingly supported the bill.[50] Now with the long-awaited floor debate seemingly imminent, Udall and Rhodes polled their House colleagues again to determine whether the bill stood a good chance of passage. On 22 August, Udall's poll revealed that 156 of his colleagues supported the bill outright, with another 70 leaning in favor of it. Calculating a "reasonably optimistic" assessment of the probables and undecided votes, Mo Udall believed that he stood a good chance of obtaining around 260 votes in support of the project, although only 218 were necessary to obtain passage.[51] Udall, Rhodes and the rest of the Arizona task force now swung into action to try to influence the probable and undecided votes through influential constituents or other methods, Udall even "nailing down" a colleague's vote with a gift of a framed picture of Grand Canyon that he paid for himself.[52]

Opponents of the dams also continued their efforts, although many of them were now resigned to the inevitability that the bill would come before the House. Richard Bradley ventured into hostile territory toward the end of July and delivered an address to the Los Angeles Town Hall to rebut Floyd Dominy, who had spoken several weeks earlier.[53] By the end of August, the Colorado Open Space Coordinating Council had helped produce and circulate two television documentaries to rebut the film produced by CAP advocates,[54] while the July–August *Sierra Club Bulletin* featured a cover photo of upper Lake Powell, with driftwood and other floating debris literally covering the reservoir's surface with the caption, "A Portent of Things to Come in Grand Canyon?"[55] Individuals also continued to lobby at the grassroots level; many people wrote the Sierra Club asking for reprints of articles to distribute to friends, including Mrs. Helen Skelton of Freemont, Indiana, who took $150.00 of her own money and placed full-page ads in two local newspapers.[56]

Preservationists also managed to rebut the attempts made by the reclamation lobby to portray them as anti-Indian, a campaign that had grown more intense as the summer progressed. Dr. Stephen Jett, who had testified against the dams during the May hearings, was asked by David Brower to discuss the Grand Canyon dams with the Navajo Tribal Council and attorney Norman Littell in July. Jett managed to convince Littell of the economic benefits a tribal park along the rim of Marble Canyon would bring. When the Navajo Council met on 1 August 1966 Littell had drafted a resolution in opposition to the dams, calling instead for the development of the reservation's vast deposits of coal. On 3 August the Tribal Council repudiated a 1961 resolution it had passed in favor of Marble Canyon Dam and overwhelmingly approved a measure condemning the Grand Canyon dams and the "tactics of the Udalls." The council also approved a contract with Peabody Coal Company to develop the reservation's coal resources for use in the WEST consortium's Four Corners and Navajo generating plants. Presidential Medal of Freedom recipient Annie Wauneka assisted in the preparation of a press release outlining the tribe's condemnation of the dams, and the national press picked up the story, demolishing the pro-dam lobby's attempt to paint the environmentalists as racist.[57]

John Saylor continued his offensive against the project, and he announced that he intended to offer an amended bill during the floor debate that would eliminate California's annual 4.4 million-acre-foot guarantee, both Grand

Canyon dams, Aspinall's Colorado projects, and the water-importation studies. Saylor argued that his proposal would "save one billion dollars—and
Grand Canyon too," offering the House of Representatives a relatively non-
controversial alternative to the CAP with the mid-term elections just over
three months away.[58]

Now that the critical proceedings in the Rules Committee were under
way, both pro- and antidam politicians stepped up the rhetoric in Congress.
During the months of July and August, the most vocal dam proponents, John
Rhodes and Morris Udall, addressed their House colleagues twelve times from
the podium and, not to be outdone, the antidam triumvirate of John Saylor,
John Dingell, and Henry Reuss of Wisconsin made thirty-seven speeches on
the floor while the Interior and Rules Committees discussed the bill.[59]

By the middle of August, when the bill still had not been released, Morris Udall began to suspect that the California representatives were obstruct-
ing the proceedings, and Udall and John Rhodes met with California water
advocates to determine whether this was the case. During a meeting on 22
August 1966 with water attorney Northcutt Ely, who still masterminded
California's water strategy three years after losing the epic Supreme Court
fight, Udall and Rhodes learned the fateful news. Ely claimed that he had spoken with some California congressmen who believed that John Saylor possessed the votes to pass his substitute bill during the upcoming floor debate.
Even worse from Arizona's perspective, Ely stated that he had obtained Wayne
Aspinall's backing because he had convinced Aspinall that if Saylor succeeded,
Henry Jackson would ram a similar bill through the Senate, and thus California and Colorado would lose the features most important to them. To prevent this from happening, Ely told Udall and Rhodes that he was using his
influence with the California members of the Rules Committee to prevent Saylor from presenting his substitution during the floor debate.[60]

Stunned, Udall and Rhodes, citing a poll Udall had completed that very
day, contended that they already had a firm commitment of three-fourths of the
votes needed to pass the legislation in its present form, along with enough
"probables" so that the bill should pass with ease. However, Ely was adamant,
so long as the possibility existed that Saylor's amended bill might gain
approval; he had instructed the two California representatives in the Rules
Committee to hold the bill indefinitely to keep it from the floor. The Arizona
representatives argued that even if Saylor succeeded, they had enough politi-

cal support to reinsert whatever Saylor managed to delete, and so there was little chance that a stripped-down version of the bill would ever pass the House.[61] For the next two weeks, with a growing desperation that never overwhelmed his sense of political pragmatism or personal tact, Morris Udall tried frantically to overcome the roadblock, even conducting a new poll on 26 August, indicating support for the bill had grown.[62] At one point John Rhodes briefly considered attaching the CAP bill as a rider to an appropriations bill, in an attempt to circumvent the Rules Committee altogether, but apparently determined that there was not enough time left in the current session to begin such a move.[63] Consequently, even though Rhodes and Udall cited strong evidence indicating that the House would pass the legislation, Ely continued to instruct the Rules Committee members from California to hold the Lower Colorado River Basin Project until it eventually died, the last gasp coming in mid-September of 1966, when Rhodes and Udall determined that the support they had obtained in August had evaporated owing to the imminence of the coming election.[64]

Did Northcutt Ely and Wayne Aspinall have legitimate reasons to fear John Saylor's threats to amend the bill to delete the Colorado/California provisions as well as the Grand Canyon dams in August of 1966? If so, it would appear as though the preservationists' campaign had bridged the public and political aspects of the Grand Canyon debate, and that environmental groups such as the Sierra Club could claim that they had saved the Canyon by stopping the dams. Environmental historians who argue that the preservationists are the primary cause of the bill's defeat base their arguments upon this presumption.[65] However, Northcutt Ely never cited any hard evidence to support his claim that John Saylor possessed the political strength to alter the bill. When pressed by Arizona's representatives, Ely could not produce any polling data and stated that his actions were based upon a "consensus" of senior California congressmen. Furthermore, when Rhodes and Udall asked Ely which congressmen he had spoken with, he refused to reveal their identities. It appears as though Ely either was unwilling or unable to demonstrate that his manipulation of the Rules Committee was based upon any hard evidence that would indicate Saylor possessed the strength to follow through on his threat.[66]

Conversely, Morris Udall and John Rhodes had been polling their House colleagues since May of 1966, and virtually all of these polls suggested that the bill stood a good chance of passage and had gained support throughout the summer of 1966 despite the public outcry against the dams. Les Alexander, of Udall's staff, reflected that it was common practice for the Speaker of the House to recommend that a bill be introduced to the floor when its sponsors could guarantee 150 solid votes in favor of it,[67] and by 22 August Rhodes and Udall could claim that they possessed well above that number. On 26 August Udall and Rhodes took a new poll that indicated they could count on 170 sure votes and 67 "probables" in their column, along with 76 members who were undecided or believed themselves uninformed who could go either way. Even Udall's worst-case assessment of how, in his opinion, each "probable" and "undecided/uninformed" member would vote yielded a majority of 228 at the very least. On the basis of this evidence, it appears that Rhodes and Udall had good reason to believe that the House would pass the proposal by a comfortable margin.

Contrary to Ely's assertions, there is no evidence to suggest that Aspinall was manipulating the Rules Committee as well to keep the bill in limbo, while there is a great deal to support the opposite conclusion. As chair of the Interior Committee, Aspinall had beaten back similar challenges from Saylor for most of the summer with ease, the bill passing by substantial margins on both the subcommittee and committee level every time Saylor attempted to contest it. Given Aspinall's position of influence, he could have killed the bill during the Interior Committee proceedings had he truly believed that Saylor could follow through with his threats. Furthermore, although Ely claimed that Aspinall shared his views, Morris Udall and John Rhodes obtained Aspinall's word on 10 September that if the bill should emerge from the Rules Committee, Aspinall would fight for it on the House floor.[68] Clearly Ely was the driving force behind the Rules Committee debacle, and though he claimed Aspinall supported him, he could not substantiate his arguments with solid evidence. In the face of strong indications that Rhodes and Udall possessed the backing to obtain House passage of the legislation as originally written, Ely apparently used the Saylor threat as an excuse to hold up the Lower Colorado River Basin legislation to accomplish some other purpose.

In order to understand Ely's actions, one must examine the Arizona/California water dispute in the aggregate. For almost five decades Arizona and California had battled over the lower-basin allocation of the Colorado River in the courts and Congress, and they came to the brink of exchanging gunfire in 1934 when Arizona Governor Benjamin Mouer called out the National Guard to prevent California from building a diversion dam on the lower reach of the river.[69] Northcutt Ely had been the mastermind behind California's water strategy since the late 1940s, and in the wake of Arizona's 1963 Supreme Court victory he was quoted widely as saying that California possessed the political power to negate the Court's decision through legislative intrigue.[70] Because of Ely's background as a water lawyer, he believed that in accordance with the doctrine of Prior Appropriation, California's 4.4 million-acre-foot allotment should receive priority over that of Arizona because California had put its allotment to "beneficial use" first. Ely geared California's strategy to attaining this objective, using the "California guarantee" as a bargaining chip with Arizona in exchange for California's political support.

But Ely was concerned with more than the mere preservation of California's 4.4 million-acre-foot allotment. In 1966 California was still using 5.2 million acre feet of water each year, 800,000 of which the Supreme Court had awarded to Arizona in 1963. After three years of negotiations and delays, Ely was apparently not really interested in passing a bill so much as in maintaining the status quo, because as long as the CAP remained unbuilt, California could go on using Arizona's water.

Although it is difficult to separate the issues from the mutual suspicions that had built up during forty-five years of subterfuge, the documentary record provides ample evidence of whether Ely was bargaining in good faith. When John Rhodes and Mo Udall met with Ely in late August to try to convince him that they had the votes to pass the project over Saylor's attempts to amend it, Ely indicated that he would be satisfied if the guarantee was preserved and stated that his fears were based upon what might happen if a bill were allowed to "go to the Senate with the 'guarantee' eliminated."[71] Believing that they could take Ely at his word, Rhodes and Udall then initiated negotiations with John Saylor in an attempt to preserve the "California guarantee," and in early September they received Saylor's counteroffer. Incredibly, John Saylor, the most strident environmentalist in Congress, wrote Arizona's representatives stating that he would support a bill that included a low dam at the Bridge Canyon site—one that would back water through the length of the national monument—and the California 4.4 million-acre-foot guarantee.[72] Here, then, would come the test of whether Ely was negotiating in good faith, for Saylor had given his word to Udall and Rhodes that he would now support the retention of the California guarantee during the floor debate.

John Saylor's counterproposal was revealing both of his own perception of strength as well as of Ely's true intentions. For Saylor to have proposed a compromise bill that included a reservoir that would stretch the entire length of Grand Canyon National Monument was indicative that Saylor believed that he stood little chance of obtaining his amendments on the floor; it was a desperate move by a shrewd politician who thought Rhodes and Udall had the votes to pass a two-dam bill. However, in the context of the Rules Committee situation, Saylor's support of one Grand Canyon dam, despite months of intense Sierra Club rhetoric, was only of secondary importance. Had Northcutt Ely been bargaining in good faith with Rhodes and Udall, Saylor's inclusion of the 4.4 million-acre-foot provision should have assuaged Ely's fears, for California's priority was now guaranteed by the very politician who had sworn to delete it. Yet when Rhodes and Udall presented the Saylor compromise to Ely, the latter balked, even though several California representatives had indicated that they would support it.[73] When Ely refused to grant his assent to Saylor's compromise, the bill's fate was sealed, because it was too late for further negotiations in the Eighty-ninth Congress. It is clear from this exchange that Northcutt Ely used the Saylor threat as a pretext to mask his true intentions—to manipulate the political process to delay the implementation of the Supreme Court decision of 1963, which he had lost, so that California could continue using 800,000 acre feet of Arizona's water allotment.

Arizona water advocates began assessing the blame for this catastrophic defeat even before the bill was officially pronounced dead in mid-September. Rich Johnson blasted California's representatives for "being unwilling to act... in good faith," a suspicion perhaps nurtured by his years of dealing with California's political and legal maneuvers.[74] One Arizona official, Larry Mehren, of the Central Arizona Project Association, named Carl Hayden as the culprit, evidently because the senator had not initiated concurrent hearings in the Senate, an assessment roundly condemned by the Phoenix newspapers and virtually everyone else associated with the project, Republicans and Democrats alike.[75] Rhodes and Udall were reluctant to blame California publicly, perhaps still viewing it as a potential source of support, and they even released a report that emphasized the positive accomplishments of 1966 that could be built upon in the next Congress.[76] Wayne Aspinall publicly blamed the defeat first and foremost upon the president for failing to back the proposal.[77]

It is difficult to determine where President Johnson stood on the issue of

dams in Grand Canyon. LBJ had a long history of supporting reclamation projects, voting in favor of the CAP both times it came before the Senate in
1950–1951, and he maintained a close friendship with Carl Hayden during his
presidency. However, Johnson also sought to avoid taking definitive positions
on controversial issues throughout his political career, and by the summer of
1966 the Grand Canyon dams had become a national issue as a result of the
Sierra Club's publicity campaign. Former Senate Majority leader Ernest McFarland, now a justice of the Arizona Supreme Court, telephoned his old Senate
ally on 1 August 1966 and spoke with him about the dams, receiving Johnson's promise not to take an opposition position before examining all the facts.
After his conversation with the president, McFarland concluded that LBJ could
be induced to support the project, but only after it emerged from the Rules
Committee and onto the House floor.[78] Stewart Udall believes that LBJ would
have supported the project had Senator Hayden asked for his support; however, Udall also warned Arizona's congressional representatives as early as 30
June that the passage of a bill including both dams would place LBJ in a
quandary.[79] In any event, President Johnson never had to make a decision
because the bill died in committee.

Despite Johnson's history of support for reclamation, many preservationists viewed him as being sympathetic to environmental issues, a perception
created by Johnson's 1964 address to Congress on the importance of preserving natural beauty and by his support of the Wilderness Act. However, most
Americans seeking to voice their concerns to the administration about Grand
Canyon communicated not with the president, but with his wife, Lady Bird
Johnson, because she had become one of the administration's chief spokesper-
sons on environmental issues as a result of her beautification campaign. Ordinary citizens concerned with the possible damming of Grand Canyon began to
write Mrs. Johnson in ever increasing numbers in 1966 as the political battle
reached its crescendo.[80]

Sharon Francis, who had collaborated with Stewart Udall in writing the
Quiet Crisis, worked for Lady Bird Johnson on beautification issues, and she
also aided the First Lady in determining an appropriate response to the Grand
Canyon dam controversy. Francis's involvement alarmed pro-dam officials
within the Interior Department. "Sharon Francis is about as 100 percent a
preservationist as they come," Orren Beaty wrote Stewart Udall in July, "and
I deeply regret her influence in Mrs. Johnson's office."[81] The First Lady com-

mented to Francis that the letters against the dams, which totaled about fifty a week, were the "highest caliber" letters she had seen on "any subject," and she insisted on answering many of them herself, rather than turning them over to the Interior Department for the standard reply because Mrs. Johnson thought that if she did so, their authors would infer that "she did not care." The First Lady believed she should take a position because to "preach natural beauty and ignore what was happening to the greatest beauty of them all— Grand Canyon," would be hypocritical. Though Mrs. Johnson never opposed the dams unequivocally, she desired that studies of alternatives be made that included an opportunity for public discussion, and she communicated these feelings to Secretary Udall.[82] Sharon Francis also discussed the possibility of having the Bureau of the Budget authorize the study of alternatives with the interior secretary, and although the amount of influence Mrs. Johnson was able to exert is a matter for conjecture, Sharon Francis believes that LBJ "deferred" to the First Lady on environmental issues.[83]

Perhaps one indication of Mrs. Johnson's influence with both the president and the public is evidenced by the efforts made by officials within the Bureau of Reclamation who, at the height of the Grand Canyon dam controversy, managed to convince the First Lady to dedicate Glen Canyon Dam, a public relations victory of the highest magnitude. Although the effect upon public perception is difficult to determine, clearly the Bureau hoped that the widely distributed photos and news accounts of Mrs. Johnson's speech atop Glen Canyon Dam would create the inference that she approved the construction of dams in Grand Canyon downstream.[84] One thing can be stated with certainty, however. Lyndon Johnson would have been forced to make a very difficult decision had Congress passed the Lower Colorado River Basin Project in 1966. Whether the president signed or vetoed the bill, he would most certainly have come under fire, either from influential pro-dam politicians, who could threaten his legislative agenda in Congress on one side, or fiscally conservative politicians, the First Lady, and an angry public on the other.

Why did the legislation fail in autumn of 1966? In their postmortems of the 1966 legislative session, Morris Udall, John Rhodes, Wayne Aspinall, and other proponents of the Grand Canyon dams tried to determine why they could not pass the legislation they had brought to the brink of success in the House. Although each of these key politicians acknowledged the preservationists' antidam offensive as important, they also indicated that it was only one of many factors that contributed to the congressional defeat of the Lower Colorado River Basin Project in 1966. The primary reason the bill failed, according to these and other participants, including veteran Senator Carl Hayden, was that the bill had become so encumbered with compromises that it bogged down when these political deals began to unravel.[85]

Water augmentation, the incentive Stewart Udall used in 1963 to gain California's support, also precipitated opposition from Henry Jackson, the Senate Interior Committee chair. Consequently, when the Pacific Northwest refused to compromise the issue of water importation from the Columbia River, a contingency that Stewart Udall and the framers of subsequent legislation had not anticipated, it placed John Rhodes and Morris Udall in an untenable position because California's support hinged upon a successful resolution of this problem. Complicating matters further, Wayne Aspinall had also become a proponent of water importation because he believed that if the CAP were built as a single project, it would take water from the upper basin; hence, he believed only through basin augmentation could the upper-basin allotment from the 1922 Compact be preserved.

The issue of interbasin water transfers brought three indispensable sources of potential support—California, Aspinall, and Jackson—into an irreconcilable conflict for which there was no politically acceptable solution. Had preservationists remained silent about the proposed Grand Canyon dams, Senator Henry Jackson would still have objected to the taking of water from his home state and would have posed an impenetrable roadblock to the Lower Colorado River Basin Project had it been passed by the House. The final blow, once the compromises had begun to unravel, was delivered by California water strategist Northcutt Ely, who used the delicate negotiations over importation studies, the Californian guarantee, and John Saylor's threatened amendments, to keep the bill bottled up in the Rules Committee, thus preserving the status quo—along with California's use of almost 800,000 acre feet of the water the Supreme Court had awarded Arizona in 1963.

Stewart Udall's grand strategy of 1963 now lay in shambles, undone by the very compromises that had held so much promise only a short time before. In early fall of 1966, the secretary realized that, in advocating a regional solution contingent upon water importation, he had unwittingly sowed the seeds of the bill's failure even though he had accomplished his initial goal of gaining California's support for the Central Arizona Project. Henry Jackson's adamant opposition to water importation placed Udall into a dilemma worse than the situation he had faced in 1963, because not only did Udall have yet to find the correct political formula to gain indispensable political support, he now had the added burden of dealing with the fallout from the recent legislative failure. Udall understood that as a federal official he had much greater latitude than did his brother or other proponents of a federal CAP because his position as interior secretary was somewhat insulated from Arizona politics as well as from the cacophony of criticism currently emanating from angry Arizona water officials and newspaper editors. Udall believed that it was his responsibility to assume once again the leadership of the effort in the wake of the failure in the House, although he realized that it would be difficult to untie this legislative Gordian knot without losing a great deal of political support. However, Udall believed a solution must be found, even if it took a change in reclamation policy, and in early September he directed his Interior Department staff to begin studying alternative proposals to dams in Grand Canyon.[86]

While the interior secretary explored alternative federal proposals, Arizona's water interests, frustrated with the lack of action by Congress when victory appeared to be within reach, revived the idea that the state should build the CAP without federal assistance. The moratorium on Arizona's FPC license application, imposed by Congress at Carl Hayden's insistence in 1964, was set to expire on 31 December 1966. Governor Sam Goddard, supported by Arizona's congressional delegation, directed the Arizona Power Authority and other state water agencies to report on the feasibility of a state-financed CAP by 1 January 1967.[87]

Although John Rhodes and Morris Udall endorsed the feasibility study of a state-funded project, they also began to formulate strategy to obtain passage of a federal CAP bill in the upcoming Ninetieth Congress. Udall and Rhodes believed that the recently defeated Lower Colorado River Basin Project bill was cumbersome and contained too many compromises and controversial provisions, and they now felt that a skeletal approach similar to the bills Carl Hayden had advocated since the 1963 Supreme Court decision would have a better chance of passage than a regional proposal. Representative George Senner predicted that a slimmed-down federal project would pass in the Ninetieth Congress, although one dam might have to be eliminated. Floyd Dominy also recommended the elimination of Marble Canyon Dam and the enlargement of Grand Canyon National Park to include Marble Canyon, an ironic position for the commissioner to take considering that he had denied that Marble Canyon was a part of Grand Canyon for so long. Nevertheless, Dominy had first broached the idea of compromise in April 1966 because he realized the difficulty of getting both dams through Congress.[88] Even Interior Secretary Stewart Udall did not oppose the feasibility studies of a state-funded CAP, although he cautioned state officials to put aside their frustrations with the federal government and look at the Arizona proposal objectively, because he believed that a federal project could still be obtained.[89]

Prominent environmental historians credit Stewart Udall with playing a major role in formulating the environmental ideology of the Kennedy and Johnson administrations during the formative period of the modern environmental movement.[90] Stewart Udall is revered by many environmentalists today as a strong advocate of preservation. However, as interior secretary he fought to reconcile his emerging preservationist consciousness with his deep belief in the Pinchotian tradition of resource conservation, and in the case of Grand Canyon this struggle became even more acute because Udall also confronted his desire to obtain the Central Arizona Project for his native state. The Interior Department archives contain hundreds of letters from environmentalists who questioned how the author of the *Quiet Crisis*, who so eloquently stated the case for preservation, could support the construction of dams in Grand Canyon. Environmental historians have argued that the preservationists' antidam campaign forced Stewart Udall to decide between development and preservation and that he chose the latter, evidence that the interior secretary experienced a shift in his own environmental consciousness.[91] However, one must remember that Udall was at heart a political pragmatist and had demonstrated this propensity throughout his congressional career and tenure as interior secretary. In 1963, Udall believed he had formulated a practical solution; he believed that he could support dams in Grand Canyon and still advocate in favor of preservation elsewhere. In autumn of 1966, the regional plan in ruins, Carl Hayden in failing health and planning to retire after the 1968 election, and believing his own tenure as interior secretary would end in early 1969, Udall realized that Arizona's disproportionately powerful political influence would end in a little over two years, after which there would be little chance of obtaining congressional approval of the CAP. "I did not reverse myself," Stewart Udall emphasized in a March 1997 interview. Rather, Udall decided to sponsor a less controversial bill while Arizona still had the politi-

cal muscle to shepherd it through Congress. In the end, Udall dropped the
Grand Canyon dams, not for preservationist reasons, but because it was the
most practical political option available to him.[92]

Udall chose the alternative he would pursue on the basis of pragmatic
reasons as well. In early September, Udall directed Assistant Secretary Kenneth Holum to spearhead an Interior Department study of alternatives to the
Grand Canyon dams, while Udall himself began to communicate the impending changes to the president and the Budget Bureau.[93] Udall kept his decision to himself as he struggled to determine which alternative constituted the
most politically practical source of power for the CAP.[94] Although the Atomic Energy Commission still trumpeted the possibilities of nuclear power, signs
were already appearing that nuclear reactors were not the panacea they had
been promised to be. Prominent preservationists had also begun to suspect
that nuclear power was an illusory solution, although they continued to use
the alternative of nuclear power to "kill the dams first" and to save Grand
Canyon, intending to mount a campaign against nuclear power later.[95] Indeed,
as Sierra Club experts such as Laurence Moss argued in favor of a nuclear-powered CAP in 1966 and again in 1967, some Sierra Club leaders had begun to
back away from their advocacy of nuclear power as early as 1963 because of rising safety concerns. Even David Brower had begun to have suspicions in the
summer of 1966.[96]

Udall remained optimistic about the potential for nuclear power through
the end of his tenure as interior secretary, but he also realized that the approval
and construction of nuclear power plants was time-prohibitive, often taking
more than ten years between conception and completion, with the gap widen-
ing every day. Although Udall believed that nuclear-powered desalinization
plants would someday provide a solution to the problem of water augmentation and he still advocated the construction of a large desalinization plant off
the Southern California coast, by mid-autumn of 1966 he realized that thermal
power constituted the most expedient means to obtain power for the Central
Arizona Project because coal plants would not take as long to build and they
relied upon existing technology.[97] In October, Udall went public and stated
that the administration was considering legislation that would offer alternatives
to the Grand Canyon dams, and by early December Udall decided to persuade President Johnson to back a CAP proposal without dams at the Bridge
and Marble Canyon dam sites.[98]

Wayne Aspinall called Udall's idea of thermal power generation "nonsense" and predicted that it would have little chance in Congress. Arizona politicians were also reluctant to relinquish the Grand Canyon dams, and in December 1966 Carl Hayden presented a new CAP strategy for the delegation to use in the upcoming Ninetieth Congress. Hayden's tactics represented a radical change from his previous position; he now advocated the introduction of bills in both houses of Congress simultaneously and endorsed a state-constructed Marble Canyon Dam. The rest of the delegation agreed with Hayden's approach and conceded that while some compromises might be necessary, they would not allow the legislation to become as cumbersome as the bill that had recently stalled in the Rules Committee.[99]

On 11 January 1967 John Rhodes, Morris Udall, and Sam Steiger, who had defeated George Senner in the November election, proposed a CAP bill that eliminated Marble Canyon Dam but included a high dam at Bridge Canyon. Wayne Aspinall introduced a bill reminiscent of the Sierra Club's proposed compromise of 1949. Instead of eliminating the Bridge-Hualapai Dam, Aspinall proposed to move the park instead, shifting the west boundary eastward to the head of Hualapai Lake and extending the east boundary a like distance to include some of Marble Canyon. The Sierra Club protested and claimed that slack water would still be present through the entire length of the national monument. Aspinall responded by suggesting that the monument should be abolished, in his mind eliminating the controversy.[100]

Other proposals also surfaced including a fantastic scheme advanced by Floyd Goss, an engineer with the Los Angeles Department of Water and Power, who argued that if Bridge Canyon Dam were constructed as a pumped storage project, it would have an annual generating capacity of 5.1 million megawatts, four times greater than that of Hoover Dam. Craig Hosmer trumpeted the project's virtues, as a means to undercut the economic arguments of the preservationists. However, the downside to the Goss proposal, which quickly sank from view, was that it required an additional dam downstream, and Bridge Canyon Dam would create tremendous surges of water, making the lower canyon, according to Floyd Dominy, "a very dangerous place."[101]

Stewart Udall presented the Interior Department's CAP proposal at a press conference on 1 February 1967. This plan eliminated both dams in Grand Canyon and advocated for the expansion of Grand Canyon National Park to include Marble Canyon, while calling upon Congress to determine the usage of the Bridge Canyon site. The new scheme was attacked from all sides by politicians, including Wayne Aspinall, who stated flatly that the administration proposal "will not pass" in Congress. Arizona's "go it alone" proponents were also disappointed because the plan included the Marble Canyon site within the proposed expansion of the national park, and they accused Udall of "double-crossing" his native state.[102]

But Udall's plan found acceptance in other circles. Henry Jackson expressed his delight with Udall's proposal and endorsed it completely. The most important development, though, was the reaction of Carl Hayden, who indicated that he might approve of the measure if it would "get the project moving."[103] This represented a landmark change on Hayden's part, for he had been the most strident advocate of building hydroelectric dams in Grand Canyon for more than twenty years.[104] However, the victory had not yet been won, for powerful political forces in the House of Representatives still advocated construction of the dams.

On 16 February 1967 Senators Carl Hayden and Paul Fannin of Arizona, and Henry Jackson of Washington, introduced CAP legislation omitting any references to hydroelectric dams in Grand Canyon. Instead, the measure called for a coal-fired steam plant to generate the power required to pump water through the proposed aqueduct. The bill came under immediate criticism from Senator Thomas Kuchel of California, who already had introduced legislation advocating a regional plan and the construction of Bridge Canyon Dam. The Hayden-Fannin-Jackson alliance proved strong enough to overcome Kuchel's opposition, and the measure passed the Senate Interior Committee easily, with the addition of one important provision—a moratorium on dam construction between Lake Mead and Grand Canyon National Park. After administrative delays and a brief debate, the Senate overwhelmingly passed the Hayden-Fannin-Jackson proposal on 7 August 1967, the third time that the Senate had passed CAP legislation.[105]

The easy passage of the CAP bill in the Senate was assured because of the influence of Senators Hayden and Jackson. In the House the measure faced stiff opposition led primarily by Wayne Aspinall and other congressmen who still saw the dams as a potential source of revenue for other reclamation projects within the Colorado Basin. Several CAP bills, which included two dams, one dam, or no dams in Grand Canyon, were introduced in the House in early 1967. The House Subcommittee on Reclamation and Irrigation held hearings in March 1967 to consider these proposals, and once again preservationists testified in opposition of the dams, reiterating their arguments of 1966. Fearing complacency caused by the introduction of dam-free bills in the Senate, the Sierra Club took out yet another full-page advertisement in the *New York Times* to revitalize its letter-writing campaign. The advertisements cautioned that the battle was not yet over and that the Canyon was still in grave danger. Additionally, the Sierra Club emphasized that it was still battling the IRS, attempting to fan the flames of public outrage generated by the revocation of June 1966.[106] Interior Secretary Udall and Dr. Stephen Jett also testified, citing the benefits that would accrue to the Navajo Tribe from the development of their coal reserves, while the Hualapai tribal chairman urged the committee to include Hualapai Dam in the bill.[107]

Representatives from Arizona and California clashed over California's insistence upon the annual 4.4 million-acre-foot guarantee and augmentation of the basin's water supply from the Pacific Northwest. The feuding contingents' only point of agreement was their opposition to Interior Secretary Udall's plan and Hayden's similar Senate proposal. Although Morris Udall and John Rhodes were now amenable to the CAP with or without dams for power generation, the hearings adjourned after five days of inconclusive debate without setting a definite date for presentation of a CAP measure to the full Interior Committee because of Wayne Aspinall's insistence that the bill include Hualapai Dam.[108] Once again the CAP had passed the Senate, but had run into stiff opposition in the House, this time because Chairman Aspinall and the California delegation had joined forces against any project without dams, provisions for water importation, and the California guarantee.[109]

Interior Secretary Udall, though he had introduced legislation recommending against the construction of additional dams on the Colorado River, still remained undecided about whether a dam should be built at the Bridge Canyon site. In June 1967 the secretary took his family and some National Park Service personnel on a guided Colorado River trip to examine the disputed dam sites firsthand. Casting off from Lee's Ferry, a river crossing established by his great-grandfather in 1872, Udall felt a sense of awe and wonder as he drifted through the Colorado gorge as well as occasional terror while riding the rapids. Writing for *Venture* magazine several months later, Udall chastised himself for making an "armchair judgement" when formulating the Pacific Southwest Water Plan in 1963 and called for the enlargement of Grand

Canyon National Park to include the site if the power could truly be provided by other means. "The burden of proof, I believe, rests on the dam-builders," Udall wrote. "If they cannot make out a compelling case, the park should be enlarged and given permanent protection."[110] Seeing the wonders of lower Grand Canyon in June of 1967 converted Udall to the preservationists' point of view.

Others, however, had yet to experience this ideological transformation, and on 2 August 1967 Wayne Aspinall decreed there would be no further action on the CAP because he planned to adjourn the Interior Committee for the remainder of the year. Despite the objections of Arizona's congressional delegation, the committee assembled a quorum and voted to adjourn during the week of 28 August 1967, and the chairman flew home to Colorado.[111] Angered by Aspinall's intractability, frustrated with California's continued opposition, and believing that they had substantial support from their House colleagues, John Rhodes and Morris Udall sought to circumvent Aspinall's opposition by bypassing the Interior Committee altogether. Knowing that the Senate was currently debating a public works appropriations bill recently passed by the House, Rhodes and Udall spoke with Carl Hayden about the possibility of attaching the CAP to the Senate version of the appropriations bill, a rarely used procedure that required enormous power and prestige in the Senate as well as a suspension of the rules.[112] But Carl Hayden had run out of patience with Aspinall, and though not a hardball politician by nature, Hayden agreed to pressure Aspinall in two different ways. First, as chair of the powerful Senate Appropriations Committee, he moved to block authorization of the Fryingpan–Arkansas Mountain Diversion Project slated for Aspinall's home state of Colorado. In addition, he threatened to attach the Central Arizona Project as a rider to the public works appropriations bill and obtained the two-thirds Senate vote necessary to suspend the normal rules of parliamentary procedure.[113] Hayden's action had the desired effect, and Aspinall scrambled back to Washington and promised Hayden that the CAP bill would be brought to a House vote when the Ninetieth Congress reconvened in January or early February of 1968.[114] By using an uncharacteristic display of raw political power, Carl Hayden won Aspinall's assurance that the CAP would be brought before the entire House of Representatives for the first time since Hayden introduced it in the Senate in 1947.

As the Ninetieth Congress reconvened for its second session, President

Lyndon B. Johnson finally endorsed the CAP publicly and called upon Congress to pass it with all possible speed. True to his word, Wayne Aspinall reopened the CAP hearings and on 26 March 1968 the Interior Committee approved the bill. Aspinall, the last influential dam proponent, had finally capitulated—the bill approved by the full Interior Committee deleted all hydroelectric dams from the project. Elated by their good fortune, Arizona's congressional delegation shepherded the CAP bill through the Rules Committee and onto the House floor for a vote. On 15 May 1968 the House of Representatives overwhelmingly passed legislation authorizing the construction of the CAP by the federal government, its electricity to be provided by an immense coal-fired power plant located in Page, Arizona. The bill contained Aspinall's five upper-basin projects and the California 4.4 million-acre-foot guarantee in perpetuity, concessions Arizona's representatives made to gain the political support of these two factions. After negotiations in the joint conference committee and approval by both houses of Congress, the final version of the CAP bill, one without hydroelectric dams in Grand Canyon and including the California guarantee in perpetuity, was ready for the president's signature.

Stooped with age, but still of dignified bearing, Carl Hayden, in his forty-seventh and last year as a senator from Arizona, shuffled into the East Room of the White House along with a host of other dignitaries, including Stewart and Morris Udall, Paul Fannin, John Rhodes, and Sam Steiger, to witness the signing of the CAP legislation by President Lyndon B. Johnson on 30 September 1968 (fig. 8). Seated in the audience was David Brower, there to witness the culmination of over five years of heated battle—the enactment of a CAP measure without dams in any portion of Grand Canyon. President and Mrs. Johnson strode into the room, and LBJ seated himself at a small desk provided for the occasion, made a few brief remarks, and signed the Colorado River Basin Project Act into law. President Johnson, smiling broadly, turned to Carl Hayden, handed him the pen used in the ceremony, and shook his hand. Carl Hayden commended past and present members of the Arizona congressional delegation and declared: "Today is the high water mark in my career as a U.S. senator."[115] With that, the dean of the Senate walked out of the room and into retirement, his CAP dream a reality at last.

Figure 8. President Lyndon Johnson, surrounded by Arizona politicians, signs the damless Central Arizona Project bill into law on 30 September 1968. *Courtesy of Special Collections, University of Arizona Library.*

In January of 1969, shortly before leaving office, President Johnson extended national monument status to Marble Canyon, bringing the dam site there within the jurisdiction of the National Park Service. Though the Central Arizona Project had been passed with a moratorium on additional dams between Lee's Ferry and Lake Mead, the Arizona Power Authority and the Hualapai Tribe continued to push for the construction of Hualapai Dam as a state project. The idea enjoyed renewed popularity during the energy crisis of the early 1970s and was occasionally mentioned well into the 1980s, but it never received enough congressional support to move beyond the committee level. In 1975, Congress enlarged Grand Canyon National Park to include the Bridge and Marble Canyon dam sites. Although the Grand Canyon National Park Expansion Act preserved the right of the secretary of the interior to authorize dams within the park,[116] the last line of defense Newton Drury had first conceived of in the early 1940s had now been extended to include all of Grand Canyon, bringing the controversy to an end, with the sanctity of the free-flowing Colorado River in Grand Canyon remaining intact.

A Mirage of Power

The power of a man...is his present means, to obtain
some future apparent good...reputation of power is
power...

—Thomas Hobbes, *Leviathan*

Scarcely had the dust settled from this, one of the most hotly contested
environmental controversies in American history in terms of public reaction, before its evaluation commenced. Environmentalists and journalists
writing to a popular audience, and historians within the academy began to
assess not only the place and meaning of the Grand Canyon dam controversy
within the overall context of the American environmental movement, but
also to determine the reasons for the defeat of the dams. Less than two years
after President Johnson signed the Central Arizona Project authorization
into law, the Sierra Club published *Grand Canyon of the Living Colorado*, a small
hardcover exhibit book that contained stunning color photographs of the
canyon and synopses of various aspects of the Grand Canyon battle, including a reprint of Stewart Udall's February 1968 *Venture* article, a discussion of
the Grand Canyon battle ads written by David Brower, and an essay summa-
rizing the political aspects of the Grand Canyon dam controversy that emphasized the pivotal role the Sierra Club played in defeating the dams, written by
Sierra Club member Roderick Nash, who also served as the editor of the
book.[1]

Even while Nash worked on this latest Sierra Club publication, he also was beginning his career as an environmental historian and professor of history at the University of California at Santa Barbara. In 1967 Nash published *Wilderness and the American Mind*, now regarded as a classic in the fields of both U.S. intellectual and environmental history. Nash gained national acclaim for his discussion of how the concept of wilderness has evolved in the American psyche over the past two hundred years; he published a second edition to *Wilderness* in 1973, which included an analysis of the Grand Canyon debate, and a third edition in 1983, in which he expanded his discussion. Taken almost verbatim from his 1970 essay in *Grand Canyon of the Living Colorado*, Nash's 1983 analysis concludes categorically that preservationists had achieved the near impossible in stopping the Grand Canyon dams. After stating that the environmental movement had gained enough influence by the 1950s and 1960s to "influence the political process," Nash elaborated further on Grand Canyon:

> The result in terms of Grand Canyon was unprecedented. Dams that originally had the full backing of the administration, the personal enthusiasm of the secretary of the interior, and nearly unanimous support from senators and representatives of the seven Colorado Basin states, as well as the determined boosting of water and power user's lobbies—dams, in other words, that seemed virtually certain of authorization—were stopped.[2]

According to Nash, environmentalists and the Sierra Club in particular constituted the decisive factor in the defeat of the dams because of both their direct influence with Congress and their ability to mobilize public opinion, which forced Congress into accepting alternative sources of power. The Sierra Club is the only environmental organization Nash mentions by name in his Grand Canyon discussion. Nash also argues that Stewart Udall's trip down the river in June of 1967 led to the secretary's change of mind, an event that he argues was also pivotal in stopping the dams. Because of his reputation as a scholar, Nash's analysis of the Grand Canyon dam controversy has scarcely been challenged by environmental historians and students of the Colorado River, most of whom accept his thesis at face value and who cite his interpretation in their own work.[3]

Outside of academe, the argument that the Grand Canyon dams had been stopped by the Sierra Club was widely disseminated in the popular press and in conservation magazines. Two popular accounts, John McPhee's *Encounters with the Archdruid*, published in 1971 after its syndication in the *New Yorker*, and Mark Reisner's *Cadillac Desert*, published in 1986, also communicated the argument that the Sierra Club had defeated the Grand Canyon dams to an enormous popular audience, and Reisner's book has recently been made into a four-part video series on western water development. Thus, the writers of popular accounts, conservation magazines, and historical scholarship have, in the three decades since the authorization of the CAP, accorded preservationists and the Sierra Club in particular an almost omnipotent ability to influence the policymaking process at that time. Most of these scholars cite the Grand Canyon dam controversy as the climactic confrontation between proponents of utilitarian water-development policy and the modern environmental movement and contend that the Sierra Club used its political influence to save the most important example of America's scenic grandeur, sending the Bureau of Reclamation into inexorable retreat. Some of these writers have gone further and argued that it was during the defense of Grand Canyon that the environmental movement "came of age."[4] All of these accounts are based upon the assumption that the Sierra Club's ability to mobilize public opinion transcended the traditional machinations of the congressional system and allowed preservationists to shape policy. Thus, across the spectrum of historical interpretation of the Grand Canyon dam controversy, the Sierra Club has emerged as the savior of Grand Canyon because of its perceived ability to effect political change.

These scholars recognize properly that the debate over Grand Canyon took place at two different levels: in the court of public opinion, and within the political process. Clearly the preservationists' campaign and the IRS revocation had a great effect upon public opinion, as judged by the volume of mail and the tremendous grassroots efforts made on behalf of the Canyon. However, to presume that a victory in the court of public opinion translated into a change of federal policy fails to take into consideration the complex political climate surrounding the issue as well as the isolated and intricate nature of the policymaking process itself, particularly the workings of the committee system, in which enormous power rests in the hands of the committee chairs. Though the committee system has become more democratic over the last four decades, according to Stewart Udall, chairmen such as Wayne Aspinall in the House and Henry Jackson in the Senate wielded power that was virtually absolute during the 1960s; it was only in rare instances when committee chairs opposed to legislation could be circumvented, either by sheer weight of numbers, or by a senior member of Congress who could command enough support to gain the two-thirds majority necessary to suspend the rules of parliamentary procedure.[5]

The complexity of the political battle to obtain the Central Arizona Project is staggering, and it can be divided into three distinct time periods, defined by shifting perceptions of what political alliances and concessions Arizona politicians deemed necessary to obtain the CAP, as well as the political barriers they believed stood in the way. Beginning in the first decades of the twentieth century, Arizona was embroiled in a bitter political battle to obtain the right to use water from the Colorado River, and the nature of that battle was determined largely by the constraints imposed by the Compact of 1922. From that point in time, Arizona and California would be pitted against each other over the allocation of lower-basin water, and while California would use its political power to obtain projects to tap the Colorado River time and time again, it also wielded this power to prevent Arizona from doing the same, a pattern that continued until the passage of the Central Arizona Project in 1968. Even when Arizona gained tremendous political influence during the first post–World War II decade, with Hayden gaining seniority in the Senate, Ernest MacFarland as Senate majority leader and John Murdock as chairman of the House Interior Committee, it was not enough to gain the passage of the Central Arizona Project and Bridge Canyon Dam over California's objections. California's large congressional bloc proved strong enough to overcome Murdock's chairmanship, foster House passage of a CAP moratorium in 1951, and throw the issue of lower-basin water allotment into the Supreme Court. As a result, Arizona representatives Stewart and Morris Udall and John Rhodes, having experienced California's raw political hubris firsthand, came to view California's support as indispensable to obtaining the Central Arizona Project on the eve of their renewed efforts begun in the early 1960s in anticipation of a favorable Supreme Court decision.

When Special Master Simon Rifkind released to the U.S. Supreme Court in 1960 his recommendations in *Arizona v California*, favoring Arizona over California, it precipitated another critical shift in the political landscape. Arizona politicians, who already worried about gaining California's support, now confronted fears raised by representatives of the upper-basin states, particularly from Colorado, through Wayne Aspinall, the autocratic House Interior Committee chairman, who feared that the construction of another large water project in the lower basin would reduce the upper basin's allotment. In addition, California, annually using close to one million acre feet of water Arizona claimed in its Supreme Court case and growing in population and political influence, continued to have a hypnotic effect upon Arizonans preparing to battle once again for the Central Arizona Project. Though Arizona's political influence arguably increased after Stewart Udall's appointment as secretary of the interior, and with Carl Hayden as the undisputed leader of the Senate, both in terms of seniority and his chairmanship of the all-powerful Appropriations Committee, the political obstacles to obtaining the CAP also looked larger than ever because now it appeared that California and Colorado, the two most populous states in the Colorado Basin, were allied against it. Though Carl Hayden believed that his influence in the Senate would be enough to gain passage of the CAP in both houses, Stewart Udall, after corresponding with Interior Committee Chairman Wayne Aspinall, adopted the idea of a regional water development designed to obviate opposition from California and the Interior Committee chairman, both of whom Udall now considered indispensable parties to obtaining passage of the project.

The political situation changed once again in the wake of the Supreme Court's landmark decision in *Arizona v California* handed down in June of 1963. Assured that Arizona now held legal title to enough water to justify pursuing the CAP, Stewart Udall stepped up his efforts to create regional water harmony. He obtained California's and Aspinall's support, but only after precipitating a division with Hayden and his supporters, who sought a bare-bones project, a rift in the Arizona effort that never healed fully during the entire period Congress debated the regional scheme. Udall's decision to pursue a regional water plan constitutes perhaps the most critical decision made during the Grand Canyon dam controversy, for in all likelihood the regional plan, though promising initially, doomed a Central Arizona Project including dams in Grand Canyon to defeat.

Udall predicated his comprehensive plan to gain California and Aspinall as allies upon obtaining the augmentation of the water supply of the Colorado Basin. Despite Udall's great optimism, desalinization constituted an uncertain alternative, and when California balked at Udall's attempt to base water-augmentation proposals upon either that technology or the diversion of northern California rivers, the secretary was forced to look to the Columbia River as a potential source of water importation or lose California's support for the entire project. Though the Columbia diversion brought with it the solidification of the Arizona-California-Aspinall alliance, it also raised the unanticipated ire of Senate Interior Committee Chairman Henry Jackson, which weakened Hayden's Senate influence. Jackson's control of the Senate Interior Committee made passage of the CAP without his support virtually impossible. Once California support had been purchased with the prospect of water importation, the high Bridge Canyon Dam became a nonnegotiable issue because it constituted the revenue source for the construction of the diversion works. Udall supported the high Bridge Canyon Dam in order to guarantee California's political backing, even though it was sure to precipitate an opposition campaign from environmentalists because of its infringement upon Grand Canyon National Park. However, from a politically pragmatic perspective, it appeared to be the correct choice, in light of California's tremendous House influence in 1963 and of the conservationists' retreat from the legislative arena in the wake of the *Harriss* decision, as well as their defeats in the recent controversies over Glen Canyon and Rainbow Bridge.

In the summer of 1966, despite the preservationists' campaign and the massive public outcry it generated, the political alliance between Arizona, California, and Wayne Aspinall unraveled because no one could find a means to bypass Henry Jackson, who refused to compromise the issue of water importation from the Columbia River. As these negotiations entered their most critical phase, California water strategist Northcutt Ely used John Saylor's threatened amendments as a pretext for holding the bill in the Rules Committee in order to delay the CAP so as to preserve California's use of Arizona's water allotment for another year, thereby nullifying the Supreme Court decree of 1963. Ely's actions sounded the death knell for the Grand Canyon dams in 1966.

In the wake of this defeat, Stewart Udall, believing Arizona's powerful political influence would end with Hayden's and his own retirements in January of 1969, sought to formulate a solution to gain approval of the CAP while Arizona still possessed the political muscle to obtain it. By the winter of 1966, Udall had conceived of the proposal that eventually passed—a bare-bones CAP without dams in Grand Canyon—thereby insuring Jackson's support in the Senate. The House Interior Committee debate of 1967, and Mo Udall's informal polling of his House colleagues, revealed strong support for the project despite objections from California, which still demanded a perpetual guarantee of its 4.4 million acre feet of water, and from Aspinall, who still desired augmentation from the Columbia River.[6] However, Carl Hayden used his senatorial prestige to force Wayne Aspinall into holding hearings in 1968, leading finally to a House floor debate and passage. Although California's guarantee and Aspinall's five upper-basin projects were added late in 1968 to gain their support, it is clear that the House would have passed the CAP over the objections of both in 1967 had Hayden followed through on his threat and attached the CAP to the 1967 Senate appropriations bill.

Although speculative, the above events beg the question of whether Secretary Udall's advocacy of a regional water plan constituted a wrong turn from the perspective of an advocate of the Grand Canyon dams. Had Udall supported Carl Hayden's bare-bones approach in 1963, the project would have incurred opposition from California and Aspinall. However, the same tactics Hayden used in 1967 to pressure Aspinall were also available to him in 1963—because of Hayden's enormous prestige in the Senate, he could have bypassed Aspinall once the latter was shown to be intractable—something that would not have been difficult to prove. Perhaps the greatest difficulty would have been convincing Hayden to engage in bare-knuckle politics at this level. Though Udall believed California's support to be indispensable, on the basis of his experiences of the 1950s, by 1960 the congressional climate had changed. Though the 1950s had not been conducive to the passage of water projects because of President Eisenhower's policy of "no new starts," this situation changed dramatically with the election of John Kennedy, who had promised to reverse this policy if elected. The Reclamation Bureau's budgets increased greatly after JFK became president, and western politicians began to move their projects through Congress once again.[7]

Though California's opposition proved pivotal during the climate of fiscal parsimony present during the 1950s, Arizona's House support increased during the Kennedy/Johnson administrations because of changed budget conditions and increasing belief on the part of House members that Arizona deserved its project in the wake of the 1963 Supreme Court decision. If Udall had not viewed California as such a crucial base of support, Arizona's representatives would have been able to negotiate over the high Bridge Canyon Dam and offer a proposal that would not have threatened the national park, a plan that would have gained enough congressional support to offset California's opposition. John Saylor, the most vociferous opponent of the high Bridge Canyon Dam, wrote Mo Udall on 7 September 1966, with the basin project stalled in the Rules Committee, and stated that he would support a bare-bones Central Arizona Project that included a Bridge Canyon Dam "lowered by ninety feet"—this after months of strident preservationist rhetoric and the Sierra Club's ad campaign.[8]

Additionally, Henry Jackson never stated that he opposed dams in Grand Canyon per se, just the threat of water importation that they represented, and Carl Hayden obtained his promise to move the bill through the Senate Interior Committee once it cleared the House. If one considers all of these factors in the aggregate, it appears as though Carl Hayden's political instincts of 1963 were correct; Arizona could have obtained passage of a bare-bones Central Arizona Project with at least a low Bridge Canyon Dam that would have backed water through the length of the national monument, and possibly Marble Canyon Dam, because it would not have raised the Jackson roadblock, while Aspinall and California's opposition could have been neutralized. Ironically, by seeking to construct a regional water project, though it offered the tantalizing possibility of gaining California and Aspinall's support, Stewart Udall actually increased the proposal's likelihood of failure with each compromise he made.

Yet, although the preservationists' campaign succeeded in generating a great public reaction and environmentalists offered exhaustive testimony during the congressional hearings, they did not constitute a decisive force in the political arena. The regional proposal contained the seeds of its own demise, and when the bill died in committee in the fall of 1966, Stewart Udall, mindful of the time constraints under which he labored, abandoned the Grand Canyon dams and the regional approach in favor of a politically practical solution. Udall based his regional plan upon pragmatics that might have worked during the 1950s, but failed in the political climate created after the 1963 Supreme Court decision because, as the events of 1967–1968 demonstrate, California and Wayne Aspinall were no longer indispensable parties. Ultimately, the machinations of the policymaking process, the continuing enmity between Arizona and California, and the cumbersome legislation of 1966 led to the defeat of the Grand Canyon dams. Stewart Udall's damless February 1967 proposal and Carl Hayden's approval of it constituted a politically pragmatic move by two practical politicians who understood that they were rapidly running out of time.

Preservationists and advocates of the Grand Canyon dams also struggled to gain public approval of their respective agendas, and though the environmentalists' efforts constituted the more vigorous campaign, the pro-dam lobby, though it focused primarily upon obtaining political backing, also appealed to the American public for support. CAP advocates tried initially to generate public appeal for the projects by emphasizing Arizona's need for water and the promise of more recreational opportunities. Supporters of the projects realized that with Congress and reclamation policy on their side, they did not have to achieve complete victory but only needed to avoid a catastrophic public relations defeat similar to the one that they had incurred during the Echo Park fight. The reclamationists made no such mistakes in the Grand Canyon fight, and sounding the theme that the preservationists were elitists, they attacked the opposition campaign in three ways.

First, whenever dam opponents advanced a technical argument, or even when a person with impressive credentials such as physicist Richard Bradley opposed the dams, Bureau or congressional experts offered rebuttals to prevent the preservationists from monopolizing the technological high ground. Despite the exhaustive expert testimony from Jeff Ingram, Alan Carlin, and Laurence Moss, the preservationists never succeeded in extracting an admission from project proponents that the Grand Canyon dams were not economically justifiable.[9] Although these experts presented figures, analyses, and alternatives of impressive scope during the congressional hearings, supporters of the project countered with their own witnesses and analyses, enabling them to maintain a semblance of balance of expert opinion, at least during the Interior Committee debates of 1965–1966, while the dams still were very much alive in the political realm.

Second, proponents of the dams intensified their public relations effort in the wake of the publication of Richard Bradley's article, "Ruin for Grand Canyon?" in the April 1966 issue of *Reader's Digest*. Although Floyd Dominy tried and failed to convince *Reader's Digest* to withdraw the article, Mo Udall and Barry Goldwater managed to partially co-opt the *Reader's Digest*–sponsored Grand Canyon symposium at the end of March 1966. In addition, Morris Udall and John Rhodes granted concessions to the Hualapai Tribe in exchange for their affirmative support of the project. By eliminating the Hualapai as potential antagonists, Arizona politicians took advantage of American society's rising concern over civil rights and racial issues to portray the preservationists as racist in addition to being elitist.

However, although the reclamationists demonstrated an awareness of the larger social context of the mid-1960s, they blundered because they ignored the Navajo Nation, leaving the door open for a preservationist rebuttal. Rich Johnson's letters, and Dr. Henry Dobyns's testimony received national publicity, but the full effect of these racial arguments was at least partly neutralized by Stephen Jett's mobilization of the Navajo Tribe, and in any event, this strategy became moot once Bridge/Hualapai Dam stalled in the Rules Committee in September of 1966. Although the Hualapai tribal chairman testified during the House Interior Committee hearings in 1967, the defeat of the Bridge/Hualapai Dam was already a foregone conclusion, and so the Hualapai Tribe became expendable in terms of pro-CAP propaganda. Completing the irony of the situation, supporters of the Central Arizona Project reversed their position and began to extol its benefits for the Navajo Tribe after coal-fired steam plants had been incorporated into the proposal.

Perhaps most important, the pro-dam lobby played a pivotal role in driving wedges between preservationist associations like the Sierra Club and Wilderness Society, on the one hand, and wildlife-oriented organizations such as the National Wildlife Federation, the largest conservation group in the world, on the other. It is largely due to the efforts of reclamation enthusiasts such as Bill Winter, of the Arizona Game Protective Association, that the conservation organizations did not achieve the same degree of unity in the case of Grand Canyon as they did during the Echo Park controversy. During the Echo Park conflict, the leadership of the National Wildlife Federation voted to oppose the dams slated for Dinosaur National Monument or any further intrusions into the national park system,[10] yet scarcely ten years later the Federation remained officially neutral despite threats to both Grand Canyon National Park and Monument and appeals from David Brower and other environmental leaders. In the case of Grand Canyon, the National Wildlife Federation committed itself only after the climax of the controversy in 1966, voting in March of 1967 to endorse congressional approval of the construction of steam plants, but if this alternative proved politically impracticable, the NWF favored the construction of a high Bridge/Hualapai Dam and moving the national park boundaries east, away from the reservoir the dam would create.[11]

Although an angry David Brower accused National Wildlife Federation President Thomas Kimball of advocating that the park be "dismembered piecemeal" in favor of economic interests,[12] the pro-dam lobby neutralized the political pressure of the Federation's two million members for the duration of the controversy, and consequently, the preservationists' effort remained fragmented.

Yet despite disunity, environmentalists managed to mobilize public opinion on an unprecedented scale, perhaps rivaled only by the outcry they generated during the Echo Park controversy. Historian Mark Harvey argues that the public pressured Congress into eventually deleting the dams from Dinosaur National Monument, an argument that by inference is based upon the assumption that environmentalists had access to the political process. According to Harvey, lobbying groups such as the Council of Conservationists, Trustees for Conservation, and the Citizens' Committee on Conservation wielded such powerful influence in Congress that when Congress finally deleted the Echo Park and Split Mountain Dams from the Colorado River Storage Project legislation, they instructed sympathetic congressmen to withdraw their opposition, thus allowing the bill to pass in 1956. Conservationists also gained other influential allies during the Echo Park controversy, including California, which opposed any further upper-basin water development, and representatives from the East and Midwest, who disliked western reclamation, and who, in a period of fiscal conservatism, attempted to hold true to President Eisenhower's policy of "no new starts." Consequently, the crucial committee vote was quite close in 1954, with the House Interior Committee favoring the dams by a vote of 13–12, while the next year, at the height of the letter-writing campaign it reversed itself and voted 20–6 to delete both dams.[13]

Conservationists fighting against the Echo Park dams also benefited from fortuitous circumstances that did not exist a decade later. In July 1966 at the height of the preservationists' offensive, the House Interior Committee voted 22–10 to approve the construction of both dams in Grand Canyon, this vote coming almost two months after the *New York Times* ads and the IRS revocation of the Sierra Club's tax-deductible status. How can this be explained? The Grand Canyon dam debate took place in a dramatically different political climate than did Echo Park. Reclamation budgets increased tremendously after 1960, and Presidents Kennedy and Johnson encouraged water development. The Colorado River Basin states were also united in support of the project, and even California voted for the bill until the compromises unraveled in the Rules Committee. If one compares the relative political influence wielded by the preservationists and the public in both controversies, one might conclude the preservationists had indeed penetrated the political system enough to influence policy in the case of Echo Park.

However, the aura of the preservationists' influence that the Echo Park victory created might also have been exaggerated because the dispute took place during a time when reclamation was under fire both from Congress and the administration. Because environmentalists contended that the construction of dams in Dinosaur National Monument would set a precedent that would threaten the national park system, an argument that had seemingly succeeded, their triumph at Echo Park greatly overemphasized the strength of this new legal basis for wilderness preservation, a fact borne out by subsequent defeats during controversies over Rainbow Bridge and Glen Canyon, where the precedent defense failed.

Preservationists were able to use these defeats as well as the victory at Echo Park to great effect during the Grand Canyon dam controversy. Echo Park took on significant importance as a situation where preservationists had defeated the reclamation interests on their own ground, while the fiscal and political climates within which Echo Park occurred were forgotten. Even the rhetoric of the Dinosaur controversy helped provide the foundation for the making of a mythological aura that would surround environmentalist campaigns for the next several decades—that through dogged determination, private citizens and organizations could effect changes in environmental policy. In June of 1954, after Brower testified and pointed out that the Bureau's experts had miscalculated the evaporation rates from the Echo Park and Glen Canyon reservoirs, Howard Zahniser sent a telegram to the Sierra Club leadership stating: "Salute him well. He surely hit the giant between the eyes with his five smooth stones."[14] The Dinosaur controversy was also significant for another reason that was to have a direct bearing upon the Grand Canyon battle, because it marked the point in time when the Sierra Club moved away from its traditional mission as the protector of the Sierra Nevada and took its place among activist conservation organizations.[15]

Thus, the main weapons at the preservationists' disposal entering the campaign to save Grand Canyon were the argument of precedent and the aura of the Dinosaur victory, while the Sierra Club and Wilderness Society had emerged as the leading activist environmental organizations seeking to influence legislation. The Wilderness Society gained this position as a result of its pursuit of a national wilderness system and was essentially a single-issue organization, whereas the Sierra Club, alone of all of the leading conservation associations, had defied the Supreme Court's *Harriss* decision of 1954 by deciding to continue lobbying for environmental causes and had created a tax-exempt foundation to fall back upon should its environmental advocacy elicit an IRS response. In 1965, with Rainbow Bridge and Glen Canyon lost, and the weakness of the argument of legal precedent exposed, the Sierra Club leadership abandoned it, except as a rhetorical riposte, and concentrated instead upon precipitating an immense public reaction by gaining access to the national media. By shifting their focus, Sierra Club leaders sought to transcend mere legal arguments and the policymaking process, hoping that a tremendous reaction in the court of public opinion would transmute into the political process and enable them to defeat the dams, just as they believed it had during Echo Park.

Ironically, preservationists received their first tangible legal weapon in 1965, when the Second Circuit Court of Appeals handed down its ruling in *Scenic Hudson Preservation Conference v Federal Power Commission*, better known as the *Storm King* decision, in which the court granted environmentalists standing to sue to preserve scenic values. *Storm King* did not affect Bureau of Reclamation projects but only governed proposals under consideration by the Federal Power Commission, so preservationists seeking to preserve Grand Canyon from the Bureau's proposals were still without legal recourse. However, *Storm King* constitutes the point at which environmentalists first gained entry into the policymaking process in addition to their right to testify during committee hearings, access that was broadened tremendously when Congress passed the National Environmental Policy Act in 1969.[16]

Although David Brower and other preservationists had not yet gained entrée to the inner workings of the political process in 1965, apart from their opportunity to testimony at congressional hearings, they understood that the symbolic importance of Grand Canyon itself offered the opportunity to unite divergent elements within the environmental movement and to gain widespread public sympathy. However, unlike "monumentalism," the term historian Alfred Runte uses aptly to describe America's preoccupation with the preservation of monumental scenery during the early years of the National

Park Service, by the 1960s Grand Canyon represented something more.[17]
Even though pure ecological arguments were easy to refute because the Grand
Canyon ecosystem had been altered by Glen Canyon Dam, it had not been
completely destroyed. The living river constituted the most visible reminder
that the forces that carved the canyon were still at work. Many people wrote
Congress, expressing that from a psychological perspective, it was important to
know that the Colorado River still flowed in the canyon and was still engag-
ing in its erosive mission. Even in the optimistic euphoria surrounding the
promise of post–World War II technological advances, Americans also understood and feared the fact that humanity now possessed the capacity to destroy
the Earth, through radiation, pollution, overpopulation, chemical residue,
and a myriad of other potential hazards difficult to combat at the individual
level.[18] Writing a letter protesting the proposed damming of Grand Canyon
offered people something tangible they could do. The tremendous outpouring of opposition is at least partially attributable not only to people's desire to
save the canyon and the forces that created it in their physical sense, but also
to each individual's desire to preserve his or her own "geography of hope,"
the knowledge that the river was still excavating the canyon, and the psychological belief that he or she was doing something to reverse the environmental depredations wrought by post–World War II technology.[19]

When Stewart Udall introduced the Pacific Southwest Water Plan in
August of 1963 the Sierra Club had just embarked upon three simultaneous
campaigns, in addition to its ongoing efforts to obtain passage of the Wilderness Bill, that were to solidify its leadership of the environmental movement:
two to establish national parks—one to protect the coastal redwoods of California and one to protect the North Cascades of Washington—and one to
oppose the construction of dams in Grand Canyon. Although all three campaigns were fought at the same time and the club used activist tactics in each
of them, it was its fight against the Grand Canyon dams that propelled the club
to the undisputed leadership of the environmental movement because the
redwoods and North Cascades efforts did not come close to generating the
public reaction of the Grand Canyon campaign. The club's success in gaining
access to the national media to broadcast the peril Grand Canyon faced not
only brought the threats to America's greatest scenic wonder to the attention
of millions of people but also informed this constituency about the organization leading the fight. If Echo Park constituted the point in time when the Sier-

ra Club took its place among national environmental organizations,[20] Grand Canyon was the event during which the Sierra Club gained recognition as the spearhead of environmental activism, not just among other environmental groups, but also with Congress and the American public.

The Sierra Club also benefited from its having experts testify during the congressional hearings of 1965, 1966, and 1967, even though the testimony of Laurence Moss, Alan Carlin, and Jeff Ingram did not appreciably affect the outcome of the controversy. Two months after the Interior Committee hearings of May 1966, when the preservationists made their most impressive technical arguments, the House Interior Committee reported the bill favorably with a sizable majority vote of 22–10, and Mo Udall's straw poll of late August demonstrated strong support in the House, support that was never mobilized because of Northcutt Ely's Rules Committee intrigue. However, the Sierra Club's experts did influence the campaign in the public arena by creating a foundation of scientific legitimacy for arguments in favor of alternative energy sources. Many letters and newspaper editorials written in opposition to the dams quote the arguments of Ingram, Moss, Carlin, and Richard Bradley. During the 1960s, Americans had become science-conscious because of the promises of the nuclear physicists, the space program, and a multitude of other scientific and technological advancements, and the public's frequent use of the expert's arguments suggests that gaining a foundation of scientific legitimacy proved crucial for the opposition campaign's widespread appeal.

On 10 June 1966 the nature and scope of the public reaction changed when the Internal Revenue Service clouded the Sierra Club's tax-deductible status because of the advertisements it placed in the *New York Times* and other national newspapers the previous day. The IRS revocation of June 1966 occurred during the tumultuous social upheavals of the civil rights, free speech, and antiwar movements, and it received front-page coverage in newspapers across the country. As a result, the Sierra Club gained an enormous windfall of sympathy from Americans concerned with civil liberties issues who resented federal meddling with the club's fundamental constitutional rights. Although Grand Canyon was of great symbolic importance and the Sierra Club's campaign generated a large response through 9 June 1966, public involvement grew exponentially after the IRS revocation of the following day. This increase in public activism is measured not only in the amount and content of the mail received by members of Congress after that date but also in the growth statistics for the Sierra Club membership and dramatic increases in small contributions. Thousands of people joined the Sierra Club to protest the IRS action, while tens of thousands more gleefully sent small contributions to aid the club in its Grand Canyon fight, many of whom wrote expressly stating how glad they were that their gifts were *not* tax-deductible.[21] In the social context of the 1960s, people viewed the Sierra Club as a "symbol of American free-dom,"[22] which continued to battle gamely onward despite federal repression, and many joined the club, not so much out of environmentalist sympathies, as to take a tangible step to protest what they perceived as infringement upon the basic constitutional rights of American citizens.

The Sierra Club emerged from the Grand Canyon dam controversy having created the public perception that through its activism, Grand Canyon remained free of dams. Thus, the aura of political influence it first attained as a result of Echo Park had been reinforced, and the public looked to the club to lead future environmental crusades. Although the political debates that had led to the unraveling of the compromises made among the basin states in August of 1966 had been well publicized—and Stewart Udall had announced his intention to study alternatives in September of 1966—the vast majority of people, along with the historians who have written about it, have ignored the political aspects of the controversy in favor of the heroic myth of the Sier-ra Club's "victory," a situation that was to have important ramifications for the future of the environmental movement.

Scholars have focused upon the Sierra Club's "triumph" at the expense of discussing other important ramifications and ironies of the final resolution to the struggle over the Grand Canyon dams. For example, the controversy sheds some new light upon how Native Americans and environmental organizations are perceived by the American public and portrayed in the historical record. Many environmentalists, critical of how American society has abused the land-scape of North America, argue that American Indians have an ecological con-sciousness that white society needs to emulate to assuage the environmental depredations that American industrial capitalism has wrought upon the land-scape for much of the twentieth century. Historians have also engaged in this debate, with scholars ranging from Calvin Martin to Shepard Krech polarized on the issue of Native Americans as environmentalists.[23] Ironically, only a few years before Iron Eyes Cody appeared on national television and through his tears admonished the American public to respect rather than destroy the natural world, both the Hualapai and Navajo Nations were seeking to construct hydroelectric dams in Grand Canyon, perhaps the most spectacular piece of nature to grace the North American continent. While the CAP debate is only one act in a much larger drama, it illuminates the difficulties that can arise when scholars attempt to lump all American Indians into one ecologically conscious camp. Furthermore, it also suggests that by doing so, historians have failed to recognize the agency American Indians have exercised in determining the use of their resources, even though in wielding it Native Americans may undermine popular stereotypes of themselves as protoenvironmentalists.

The campaign to gain Native American support and manipulate public opinion is also illustrative of the Machiavellian tactics Central Arizona Project proponents and environmentalists used during the Grand Canyon dam controversy. The CAP supporters promised enormous economic benefits to the Hualapai Nation for much of the debate. Yet they revealed their true colors as political pragmatists when, faced with Carl Hayden's and Stewart Udall's impending retirements in January of 1969, they abandoned the Hualapai after it became politically expedient to delete the dams, and instead sided with the Sierra Club in publicizing the benefits that would accrue to the Navajo Tribe. Their lofty pronouncements about aiding the Hualapai notwithstanding, the Department of the Interior and Arizona state and federal officials instead left the Hualapai people with heightened expectations about economic uplift that never came to pass.

Additionally, environmentalists enlisted the Navajo people in their opposition to the Grand Canyon dams, and argued that scenic tourism to Marble Canyon would constitute an important source of revenue for the tribe. But today the Navajo Rim remains relatively unpublicized and undeveloped. And in perhaps the supreme irony of the campaign, the Sierra Club, by courting the Navajo people and obtaining their opposition to the dams and support for coal-fired power plants, became a party to environmental devastation on a large scale. Peabody Coal Company has destroyed vast areas of Navajo country through strip mining, and the air pollution from the Four Corners and Navajo power plants now frequently obscures the view across Grand Canyon, the very place the club fought so stridently to preserve. In the end, both supporters and opponents of the Grand Canyon dams failed to anticipate the environmental and human consequences of their actions and compromised their idealistic rhetoric by choosing political pragmatism over human concerns.

Despite the weakness of the preservationists' political influence, the Grand Canyon dam controversy helped create public perceptions that the Sierra Club possessed the ability to influence the policymaking process for two reasons: the controversy's ultimate result, and the context of the times. Had the CAP passed containing even one Grand Canyon dam, it would have continued the string of defeats begun with Rainbow Bridge and Glen Canyon and possibly undermined the preservationists' illusion of political strength. When the threats to Grand Canyon first arose, Ira Gabrielson, the "grand old man of conservation," admonished his fellow conservationists with the rhetorical question: "If you can't save Grand Canyon, what the hell can you save?"[24] Had the environmentalists lost the Grand Canyon fight it would have been catastrophic because nothing less than the credibility of the entire preservationist agenda was at stake, while to defeat the dams—or to create the perception of doing so—would enhance the illusion of political power begun at Echo Park. Thus, when the dams were defeated as a result of political intrigue, preservationists took credit for it so that they could continue to make public appeals from the position of having actually effectuated political change. Because of Grand Canyon's status as an American national treasure and one of the seven wonders of the natural world, for the Sierra Club to claim the mantle of having saved it conferred upon the club a tremendous amount of legitimacy and prestige among environmentalists and the public alike.

However, for the club's perception of strength to be legitimate, the public had to be willing to accept the preservationists' version of events. After the IRS revocation, when the Sierra Club's Grand Canyon fight became national news, hundreds of thousands of people wrote Congress, and undoubtedly, millions more sympathized with the club over the issue of repression of its rights of speech and petition. After a decade of social unrest and amid fears of increasing governmental interference, many Americans viewed the passage of the CAP in 1968 without dams as a victory not only for preservationists but also for democracy itself, because it was perceived as an example of how dedicated citizens could halt the machine of tyranny through hard work and sacrifice and thus preserve the ideals upon which the Republic was ostensibly based. In the final analysis, the Sierra Club was able to perpetuate the illusion of political strength in the immediate aftermath of the Grand Canyon dam controversy because large numbers of American citizens in 1968 wanted desperately to believe that private individuals and organizations could still affect political outcomes through grassroots involvement in the democratic process.

Just over one year after the controversy ended, Congress passed the National Environmental Policy Act (NEPA), and President Richard Nixon signed it into law. Although with the passage of NEPA the public gained unprecedented opportunities to participate in environmental policymaking, having access to the political system did not guarantee that organizations or individuals could effect change. Hence, the American public's perception of the Sierra Club's ability to influence policy became very important in the immediate post-NEPA era because the club's leadership was able to translate this illusion of strength, which was at its peak in the wake of the club's having just "saved" Grand Canyon, into real political power, once Congress granted environmentalists legal avenues through which they could express their concerns.

The Grand Canyon dam controversy represents the point in time when the Sierra Club was able to reap the benefits of the leadership position it gained among environmental organizations because of its directors' 1960 decision to assign greater importance to public environmental activism than to the club's tax-deductible status. By trying to influence legislation despite the IRS threat, the Sierra Club not only gained a tremendous amount of public visibility but it also placed itself in a position to capitalize upon fortuitous circumstances should they occur. Although it may be serendipitous from the club's perspective that the controversy over the construction of dams in Grand Canyon took place in such a turbulent social climate, it was certainly not a chance occurrence that the Sierra Club was in position to take advantage of it. Though the preservationists' political influence and legal arguments were illusory in the case of Grand Canyon, the aura gained from the public perceptions that environmentalists saved America's greatest scenic wonder enabled subsequent Sierra Club leaders to translate its mirage of power into actual political potency, once environmentalists gained access to the inner sanctum of the policymaking process.

① Notes

Introduction

1. John McPhee, *Encounters with the Archdruid* (New York: Farrar, Straus and Giroux, 1971), 153–245.

2. For examples of these arguments please see Roderick Nash, *Wilderness and the American Mind*, 3d ed. (New Haven: Yale University Press, 1982), 227–37 (all following citations are to the 3d ed. unless otherwise noted); and Roderick Nash, ed. *Grand Canyon of the Living Colorado* (New York: Ballentine Books, 1970), 99–107; see also Alfred Runte, *National Parks: The American Experience*, 2d ed. (Lincoln: University of Nebraska Press, 1987), 191, which originated as a dissertation under the direction of Dr. Nash; and Philip Fradkin, *A River No More* (Tucson: University of Arizona Press, 1984), 228–34; see also Russell Martin, *A Story That Stands Like a Dam: Glen Canyon and the Struggle for the Soul of the West* (New York: Henry Holt, 1989), 250–74. Fradkin cites both *Wilderness and the American Mind* and *Grand Canyon of the Living Colorado* as support for his argument, while Martin cites *Wilderness*, and Fradkin. Stephen Fox also cites *Wilderness*, along with some primary sources in *The American Conservation Movement, John Muir and His Legacy* (Madison: University of Wisconsin Press, 1981), 320, but holds to Nash's conclusion that the Sierra Club stopped the dams.

Marc Reisner's *Cadillac Desert* (New York: Penguin Books, 1987), 281–301, though a more journalistic account, also discusses the political aspects of the controversy in much greater detail than the aforementioned historiography. However, Reisner, too, concludes that the dams were deleted because of the Sierra Club's campaign. See also Hal Rothman, *The Greening of a Nation?* (New York: Harcourt Brace, 1998), 75–79, and John Opie, *Nature's Nation: An Environmental History of the United States* (New York: Harcourt Brace, 1998), 393–94, both of whom echo Nash's arguments. See also Helen Ingram, *Water Politics, Continuity and Change*, (Albuquerque: University of New Mexico Press, 1990), 55–56, 59; and Michael Cohen, *The History of the Sierra Club, 1892–1970*, (San Francisco: Sierra Club Books, 1988), 178, 315, 357–65. Possibly the only publication that does not credit the Sierra Club with the victory is Rich Johnson's *The Central Arizona Project: 1918–1968*, (Tucson: University of Arizona Press, 1977).

3. Nash, *Wilderness*, 200; and Fox, *American Conservation Movement*, 289. Mark Harvey, a leading historian of the Echo Park controversy disagrees with these interpretations and argues that little was resolved by the outcome if one examines it in the light of subsequent controversies over the Colorado River and other western water resources. Please see Mark Harvey, *A Symbol of Wilderness* (Albuquerque: University of New Mexico Press, 1994), 294.

4. For a detailed discussion of the events surrounding the Sierra Club's decision to risk its tax-deductible status please see the author's Ph.D. dissertation: Byron Pearson, "People above Scenery, the Struggle over the Grand Canyon Dams, 1963–1968" (Ph.D. diss., University of Arizona, 1998), 147–53; 177–78.

5. Reisner, *Cadillac Desert*, 295; and Nash, *Wilderness*, 235. The quote is taken from Reisner.

6. President Richard Nixon signed NEPA into law on 1 January 1970.

Chapter 1

1. Thomas Jefferson, *Notes on Virginia*, in *The Life and Selected Writings of Thomas Jefferson* (New York: Random House, 1972), 192–93.

2. Joseph C. Ives, *Report upon the Colorado River of the West*, (Washington: Government Printing Office, 1861), 110.

3. Norris Hundley, *Water and the West* (Berkeley and Los Angeles: University of California Press, 1975), 9–10; see also Reisner, *Cadillac Desert*, 112–18 passim.

4. For an in-depth discussion of the Hetch Hetchy controversy, please see Cohen, *The History of the Sierra Club*, 22–31 passim; and Holoway R. Jones, *John Muir and the Sierra Club: The Battle for Yosemite* (San Francisco: Sierra Club, 1965), 6–8; see also Gifford Pinchot, *The Fight for Conservation* (Garden City, N.Y.: Harcourt Brace, 1910), 42–50; and Roderick Nash, *Wilderness*, 134–39; see also Fox, *American Conservation Movement*, 139–46.

5. Runte, *National Parks*, 77–82; see also Cohen, *History of the Sierra Club*, 22–31.

6. Runte, *National Parks*, 100–105. Olmsted wrote the Park Service's statement of purpose, calling for the preservation of scenic values, and he later argued against the inundation of Grand Canyon in the early 1940s. Mather was a self-made millionaire businessman and first director of the Park Service, who may have provided the pivotal argument before Congress, arguing that scenic preservation would create economic opportunity on the periphery of the parks. Albright, an attorney, served as Mather's trusted assistant until Mather's death in 1930, when he succeeded him as Park Service director.

7. *New York Sun*, 7 May 1903.

8. E. C. La Rue, *Colorado River and Its Utilization: Water Supply Paper 395* (Washington, D.C.: Government Printing Office, 1916), 179–80. La Rue conducted some of his analysis from the rim of the canyon and did not examine the sites closely until the 1923 survey, referenced later in this narrative.

9. *Grand Canyon National Park Establishment Act, U.S. Code,* vol. 16, sec. 221 (1919); see also Steven Carothers and Bryan T. Brown, *The Colorado River Through Grand Canyon* (Tucson: University of Arizona Press, 1991), 6.

10. For a comprehensive discussion of the Colorado River Compact see Norris Hundley, *Dividing the Waters* (Berkeley and Los Angeles: University of California Press, 1966), 48–51; see also U.S. Department of the Interior, Bureau of Reclamation, *The Colorado River: A Natural Menace Becomes a National Resource: A Comprehensive Report on the Development of the Water Resources of the Colorado River Basin for Irrigation, Power Production, and Other Beneficial Uses in Arizona, California, Colorado, Nevada, New Mexico, Utah, and Wyoming* (March 1946), 59–66. The six states that ratified the Colorado River Compact of 1922 were: Wyoming, Idaho, Colorado, Utah, New Mexico, and California. Arizona did not ratify the compact until 1944.

11. National Academy of Sciences, *Water and Choice in the Colorado Basin: An Example of Alternatives in Water Management* (Washington, D.C.: Printing and Publishing Office: National Academy of Sciences, 1968), 21.

12. E. C, La Rue, *Water and Flood Control of Colorado River Below Green River, Utah: Water Supply Paper 556* (Washington: Government Printing Office, 1925), 134–64; see also *New York Daily Tribune,* 12 December 1923; and *Washington Post,* 11 November 1923; see also the Diary of Emery Kolb, 1923 passim, Emery Kolb Papers, Special Collections, Cline Library, Northern Arizona University, hereinafter cited as (SCNAU). River miles are calculated both up- and downstream from Lee's Ferry, which is mile zero. There are three Marble Canyon dam sites; the original site was located four miles upstream of Lee's Ferry, with an alternate site at mile fifteen, where Glen Canyon Dam was eventually built. The Marble Canyon dam site that elicited the intense environmental protests of the 1960s was located downstream of Lee's Ferry in Marble Canyon at mile 39.5. The Bridge Canyon site was located at mile 237.5. Boulder (Hoover) Dam, originally planned for the Boulder Canyon site, was eventually built at the Black Canyon site several miles downstream, but retained the name Boulder Dam. The Red-Wall site was renamed the Marble Canyon site during the mid 1930s, and all references to Marble Canyon Dam after this time refer to a proposal for this location. La Rue's original Marble Canyon site was renamed the Glen Canyon site at about the same time, and is where Glen Canyon Dam is located today.

13. Reisner, *Cadillac Desert,* 130; and Fradkin, *A River No More,* 272.

14. Joseph E. Stevens, *Hoover Dam* (Norman: University of Oklahoma Press, 1988), 46, 53. The project originally was planned for Boulder Canyon, and when construction commenced at a superior site in Black Canyon, the name stuck. When finished, the dam stood 726.4 feet high. See also Russell Martin, *Story That Stands Like a Dam,* 3.

15. George Hartzog to Stewart Udall, 27 January 1964; and R. F. Walter to Dr. Elwood Mead, commissioner of Reclamation, 7 June 1932 in GRCA-04848 (GCNPMC); see also Jerome Kirwin, *Federal Water Power Legislation* (New York:

Columbia University Press, 1926), 380. The legal authority for the construction of water projects in Grand Canyon up through 1932 is as follows: Hayden's reclamation provision of 1919; the 1920 Federal Power Act, which opened all parks and monuments to water development; and the repeal of certain sections of it 3 March 1921 that only forbade construction in *existing* parks and monuments. If Congress intended to keep water projects out of parks and monuments created after 1920, it included specific language to that effect within the specific enabling legislation. However, Congress left a loophole in the law, for no provision existed to protect monuments created by presidential proclamation. Therefore, the Grand Canyon National Monument Hoover established in 1932 was not protected from water projects, nor could it have been unless Congress acted specifically to do so.

16. Mead to Albright, 14 June 1932; Albright to Roger Toll, 3 August, 1932; Albright to Mead, 11 January 1933; all in GRCA-04848, (GCNPMC).

17. Peter Wiley and Robert Gottlieb, *Empires in the Sun: The Rise of the New American West* (Tucson: University of Arizona Press, 1982), 165–90 passim. To obtain an idea of the scale to the Bureau's postwar program in the aggregate, see Reisner, "The Go Go Years," in *Cadillac Desert*, 151–75 passim.

18. Department of the Interior, Bureau of Reclamation, *The Colorado River: A Natural Menace Becomes a National Resource*, 168–84; and U.S. Department of the Interior, Bureau of Reclamation, "Memorandum Report on Reconnaissance Studies, Marble Canyon–Kanab Creek Power Development." (Boulder City, Nevada: October 1961), passim; and John S. McLaughlin to the director of the National Park Service, 24 October 1961, fiche L7423, "Marble Canyon–Kanab Creek Project 1961–1962,"(GCNPRL).

19. U.S. Department of the Interior, *The Colorado River*, 168. The 6.664 billion figure is derived from the estimated outputs of the Marble Canyon power plant (164 million kwh), and of the Kanab Creek power plant (6.5 billion kwh). See also Frederick Law Olmsted, "Preliminary Survey," passim, folder (GCNP), box 8, Drury Records, CCF/NPS, RG-79.

20. Byron Pearson, "Newton Drury of the National Park Service, a Reappraisal," *Pacific Historical Review* 68, no. 3 (fall 1999), 402–5.

21. *Los Angeles Times*, 30 July 1945; and Scoyen to Director, 6 August 1945, GRCA-04848 (GCNPMC). A proposed silt-control dam on the Little Colorado River also threatened Wupatki National Monument.

22. Fred Packard, "Grand Canyon Monument in Danger," in *National Parks Magazine*, July-September 1949, 3–8; and Fred Packard, "Grand Canyon National Park and Dinosaur Monument in Danger," *National Parks Magazine*, October-December 1949, 11–12. See also Fox, *American Conservation Movement*, 203–4.

23. Director of the National Park Service to the Director of Information, 10 May 1949, in folder (GCNP), box 8, Drury Records, RG-79; see also, Minutes, Sierra Club Board of Directors, 4 September 1949, in folder 20, carton 3, SCR.

24. Minutes, Special Meeting of the Board of Directors, 12 November 1949, folder 20, carton 3, SCR.

25. Newton B. Drury to Richard Leonard, 15 February 1950, fiche L-7423, "Dams on the Colorado River 1948–1954," (GCNPRL).

26. Samuel Hays, "From Conservation to Environment: Environmental Politics Since World War Two," *Environmental Review* 6 (fall 1982): 14–41 passim.

27. Smith to Hayden, 20 February 1950, folder 12, box 19, Carl Hayden Papers; and Drury to McFarland, 7 February 1950; director to Assistant Director Wirth, 15 February 1950, folder (GCNP), box 8, Drury Records, CCF/NPS, RG-79; see also Fred Packard to Senator Matthew M. Neeley, 9 February 1950, folder "Colorado River 1947–1959," box 6:102, Wilderness Society Papers; and U.S. Congress, Senate, Subcommittee on Irrigation and Reclamation of the Committee on Interior and Insular Affairs, *Colorado River Storage Project: Hearings before the Subcommittee on Irrigation and Reclamation of the Committee on Interior and Insular Affairs,* 84th Cong., 1st sess., 28 February–5 March 1955, 692; see also Johnson, *Central Arizona Project,* 70–71.

28. Minutes, Special Meeting of the Sierra Club Board of Directors, 12 November 1949, folder 19, carton 3, SCR; and Johnson, *Central Arizona Project,* 71.

29. Harvey, *Symbol of Wilderness,* 74–77; and Reisner, *Cadillac Desert,* 145–46.

30. Harvey, *Symbol of Wilderness,* 80–91.

31. Leonard to Zahniser, 1 August 1950; and William Voigt to Leonard, 9 August 1950, folder "Colorado River 1947–1959," box 102:6, Wilderness Society Papers; see also, Minutes, Sierra Club Board of Directors, 3 September 1950, folder 20, carton 3, SCR.

32. Harvey, *Symbol of Wilderness,* 95–105. Mark Harvey argues that although the exact situation surrounding the resignation of Drury has never been clarified, the clash between the interior secretary and Park Service director was inevitable, given Drury's preservationist ideology and Chapman's support for the Bureau.

33. David Brower, interview with the author, 27 July 1997.

34. U.S. Congress, Senate, *A Bill Authorizing the Construction, Operation and Maintenance of a Dam and Incidental Works in the Main Stream of the Colorado River at Bridge Canyon, Together with Certain Appurtenant Dams and Canals, and for Other Purposes.* 82d Cong., 1st sess., 1951, S. 75., fiche L7423, "Dams on the Colorado River, 1948–1954," (RLGCNP).

35. U.S. Congress, House, Committee on Interior and Insular Affairs, *Central Arizona Project: Hearing before the Committee on Interior and Insular Affairs,* 82nd Cong., 1st sess., 18 March 1951, passim.

36. Harvey, *Symbol of Wilderness,* 186–87, 201–2.

37. Senate Subcommittee, *Colorado River Storage Project,* 692.

38. U.S. Congress, House, Subcommittee on Irrigation and Reclamation of the Committee on Interior and Insular Affairs, *Colorado River Storage Project: Hearings*

before the Subcommittee on Irrigation and Reclamation of the Committee on Interior and Insular Affairs, 84th Cong., 1st sess., 17–19 March 1955, 733, 797.

39. Ibid., 1132–33.

40. Director, National Park Service to , Bureau of Reclamation, 4 August 1949, Fiche 7423, "Dams on the Colorado River 1938–1954, (GCNPRL).

41. *U.S. v Harriss,* 74 S.C. 808, 814.

42. Ibid., 814.

43. Ibid., 808, 813, 815.

44. Ibid., 814–15; for a good account of the confusion that the 1954 decision wrought within the Wilderness Society leadership, please see Mark W. T. Harvey, "Paying the Taxpayer: The Internal Revenue Service and the Environmental Movement," paper delivered at the American Society of Environmental History convention, Baltimore, Maryland, 6 March 1997, copy in author's possession.

45. *Martha Hubbard Davis v Commissioner of Internal Revenue,* 22 T. C. No. 131; see also John Skinner, Esq., to Leonard, 1 December 1954, in folder 15, carton 86, Richard Leonard Papers, Sierra Club Members Collection, Bancroft Library, University of California Berkeley, (hereinafter cited as Richard Leonard papers); and David Brower, "Environmental Activist, Publicist and Prophet," interview by Susan Schrepfer, (Sierra Club History Committee, 1974–1978), 136, Regional Oral History Office, Bancroft Library, University of California Berkeley.

46. Richard Leonard, "Mountaineer, Lawyer, Environmentalist," interview by Susan R, Schrepfer, (Sierra Club History Committee, 1975), 144. Regional Oral History Office, Bancroft Library, University of California Berkeley.

47. Leonard, "Mountaineer, Lawyer, Environmentalist," 144.

48. Minutes, Sierra Club, Special Meeting of the Board of Directors, 21 November 1954, folder 25, carton 3, SCR.

49. Richard Leonard's papers are filled with correspondence dated 1954–1960 between Leonard and concerned conservation leaders, to whom he invariably urged caution. For an example, please see Leonard to Zahniser, 3 January 1958, folder 5, carton 86, Richard Leonard Papers.

50. For a general account of the election of 1960, see Robert Dallek, *Lone Star Rising: Lyndon Johnson and His Times, 1908–1960* (New York: Oxford University Press, 1991), 564–75 passim; on Udall's role see Floyd Dominy, interview with author, Bellview Farm Virginia, 1 November 1996, tape and transcript in author's possession.

51. John F. Kennedy, "Special Message on Natural Resources," 23 February 1961, folder 4, box 90, Stewart Udall Papers; Stewart Udall, interview with Charles Coate, Santa Fe, New Mexico, 23 April 1997, transcript in author's possession.

52. Floyd Dominy, interview with author, 1 November 1996; and Stewart Udall, interview by W. W. Moss, 12 January 1970, transcript John F. Kennedy Library, Boston, Mass.; and Stewart Udall, interview by Chuck Coate, 23 April 1997.

53. Stegner's catchphrase, "geography of hope," is quoted in Cohen, *History of the*

Sierra Club, 261; and Ibid., 243, 260; see also Sharon Francis, telephonic interview by author, 14 August 1997, tape and transcription in author's possession; and Ansel Adams to Stewart Udall, 15 December 1960, folder 1, box 190, Stewart Udall Papers.

54. Stewart Udall, *The Quiet Crisis and the Next Generation*, (Salt Lake City: Peri-grine Smith Books, 1988), 173–87.

55. A special master is a legal expert the court appoints to hear cases in technical areas of the law such as water law.

56. Stewart Udall, *Quiet Crisis and the Next Generation*, 179; and Stewart Udall, inter-view with author, 13 March 1997.

57. Minutes, Sierra Club Board of Directors, 5–6 December 1959, folder 25, car-ton 3, SCR; David Brower, interview by author, 27 July 1997.

58. Brower, "Environmental Activist, Publicist, and Prophet," 153–54; and "Tran-script of Remarks before Sierra Club Executive Committee in Spring 1960 leading to the organization of the Sierra Club Foundation," by David Brower, dated 24 February 1961, folder 4, Box 55, SCMP; see also Edgar Wayburn, "Sierra Club Statesman," interview by Ann Lage and Susan Schrepfer, (Sierra Club History Committee, 1976–1981) 290–91, Regional Oral History Office, University of California, Berke-ley. The quote regarding Brower's freedom to lobby is from Leonard, "Mountaineer, Lawyer, Environmentalist," 144. Sierra Club historian Michael Cohen also describes the concern of the club's leadership over the potential IRS threat in *History of the Sierra Club*, 163–66, 277.

59. Udall to Charles Reed—Wayne Akin—Rich Johnson, (memo unsent but shared with Morris Udall), folder 3, box 166, Stewart Udall Papers.

60. Stewart Udall, interview with author, 13 March 1997.

61. Floyd Dominy, author interview, 1 November 1996; and Stewart Udall, inter-view with author, 13 March 1997.

62. Stewart Udall, interview with the author, 13 March 1997; and Stewart Udall, *The Myths of August: A Personal Exploration of Our Tragic Cold War Affair with the Atom*, (New York: Pantheon Books, 1994), 250–71 passim; and Floyd Dominy to the Secretary of the Interior, 9 November 1962, folder 4, box 162, Stewart Udall Papers; see also *New York Times*, 9 September 1961. The saline water program was begun with a modest budget of $2 million in 1952 and fell under the jurisdiction of the Interior Department. Congress had approved of five test plants, each designed to refine a dif-ferent desalinization process, and these test plants started to go on line in 1961.

63. Aspinall to Udall, 27 November 1962, folder 7, box 166, Stewart Udall Papers; and Stewart Udall, interview with author, 13 March 1997.

64. Udall to Aspinall, 18 January 1963, folder 7, box 166, Stewart Udall Papers.

65. Udall to Governor ____, 12 June 1963, attached to Udall to Hayden, 12 June 1963, folder 8, box 166, Stewart Udall Papers.

66. The phrase "think big" had come to symbolize the Interior Department's con-servation program under President Kennedy, and was widely used in national publi-cations by 1962.

Chapter 2

1. David Brower, *For Earth's Sake: The Life and Times of David Brower* (Salt Lake City: Peregrine Books, 1990), 347; see also Martin, *Story That Stands Like a Dam*, 208; and David Brower, interview by author, 27 July 1997.

2. "Wild By Law," *The American Experience Series*, 35 min., Corporation for Public Broadcasting, 1991, videocassette.

3. According to Marc Reisner, Brower's friends worried that he would commit suicide over the loss of Glen Canyon; see Reisner, *Cadillac Desert*, 295.

4. *New York Times*, 22 January 1963; and *Portland Oregonian*, 12 September 1962; see also David Brower, interview by author, 27 July 1997.

5. *New York Times*, 22 January 1963; and *Portland Oregonian*, 12 September 1962; see also David Brower, interview with author, 27 July 1997.

6. Stewart Udall, interview by author, 13 March 1997; and "Statement of the President," 26 October 1964, folder 4, box 162 Stewart Udall Papers; see also Stewart Udall, interview by W. W. Moss, 12 January 1970, 480, John F. Kennedy Library, Boston, Massachusetts.

7. *New York Times*, 22 January 1963; and *Portland Oregonian*, 12 September 1962.

8. *New York Times*, 27 August 1963.

9. Commissioner of Reclamation to Secretary of the Interior, 14 February 1962, folder 4, box 166, Stewart Udall Papers.

10. Brower, "Environmental Activist, Publicist, and Prophet," 122.

11. Before the Federal Power Commission, "Answer and Objection of Arizona Power Authority to Petition for Intervention, Motion for Leave out of Time, Motion for Re-Opening the Record for Presentation of Evidence of Stewart L. Udall, Secretary of the Interior," (Washington, D.C., 10 October 1962); and U.S. Federal Power Commission, "Order Granting Limited Intervention Out of Time," (Washington, D.C. November 2, 1962), fiche 7423, "Bridge Canyon Dam, 1954–1966," (GCN-PRL); see also *Arizona Republic*, 11 January 1963; and *Arizona Republic*, 24 January 1963.

12. Johnson, *Central Arizona Project*, 127–32.

13. *Arizona Republic*, 26 January 1963; and *Phoenix Gazette*, 26 January 1963; see also Barry Goldwater to Senator Henry M. Jackson, 16 April 1963; and "Sequence of Senator Hayden's Action," folder 2, box 321, Carl Hayden Papers; see also "Statement by Senator Carl Hayden Regarding S. 502," folder 1, box 321, Carl Hayden Papers; and Carl Hayden and John Rhodes to Rich Johnson and others, 19 March 1964, folder 4, box 321, Carl Hayden Papers; and Johnson, *Central Arizona Project*, 132.

14. Orren Beaty, assistant to the secretary, "Memo to the Files," 6 February 1963, folder 2, box 321, Carl Hayden Papers. The Arizona Interstate Stream Commission was the state agency responsible for Arizona's CAP and Colorado River strategies.

15. Ibid., 5–6.

16. Ibid., 2–3, 7.

17. Ibid., 1–2.

18. Ibid., 4; and Carl Hayden's handwritten notes from the meeting of 6 February 1963, folder 2, box 321, Carl Hayden Papers.

19. Johnson, *Central Arizona Project*, 131; and secretary of the interior to Assistant Secretary Holum, 1 May 1963, folder 7, box 166, Stewart Udall Papers.

20. Cohen, *History of the Sierra Club*, 318–19; and Eliot Porter, *The Place No One Knew* (San Francisco: Sierra Club Books, 1963), 7; see also David Brower, interview by author, 27 July 1997.

21. David Brower, quoted in Porter, *Place No One Knew*, 5.

22. Minutes, Sierra Club Board of Directors, 4 May 1963, folder 2, carton 4, SCR; and Martin Litton, "Sierra Club Director and Uncompromising Preservationist, 1950s–1970s," interview by Ann Lage, (Sierra Club Oral History Series, 1980–1981), 73, Regional Oral History Office, Bancroft Library, University of California Berkeley; see also Brower, "Environmental Activist, Publicist and Prophet," 143.

23. Dwight Eugene Mayo, "Arizona and the Colorado River Compact" (Master's thesis, Arizona State University, 1964). A special master is a person of technical expertise whom the court appoints to try the merits of extremely specialized cases. The master then reports his or her findings to the court, which may or may not rely upon them in rendering its decision. Arizona had also won one lawsuit in 1935.

24. U.S. Supreme Court, *Arizona v California*, "Special Master's Report," Washington, D.C.: U.S. Supreme Court, 5 December 1960.

25. For a detailed account of the *Arizona v California* saga, see Johnson, *Central Arizona Project*, 87–124 passim.

26. Ibid., 120–21. According to the Colorado River Compact of 1922, the lower basin was to receive 7.5 million acre feet of water every year. The key to the Gila River controversy is that it flows into the Colorado hundreds of miles downstream from Lee's Ferry, the point at which the Colorado River is measured. Had California succeeded in convincing the court that the Gila should be included in Arizona's allotment from the 7.5 million acre foot Compact amount, it would have, in effect, created an additional 1 million acre feet of water to draw from the lower-basin allotment, and California was already using close to 1 million acre feet to which Arizona was entitled.

27. *Arizona v California*, 83 S. Ct. 1468. See also, Johnson, *Central Arizona Project*, 140.

28. Ted Riggins, *An Ode—From California*, folder 9, box 174, Stewart Udall Papers.

29. Memorandum, Orren Beaty to Stewart Udall, 5 June 1963; and Memorandum, Hayden to Arizona Congressional Delegation, 10 May 1963, folder 8, box 166, Stewart Udall Papers.

30. Memorandum, Hayden to Arizona Congressional Delegation, 10 May 1963, folder 8, box 166, Stewart Udall Papers.

31. Secretary of the Interior, Report to the President, 11 June 1963, folder 7, box 107, Stewart Udall Papers; see also Udall to Hayden, 12 June 1963, folder 8, box 166 Stewart Udall Papers; and Udall to Hayden, 22 July 1963, folder 10, box 166, Stewart Udall Papers.

32. Keith Brown, Arizona Republican Party chairman, "Press Release," 21 June 1962, folder 8, box 166, Stewart Udall Papers.

33. *New York Times*, 12 June 1963.

34. Brower to Udall, 22 June 1963; Brower to Udall, 24 June 1963, folder 4, box 321, Carl Hayden Papers.

35. *New York Times*, 22 August 1963.

36. *New York Times*, 22 August 1963; and *New York Times*, 27 August 1963.

37. *New York Times*, 22 January 1963.

38. *New York Times*, 22 January 1963; and *New York Times*, 27 August 1963; see also *Arizona Republic*, 27 August 1963.

39. Assistant Regional Director, Resource Planning to Acting Superintendent, Grand Canyon National Park, 5 July 1963, fiche 7243, "Bridge Canyon Dam, 1954–1966," (GCNPRL); and Wirth to the Secretary of the Interior, 13 August 1963.

40. Department of the Interior, Bureau of Reclamation, "Marble Canyon–Kanab Creek," (GCNPRL).

41. Superintendent, Grand Canyon National Park to Regional Director, Region Three, 21 November 1957; and Regional Director, Region Three to Director, 27 November 1957, fiche 7423, "Bridge Canyon Dam, 1954–1966," (GCNPRL).

42. Anthony Wayne Smith, "The Mighty Colorado," *National Parks Magazine*, October 1963, 2; and Weldon Heald, "Colorado River of the West," *National Parks Magazine*, October 1963, 4–9.

43. Clyde Thomas, "The Last Days of Grand Canyon Too?" *Sierra Club Bulletin*, October 1963, 2–4. According to Sierra Club historian Michael Cohen, Martin Litton wrote this article under the pseudonym of Clyde Thomas.

44. Hayden to Udall, 7 February 1964, folder 6, box 167, Stewart Udall Papers; Johnson, *Central Arizona Project*, 146.

45. *Los Angeles Times*, 13 November 1963; and Hayden to Udall, 5 December 1963, folder 3, box 167, Stewart Udall Papers.

46. Johnson, *Central Arizona Project*, 147.

47. Stewart Udall to LBJ re: PSWP, n.d. folder 3, box 174, Stewart Udall Papers. Although this document is undated, its content suggests that it was written as an informational document to LBJ during the first three months of his presidency. It is important because Kennedy never endorsed the PSWP publicly, yet in this memo Udall states that he had obtained Kennedy's "concurrence" in favor of the PSWP.

Chapter 3

1. Stewart Udall, "En route Back to Washington," handwritten notes taken aboard the cabinet plane, 22 November 1963, folder 3, box 109, Stewart Udall Papers.

2. Ibid., passim; and Robert Caro, *The Years of Lyndon Johnson*, vol. 1, *The Path to Power* (New York: Alfred Knopf, 1982) 458–68 passim; see also Dallek, *Lone Star Rising*, 175, 179–81; and Stewart Udall, interview by author, 13 March 1997, see also McFarland to the President, 1 August 1966, folder 2, box 476, Morris Udall Papers.

3. Caro, *Path to Power*, 552; see also Robert Caro, *The Years of Lyndon Johnson*, vol. 2, *Means of Ascent* (New York: Alfred Knopf Inc., 1990), 77–78, 125.

4. Udall to Moyers and attached "Memo to the President," 27 November 1963, folder 9, box 197, Stewart Udall Papers.

5. *Arizona Daily Star*, 12 December 1963; and *Arizona Daily Star*, 30 December 1963; see also Udall to Hayden, 19 December 1963, folder 2, box 167, Stewart Udall Papers.

6. Remarks by Commissioner Floyd E. Dominy, Bureau of Reclamation, Tucson, Arizona, 11 December 1963; see also Floyd Dominy, interview by author, 1 November 1996.

7. Beaty to Udall, 16 December 1963, folder 2, box 167, Stewart Udall Papers.

8. *Arizona Republic*, 27 December 1963; and *Arizona Republic*, 29 December 1963; see also Carl Hayden, Telegram to Stewart Udall, 30 December 1963; and *New York Times*, 15 February 1964; see also Stewart Udall interview by author, 13 March 1997.

9. Assistant Secretary—Public Land Management to Secretary of the Interior, 6 January 1964, part 1, box 125, D of I/CCF, RG 48.

10. Assistant Secretary—Public Land Management to Secretary of the Interior, 6 January 1964, part 1, box 125, D of I/CCF, RG 48.

11. McLaughlin to Director, 13 December 1963; and McLaughlin to Director, 4 February 1964, fiche 7423, "Bridge Canyon Dam, 1954–1966," (GCNPRL.)

12. Director Hartzog to the Secretary of the Interior, 27 January 1964, fiche 7423, "Bridge Canyon Dam, 1954–1966," (GCNPRL).

13. Carl Hayden to George B. Hartzog, 17 February 1964; and Superintendent McLaughlin to his staff, 26 February 1964; see also John A. Carver, Jr. to Carl Hayden, 6 March 1964; and Regional Director National Park Service to Southwest Region Superintendents, 16 March 1964; fiche 7423, "Bridge Canyon Dam, 1954–1966," (GCNPRL); and *Arizona Daily Sun*, 20 February 1964; see also *Arizona Republic*, 20 February 1964.

14. Brower, "Environmental Activist, Publicist and Prophet," 61; and George Hartzog, interview by author, 2 November 1996.

15. George Hartzog, interview by author, 2 November 1996.

16. E. C. La Rue's 1923 report included several dam site assessments within Grand Canyon National Park.

17. U.S. Department of the Interior, "National Park Service Appendix to Pacific Southwest Water Plan," August 1963, box 172, Stewart Udall Papers.

18. *Grand Canyon National Park Establishment Act, Statutes at Large* 40, sec. 1, 1178; and Jasperson to Brower, 28 April 1964, folder 13, box 21, SCMP.

19. *Arizona Republic,* 29 December 1963.

20. Regional Director to Southwest Region Superintendents, 26 March 1964, fiche 7423, "Bridge Canyon Dam, 1954–1966," (GCNPRL).

21. O. N. Arrington, Chief AZGF Special Services Division, to Governor Fannin, 20 March 1964, folder 6, box 167, Stewart Udall Papers..

22. Morley Fox, "A Report on Conservation Groups," 1965, folder 9, box 478, Morris Udall Papers. Fox was the Washington Representative for the Central Arizona Project Association, a pro-CAP lobbying organization.

23. Transcript of Udall/Hayden exchange at the CAP hearings before the Senate Committee on Interior and Insular Affairs, prepared by Floyd Dominy, file 7, box 167, Stewart Udall Papers; and Udall to Senator Henry Jackson, 9 April 1964, folder 8, box 167, Stewart Udall Papers.

24. Stewart Udall, "Before the Subcommittee on Irrigation and Reclamation, Committee on Interior and Insular Affairs," U.S. Senate, 9 April 1964, folder 1, box 2, CAP/88, John Rhodes Papers. Grand Canyon National Park was created out of the original national monument. President Hoover created a new national monument in 1932.

25. Mead to Albright, 14 June 1932; Albright to Roger Toll, 3 August, 1932; Albright to Mead, 11 January 1933; GRCA-04848, (GCNPMC).

26. The reference to the Bureau's reluctance to build a high dam is contained in a letter from Grand Canyon National Park Superintendent M. R. Tillotson to Director, National Park Service, of 27 June 1938 commenting upon a speech given by Assistant Reclamation Commissioner E. B. Debler, 27 June 1938, GRCA-04848, (GCNPMC). The Bureau's repudiation of this earlier position can be found in U.S. Department of the Interior, Bureau of Reclamation, "Preliminary Report on Colorado River–Phoenix Diversion Project, Arizona," (March 1944), 3–4, 10.

27. Staats to Udall, 20 January 1964, folder 5, box 167, Stewart Udall Papers; and Joe Califano, Department of the Army, to Kermit Gordon, 1 April 1964; see also Staats to Udall, 25 April 1964, folder 8, box 167, Stewart Udall Papers; and Staats to Udall, 11 March 1964, folder 3, box 1, CAP/88, John Rhodes Papers.

28. Udall to LBJ, 14 February 1964, folder 1, box 476, Morris Udall Papers; and *Arizona Republic,* 16 April 1964; see also Stewart Udall "Reports to the President," 2 January, 2 February, 3 March, 24 March, 7 April 1964, folders 7–9, box 115, Stewart Udall Papers; and Carl Hayden to the President, 5 May 1964, folder 1, box 168, Stewart Udall Papers; see also Stewart Udall, interview by author, 13 March 1997.

29. *Newsletter,* Central Arizona Project Association, August 1964, 1; and *Phoenix Gazette,* 28 July 1964; see also Johnson, *Central Arizona Project,* 143–44.

30. Johnson, *Central Arizona Project*, 143–44, 2; and Reisner, *Cadillac Desert*, 289.

31. *Arizona Republic*, 20 June 1964.

32. Stephen Raushenbush, "A Bridge Canyon Dam Is Not Necessary," *National Parks Magazine*, April 1964, 4–9.

33. Anthony Wayne Smith, "The Editorial Page," *National Parks Magazine*, April 1964, 2.

34. David Brower, "The New Threat to Grand Canyon: Action Needed," *Sierra Club Bulletin*, January 1964, 18; and David Brower, "Gigantic Southwest Water Plan Offers More Reservoirs than Water," *Sierra Club Bulletin*, September 1964, 12–13; see also Luna Leopold "Confidential" to Bradley and Brower, 10 November 1964, folder 12, box 21, SCMP. The signature on this letter is blocked out in the Sierra Club files, but Leopold's signature appears on the copy located in Richard Bradley's papers.

35. *Arizona Republic*, 28 February 1964; and Francois Leydet, *Time and the River Flowing* (San Francisco: Sierra Club, 1964), passim; see also David Brower, "Our Special Grand Canyon campaign needs...," 1964, folder "Grand Canyon General," box 209, SCMP; and *New York Times*, 9 November 1964; and *New York Times*, 10 November 1964.

36. Harvey, *Symbol of Wilderness*, 162–66; and David Brower Tape, untitled, 1977, (GCNPMC).

37. Richard Bradley, "The Controversial Colorado," 24 September 1964, folder "The Controversial Colorado," box 1 "Grand Canyon Dams," Richard Bradley Papers, Conservation Collection, Western History/Genealogy Department, Denver Public Library, Denver, hereinafter cited as Richard Bradley Papers.

38. Luna Leopold "Confidential" to Bradley and Brower, 10 November 1964, folder 12, box 21, SCMP; and Bradley to Saylor, 15 November 1964, folder 12, box 21, SCMP.

39. *Denver Post*, 25 September 1964; and Dominy to Bradley, 26 October 1964, folder 12, box 21, SCMP; see also *Denver Post*, 19 October 1964; and Richard C. Bradley, "Attack on Grand Canyon," *The Living Wilderness*, winter 1964–65, 3–6; see also Richard C. Bradley, "Grand Canyon of the Controversial Colorado," *Sierra Club Bulletin*, December 1964, 73–78.

40. Rhodes to Governor Fannin, Mo Udall and others regarding the November field hearings, 3 September 1964, folder 2, box 477, Morris Udall Papers; and Larry Mehren to Morris Udall, 1 September 1964, folder 2, box 2, CAP/88, John Rhodes Papers.

41. Roy Webb, *If We Had a Boat*, (Salt Lake: University of Utah Press, 1986), 131; and U.S. Department of the Interior, Bureau of Reclamation, *Bridge and Marble Canyon Dams and Their Relationship to Grand Canyon National Park and Monument* (Washington, D.C.: Government Printing Office, 1964), passim.

42. Science Advisor to the Secretary, 10 April 1964, folder 4, box 162, Stewart Udall Papers; and Commissioner of Reclamation to the Secretary, 29 October 1964, folder 1, box 168, Stewart Udall Papers.

43. Assistant Secretary, Water and Power Development to Secretary of the Interior, 30 December 1964; and Holum to Jackson, 11 December 1964, folder 2, box 168, Stewart Udall Papers.

44. Orren Beaty to Udall, 31 December 1964, folder 2, box 168, Stewart Udall Papers. *Phreatophytes* are plants that consume enormous quantities of water.

45. Joe Jensen, "Confidential Report to M. W. D. Directors," 15 December 1964, folder 2, box 168, Stewart Udall Papers. California, of course, desired that the 4.4 million-acre-foot guarantee be given in perpetuity.

Chapter 4

1. William O'Neil, *Coming Apart* (New York: Times Book Company, 1971), 278–87; and Barbara Brower to author, 19 December 1997.

2. *Brandenburg v Ohio*, 89 S. Ct. 1827; and *New York Times Co. v United States*, 91 S. Ct. 2140. The Court in *Brandenburg* overturned an Ohio statute that forbade the advocacy of the use of force to implement political reform.

3. For interpretations of these and other social movements of the 1960s, please see O'Neil, *Coming Apart*, passim; and Stewart Burns, *Social Movements of the 1960s* (Boston: Twayne Publishers, 1990); for a leading interpretation of the importance of Rachel Carson's book see Fox, *American Conservation Movement*, 296–98.

4. *Los Angeles Times*, 15 December 1964; and Orren Beaty, "Memorandum to the Secretary," 31 December 1964, folder 2, box 108, Stewart Udall Papers.

5. Johnson, *Central Arizona Project*, 149–50.

6. Ibid., 152.

7. U.S. Department of the Interior, *Lake Powell: Jewel of the Colorado* (Washington, D.C.: Government Printing Office, 1965), passim.

8. Ibid., inside front cover; and John Wesley Powell, *The Exploration of the Colorado River and Its Canyons* (New York: Dover Publications, 1961), 233; see also Assistant Director, Resource Planning to Departmental Task Force—Lower Colorado River, box 321, folder 4, Carl Hayden Papers.

9. United States Department of the Interior, "National Park Service Appendix to Pacific Southwest Water Plan," August, 1963.

10. Michael Nadel, editor of *The Living Wilderness*, to Mrs. Alfred Hudson, 21 May 1965, folder "Colorado River, 1960–1965," box 106, Wilderness Society Papers; and *New York Times*, 20 December 1964; see also Russell Butcher to Brooks Alexander, 28 April 1965, folder 32, box, 11, SCMP; and "Grand Canyon 'Cash Registers,'" *Life Magazine*, 7 May 1965; see also Bradley to Brower, 8 January 1965, folder 29, box 19, SCMP; and Bradley to Wallace Stegner, n.d. 1965, folder "Atlantic," box 1 "Grand Canyon Dams," Richard Bradley Papers.

11. Bradley to Charles Morton, editor, *The Atlantic Monthly*, 10 March 1965; and Bradley to Wallace Stegner, fall 1965; see also Stegner to Bradley, 25 November 1965, folder "Atlantic," box 1 "Grand Canyon Dams," Richard Bradley Papers; and "Pro-

ceedings: Project Rescue, A Seminar on the Central Arizona Project," Co-sponsored by the Arizona State University and the Central Arizona Project Association, 6, 8, 10 July 1964, folder 5, box 3, CAP/88, John Rhodes Papers.

12. David Brower, "The Chips Are Down for Grand Canyon," *Sierra Club Bulletin*, February 1965; and Carlin to Brower, 8 March 1965, folder 9, box 21, SCMP; see also David Brower, interview by author, 27 July 1997.

13. *Phoenix Gazette*, 30 April 1965; and *Phoenix Gazette*, 10 May 1965; see also *Arizona Republic*, 11 May 1965; and Assistant Secretary—Water and Power to Secretary of the Interior, 3 November 1964, folder 2, box 168, Stewart Udall Papers; see also Staats to Stewart Udall, 18 March 1965, folder 4, box 164, Stewart Udall Papers.

14. Stewart Udall to Aspinall, 17 May 1965; and Udall to Budget Director, 15 April 1965, folder 5, box 168, Stewart Udall Papers; for Rhodes's and Dominy's perspectives see also Johnson, *Central Arizona Project*, 155.

15. *Portland Oregonian*, 18 July 1965; Marc Reisner also discusses Jackson's action in *Cadillac Desert*, 289.

16. Johnson, *Central Arizona Project*, 161–63. The CAP would have created a water deficit in the upper basin because the river was overallocated. If the CAP were built, it would bring the lower basin's total use close to its 7.5-million-acre-foot allotment under the 1922 compact. Since the compact supposedly divided the annual flow equally between the basins, for the lower basin to put its entire compact allotment to use would necessarily create shortfalls upstream.

17. U.S. Congress, House, Subcommittee on Irrigation and Reclamation of the Committee on Interior and Insular Affairs, *Lower Colorado Basin Project: Hearings before the Subcommittee on Irrigation and Reclamation of the Committee on Interior and Insular Affairs*, 89th Cong., 1st sess., 23–31 August, 1 September 1965, 109, 166–88, 736; and Floyd Dominy, interview by author, 1 November 1996. According to Dominy two of these scale models were actually built.

18. U.S. Congress, House, Subcommittee on Irrigation and Reclamation of the Committee on Interior and Insular Affairs, *Lower Colorado Basin Project: Hearings before the Subcommittee on Irrigation and Reclamation of the Committee on Interior and Insular Affairs*, 89th Cong., 1st sess., 23–31 August, 1 September 1965, 201–10.

19. Ibid., iv–vi; and Richard Lamm, "Report to the Colorado Open Space Coordinating Council on Testifying before the House Interior and Insular Affairs Subcommittee on Irrigation and Reclamation," 1 September 1965, folder 21, box 20, SCMP; see also Bradley to Charles Morton, 3 April 1966, folder "Atlantic," box 1 "Grand Canyon Dams," Richard Bradley Papers.

20. U.S. Congress, House, Subcommittee on Irrigation and Reclamation of the Committee on Interior and Insular Affairs, *Lower Colorado Basin Project: Hearings before the Subcommittee on Irrigation and Reclamation of the Committee on Interior and Insular Affairs*, 89th Cong., 1st sess., 23–31 August, 1 September 1965, 716–19, 751–52.

21. Ibid., 872; and Lamm, "Report," 1–3.

22. U.S. Congress, House, Subcommittee on Irrigation and Reclamation of the Committee on Interior and Insular Affairs, *Lower Colorado Basin Project: Hearings before the Subcommittee on Irrigation and Reclamation of the Committee on Interior and Insular Affairs*, 89th Cong., 1st sess., 23–31 August, 1 September 1965, 800–808; and "'Time and the River Flowing,' An Analysis by Representative Morris K. Udall of Francois Leydet's book on the Grand Canyon of the Colorado," box 321, folder 5, Carl Hayden Papers.

23. U.S. Congress, House, Subcommittee on Irrigation and Reclamation of the Committee on Interior and Insular Affairs, *Lower Colorado Basin Project: Hearings before the Subcommittee on Irrigation and Reclamation of the Committee on Interior and Insular Affairs*, 89th Cong., 1st sess., 23–31 August, 1 September 1965, 809–10.

24. Ibid., 644–45.

25. Ibid., 646–53.

26. Johnson, *Central Arizona Project*, 170–74.

27. U.S. Congress, House, Subcommittee on Irrigation and Reclamation of the Committee on Interior and Insular Affairs, *Lower Colorado Basin Project: Hearings before the Subcommittee on Irrigation and Reclamation of the Committee on Interior and Insular Affairs*, 89th Cong., 1st sess., 23–31 August, 1 September 1965, 757–58, 803.

28. Ibid., 646–53.

29. Udall to Dominy, 28 August 1965, folder 5, box 477, Morris Udall Papers; and Mo Udall to Stewart Udall, 20 January 1966, folder 6, box 166, Stewart Udall Papers.

30. U.S. Congress, House, Subcommittee on Irrigation and Reclamation of the Committee on Interior and Insular Affairs, *Lower Colorado Basin Project: Hearings before the Subcommittee on Irrigation and Reclamation of the Committee on Interior and Insular Affairs*, 89th Cong., 1st sess., 23–31 August, 1 September 1965, 147; and Lamm, "Report," 1.

31. Lamm, "Report," 1.

32. Ibid., 2–3.

33. U.S. Congress, House, Subcommittee on Irrigation and Reclamation of the Committee on Interior and Insular Affairs, *Lower Colorado Basin Project: Hearings before the Subcommittee on Irrigation and Reclamation of the Committee on Interior and Insular Affairs*, 89th Cong., 1st sess., 23–31 August, 1 September 1965, 201, 736; and David Brower, "Grand Canyon: Department of Amplification," *Sierra Club Bulletin*, December 1965, 14–15.

34. Hartzog to a Mr. Larry Hadley, 11 December 1964, folder 266, box 36, George Hartzog Papers; and Hartzog to a Mr. Frank Harrison, 6 October 1965, folder 269, box 36, George Hartzog Papers; see also Director to all Regional Directors, 18 October 1965, folder 1, box 169, Stewart Udall Papers.

35. The influx of mail is difficult to measure; however, my assessment of approximately two thousand letters contained in the collections of Carl Hayden, Stewart

Udall, Morris Udall, John Rhodes, Interior Department, National Park Service, and John Saylor reveals that the number of letters increased dramatically after the August-September 1965 hearings, tapered off for the first quarter of 1966, and increased again after the May 1966 hearings, the Sierra Club's ad campaign, and the IRS revocation of 9 June 1966.

36. Griffin to Brower, 10 August 1965, folder 19, box 29, SCMP.

37. Richard Lamm to David Brower, 28 October 1965; and Mrs. Hasse Bunnelle to Lamm, 29 October 1965; see also Dr. Estella Leopold to Hasse Bunnelle, 15 October 1965; and Hasse Bunnelle to Leopold, 29 October 1965, folder 10, box 21, SCMP.

38. "Activity Highlights 1965–1966: Future Goals," Colorado Open Space Coordinating Council, Inc., 24 September 1966, folder "Colorado Mountain Club," box 1 "Grand Canyon Dams," Richard Bradley Papers.

39. Bradley to Stegner, n.d. 1965; and Stegner to Bradley, 25 November 1965, folder "Atlantic," box 1 "Grand Canyon Dams," Richard Bradley Papers; see also Vosburgh to Bradley, 6 August 1965, folder "Audubon," box 1 "Grand Canyon Dams," Richard Bradley Papers.

40. Rich Johnson, "Minutes: Meeting of Joint Public Relations Committee," 23 September 1965, folder 1, box 3, CAP/89, John Rhodes Papers.

41. "Memo on CAP hearings from MKU," 28 August 1965, folder 2, box 3, CAP/89, John Rhodes Papers; and *Arizona Republic*, 27 October 1965; see also *Arizona Daily Star*, 14 December 1965; and Smith to the National Parks Association Board of Trustees, 28 September 1965, folder 34, box 11, SCMP.

42. Mark W. T. Harvey, "Defending the Park System: The Controversy over Rainbow Bridge," *New Mexico Historical Review* 73 (January 1998): 45, 47, 49, 53, 55, 56, 59, 60.

43. Richard Bradley to Wallace Stegner, n.d. 1965, folder "Atlantic," box 1, "Grand Canyon Dams," Richard Bradley Papers; and Bruce Stewart, "Think Big," *Harper's*, August 1965, 62–63; see also Estella Leopold to Hasse Bunnelle, 15 October 1965, folder 10, box 21, SCMP.

Chapter 5

1. Morris Udall, *Too Funny to Be President* (New York: Henry Holt and Company, 1988), 92. Mo Udall lost his eye as a result of a childhood accident; however, in typical good humor, he made light of it throughout his political career.

2. "Notes on March 15 Conference," folder 2, box 476, Morris Udall Papers.

3. U.S. Congress, House, Subcommittee on Irrigation and Reclamation of the Committee on Interior and Insular Affairs, *Lower Colorado Basin Project: Hearings before the Subcommittee on Irrigation and Reclamation of the Committee on Interior and Insular Affairs*, 89th Cong., 1st sess., 23–31 August, 1 September 1965, 646–53.

4. "Minutes of Meeting held at 10:00 o'clock, A.M., January 4, 1966 in the Arizona

Room of the Hotel Adams, Phoenix, Arizona," 4–5, 7, folder 4, box 1, CAP/89, John Rhodes Papers.

5. Marks to Rhodes, 19 June 1963; and Rhodes to Marks, 26 June 1963, folder 1, box 1, CAP/88, John Rhodes Papers; see also Lazarus to Stewart Udall, 4 October 1963, folder 2, box 1, CAP/88, John Rhodes Papers.

6. Douglas Wall, chairman, Arizona Interstate Stream Commission, "Confidential Memorandum," forwarded to John Rhodes by Ray Killian, secretary, Arizona Interstate Stream Commission, 8 March 1965, folder 1, box 2, CAP/88, John Rhodes Papers.

7. Acting Commissioner of Reclamation to Morris Udall, 12 October 1965, folder 5, box 477, Morris Udall Papers. The terms of the Hualapai contract with the APA, adjusted for inflation between 1960 and 1965, called for a payment of $150,000 upon execution of the agreement; $2000/month; a lump-sum payment of between $1.05 and $1.37 million; and annual royalties of between $402,000, and $794,400 for the life of the project. Please see "Statement of Arthur Lazarus: Re Interest of Hualapai tribe In CAP," attached to Udall to Rhodes and Senner, 18 March 1965, folder 5, box 477, Morris Udall Papers.

8. The legal issues surrounding Hualapai and Navajo claims to the Bridge and Marble Canyon dam sites are complex. For a detailed analysis please see Byron Pearson, "'We Have Almost Forgotten How to Hope:' The Hualapai, the Navajo, and the Fight for the Central Arizona Project, 1944–1968," *Western Historical Quarterly* 31 (autumn 2000): 297–316.

9. Johnson to Morris Udall, 25 December 1965; and Marks to Rhodes, Udall, and Senner, 17 January 1966; see also Morris Udall to Stewart Udall, 20 January 1966, folder 5, box 477, Morris Udall Papers.

10. Assistant Secretary—Public Land Management to Secretary Udall, 14 March 1966, folder 6, box 169, Stewart Udall Papers; and Les Alexander, "Memo to the files," 30 March 1966, folder 1, box 169, Stewart Udall Papers.

11. *New York Times*, 28 August 1963; and *New York Times*, 17 January 1966.

12. Richard Bradley to Barbara Walton, curator of the Western History Collection at the Denver Public Library, 1995, box 1 "Grand Canyon Dams," Richard Bradley Papers; *Audubon*, January-February 1966, 34–41.

13. Nicholson to Bradley, 27 January 1966, folder "Reader's Digest Article," box 1 "Grand Canyon Dams," Richard Bradley Papers; Nancy Weston to David Brower, 28 July 1959, folder 47, box 11, SCMP.

14. Acting Commissioner Bennett to Regional Director, Boulder City, 23 March 1966, folder 9, box 478, Morris Udall Papers; and Bradley to Brower, 1 March 1966, folder 32, box 19, SCMP

15. *Denver Post*, 6 March 1966; and "COSCC: Activity Highlights, 1965–1966," 24 September 1966, folder "Colorado Mountain Club," box 1 "Grand Canyon Dams," Richard Bradley Papers.

16. *Arizona Republic*, 27 March 1966; and Bill Winter to John Rhodes, 6 June 1966, in folder 4, box 3, CAP/89, John Rhodes Papers.

17. Rich Johnson, Memorandum, 1 April 1966, folder 9, box 478, Morris Udall Papers; and Commissioner of Reclamation to Regional Director, Boulder City Nevada, 23 March 1966, folder 9, box 478, Morris Udall Papers; see also Brower to a Mr. Robert Kellogg, 28 April, 1966, folder 16, box 22, SCMP.

18. Brower to Udall, 30 March 1966, folder 6, box 6, SCMP. This document does exist, and can be found at the Grand Canyon National Park Archive. See Regional Director to Southwest Region Superintendents, 16 March 1964, fiche 7423 "Bridge Canyon Dam, 1954–1966, (GCNPRL).

19. Johnson, *Central Arizona Project*, 182; and Northcutt Ely to Sterling Fisher of *Reader's Digest*, 19 April 1966, folder 1, box 5, CAP/89 John Rhodes Papers; see also Jeff Ingram, interview by author, 12 March 1998 in which Ingram confirmed Ely's version of events; and Rich Johnson, Memorandum, 1 April 1966, folder 9, box 478, Morris Udall Papers; see also Brower to Kellogg, 28 April, 1966, folder 16, box 22, SCMP; and Floyd Dominy, interview by author, 1 November 1996.

20. According to Bureau of Reclamation historian Dr. Brit Storey and Floyd Dominy. See Floyd Dominy, interview by author, 1 November 1996.

21. Brower to Kellogg, 28 April 1966, folder 16, box 22, SCMP; and Rich Johnson, Memorandum, 1 April 1966, folder 9, box 478, Morris Udall Papers; see also Ingram to Richard Bradley, 8 April 1966, folder "Reader's Digest article," box 1 "Grand Canyon Dams," Richard Bradley Papers.

22. George Steck, interview by Michael Quinn, 3 September 1995, (Grand Canyon National Park Museum, Grand Canyon National Park); and Harold Bradley to Brower, 16 April 1966, folder 26, box 22, SCMP; see also *Reader's Digest*, "Press Information and Itinerary," 31 March 1966, fiche 7423, "Bridge Canyon Dam 1954–1966," GCNPRL; and *"Reader's Digest* Enlists in the Fight to Save Grand Canyon," *Sierra Club Bulletin*, May 1966, 6–7; see also *Arizona Republic*, 31 March 1966. Toroweap is the point on the north rim where the greatest vertical face in all the canyon exists, dropping some thirty-five hundred feet from rim to river.

23. The term is used frequently by Richard Bradley in his correspondence regarding the conference. For an example, please see Bradley to Brower, 12 April 1966, folder 33, box 19 SCMP.

24. Stephen Jett to author, 6 February 1998; see also Brower to Kellogg, 28 April 1966, folder 16, box 22, SCMP.

25. Perhaps Morris Udall's reluctance to raise the debate beyond policy considerations is indicative of something that the senior Bureau officials had expressed to their subordinates just two weeks previously, that the safest argument against alternative energy proposals was to couch it in terms of policy. Minor Bureau officials were cautioned to "not go beyond" issues of policy, for fear that if they did so that it would weaken the case for hydropower. See Commissioner to Regional Director, Boulder City, 23 March 1966, folder 9, box 478, Morris Udall Papers.

26. *Arizona Republic*, 1 April 1966; and Stephen Jett to author, 6 February 1998; see also Brower to Kellogg, 28 April 1966, folder 16, box 22, SCMP.

27. Richard Bradley to Brower, 12 April 1966, folder 33, box 19, SCMP; and Ingram to Richard Bradley, 8 April 1966, folder "Reader's Digest article," box 1 "Grand Canyon Dams," Richard Bradley Papers; see also Clifton Merritt to Stewart Brandborg, 20 April 1966, folder "Colorado River," box 6:102, Wilderness Society Papers; and Larry Stevens, *The Colorado River in Grand Canyon: A Guide*, 3rd ed. (Flagstaff, Ariz.: Red Lake Books, 1990), 90; see also Colorado Open Space Coordinating Council, "Open Space Report," 15 April 1966, folder, "Reader's Digest Conference News," box 1, "Grand Canyon Dams," Richard Bradley Papers. Reactions of members of the eastern press are typified by the comments of Mrs. Jean Ensign, general manager of radio station WVIP in suburban New York, who wrote: "The workshops were certainly informative, but it was the Canyon itself (which I had never seen) that spoke to me most eloquently." See Mrs. Jean T. Ensign to Brower, 3 June 1966, folder 34, box 19, SCMP.

28. Morris Udall, *Too Funny To Be President*, 59.

29. Johnson, *Central Arizona Project*, 183; and Floyd Dominy, interview by author, 1 November 1996; see also Robert Gray to John Rhodes, 26 April 1966, folder 4, box 3, CAP/89, John Rhodes Papers; and *Congressional Quarterly*, December 1965, for information about Washington lobbyists; see also *Arizona Republic*, 29 May 1966; and William and Elisabeth Layton to Stewart Udall, 6 May 1966, folder 33, box 19, SCMP.

30. John W. Ragsdale, "Anno Dominy MCMLXVI," *Biophilist* (March-April 1966), copy in folder 2, box 012, Carl Hayden Papers; and Burns to Brower, 11 May 1966, folder 16, box 22, SCMP; see also "Knight Errant to Nature's Rescue," *Life*, 27 May 1966; and "Dam the Canyon?" *Newsweek*, 30 May 1966.

31. "The Entire Grand Canyon Must Be Protected," *Sierra Club Bulletin*, May 1966, 8–9; and *Arizona Republic*, 17 April 1966.

32. Johnson, *Central Arizona Project* 185; and *Arizona Republic;* 3 April 1966; see also *New York Times*, 2 May 1966; and Ozell Trask, "Memo to the Files," 29 April 1966, folder 2, box 476, Morris Udall Papers.

33. Johnson, *Central Arizona Project*, 172; and Ray Killian, "Memorandum to the Files," 6 April 1966, folder 2, box 476, Morris Udall Papers.

34. Winter to Rhodes, 6 June 1966, folder 4, box 3, CAP/89, John Rhodes Papers.

35. U.S. Congress, House, Subcommittee on Irrigation and Reclamation of the Committee on Interior and Insular Affairs, *Lower Colorado Basin Project: Hearings before the Subcommittee on Irrigation and Reclamation of the Committee on Interior and Insular Affairs*, 89th Cong., 2d sess., 9–13, 18 May 1966, 1086, 1378, 1390; and Joe Jensen, "Confidential Report to M. W. D. Directors," 15 December 1964, folder 2, box 168, Stewart Udall Papers.

36. U.S. Congress, House, Subcommittee on Irrigation and Reclamation of the

Committee on Interior and Insular Affairs, *Lower Colorado Basin Project: Hearings before the Subcommittee on Irrigation and Reclamation of the Committee on Interior and Insular Affairs,* 89th Cong., 2d sess., 9–13, 18 May 1966, 1086; and Johnson, *Central Arizona Project,* 186.

37. Johnson, *Central Arizona Project,* 188; and U.S. Congress, House, Subcommittee on Irrigation and Reclamation of the Committee on Interior and Insular Affairs, *Lower Colorado Basin Project: Hearings before the Subcommittee on Irrigation and Reclamation of the Committee on Interior and Insular Affairs,* 89th Cong., 2d sess., 9–13, 18 May 1966, 1362–65, 1380.

38. David Brower, "Environmental Activist, Publicist, and Prophet," 150.

39. For Hosmer's treatment of opposition witnesses, see U.S. Congress, House, Subcommittee on Irrigation and Reclamation of the Committee on Interior and Insular Affairs, *Lower Colorado Basin Project: Hearings before the Subcommittee on Irrigation and Reclamation of the Committee on Interior and Insular Affairs,* 89th Cong., 2d sess., 9–13, 18 May 1966, 1429 to the end of the record.

40. Ibid., 1488, 1491, 1493. Ingram also pointed to studies that seemed to indicate that silt from the Paria River would render Marble Canyon Dam useless in a relatively short period of time, although this data was relatively incomplete. Representative Hosmer objected, stating that "the mathematician seems not to be aware of where the water comes from that is going to Marble Canyon Dam. It is already desilted by Lake Powell." Hosmer, unable to rebut Ingram's figures, also demonstrated his ignorance of geography in this exchange, for the Paria River is *downstream* from Glen Canyon Dam and would not flow into Lake Powell at all.

41. The Bureau argued throughout the controversy that the dams were needed for peaking power. By increasing the flow of water through the generators, dams can meet spikes in power demand in an instant, something that steam and nuclear plants are not as efficient at doing. However, by including pumped storage plants in his analysis, Carlin presented an alternative that could match the peaking capacity of the Grand Canyon dams. Pumped storage simply refers to the construction of an upper and lower reservoir with a hydro dam in between them, a system that can be built in canyons of low scenic value. Water can be brought in from outside. During periods of low demand, the power generated by the dam can be used to pump water from the lower reservoir back upstream. During periods of high demand for power, the water is released from the upper reservoir at a faster rate, providing all the peaking advantages of hydropower.

42. U.S. Congress, House, Subcommittee on Irrigation and Reclamation of the Committee on Interior and Insular Affairs, *Lower Colorado Basin Project: Hearings before the Subcommittee on Irrigation and Reclamation of the Committee on Interior and Insular Affairs,* 89th Cong., 2d sess., 9–13, 18 May 1966, 1497–1538.

43. Ibid., 1540–76.

44. Morris Udall to Les Alexander, 26 April 1966, folder 2, box 476, Morris Udall

Papers; and John Rhodes, Memorandum, 18 April 1966, folder 4, box 3, CAP/89, John Rhodes Papers; see also U.S. Congress, House, Subcommittee on Irrigation and Reclamation of the Committee on Interior and Insular Affairs, *Lower Colorado Basin Project: Hearings before the Subcommittee on Irrigation and Reclamation of the Committee on Interior and Insular Affairs,* 89th Cong., 2d sess., 9–13, 18 May 1966, 1294.

45. Eugene Weiner to Henry Dobyns, 2 April 1966; and Dobyns to Weiner, 6 April 1966, folder 4, box 3, CAP/89, John Rhodes Papers.

46. U.S. Congress, House, Subcommittee on Irrigation and Reclamation of the Committee on Interior and Insular Affairs, *Lower Colorado Basin Project: Hearings before the Subcommittee on Irrigation and Reclamation of the Committee on Interior and Insular Affairs,* 89th Cong., 2d sess., 9–13, 18 May 1966, 1577, 1579; and Ray Killian to Rich Johnson, 18 April 1966; see also John Rhodes to Henry Dobyns, 20 April 1966, folder 4, box 3, CAP/89, John Rhodes Papers; and *Arizona Republic,* 8 May 1966; see also U.S. Congress, House, Speech of Morris K. Udall, "The Conservation Plot That Failed," *Congressional Record* (10 May 1966), A2507–8.

47. U.S. Congress, House, Subcommittee on Irrigation and Reclamation of the Committee on Interior and Insular Affairs, *Lower Colorado Basin Project: Hearings before the Subcommittee on Irrigation and Reclamation of the Committee on Interior and Insular Affairs,* 89th Cong., 2d sess., 9–13, 18 May 1966, 1581–87; and Stephen Jett to author, 28 December 1997; see also Jett to author, 6 February 1998, in author's possession.

48. Stewart Udall, interview by author, 15 March 1997; and Mo Udall, "Rules Headcount," 2 May 1966; see also Mo Udall, "Summary of 1st Headcount," 2 May 1966, folder 11, box 480, Morris Udall Papers; and Rhodes to Lewis Douglas, 26 May 1966, folder 4, box 3, CAP/89, John Rhodes Papers. Morris Udall's analysis of early May, just prior to the hearings, reveals a strong predisposition toward passage on the part of the House members. Udall's tally of the 435 members of Congress breaks down as follows: in favor—68; probable—202; undecided—159; opposed—6. A total of 218 votes were needed for passage, and Mo's tally shows that 270 members were at least leaning in favor of the bill.

49. Morris Udall to "Dear Colleague," 3 June 1966; and Lex Alexander to Task Force, 8 June 1966, folder 4, box 477, Morris Udall Papers; see also Morris Udall, "June 8 Luncheon," folder 5, box 477, Morris Udall Papers; and Udall to Les Alexander, of the CAPA, 7 June 1966, folder 2, box 476, Morris Udall Papers.

50. L. M. Alexander, "Memorandum—A Lobbying Plan," 8 June 1966, and L. M. Alexander, "Subject: A Lobbying Plan (Ref. June 8, 1966 Memo)," 6 July 1966, folder 5, box 477, Morris Udall Papers.

51. L. M. Alexander, "Memorandum—A Lobbying Plan," 8 June 1966, and L. M. Alexander, "Subject: A Lobbying Plan (Ref. June 8, 1966 Memo)," 6 July 1966, folder 5, box 477, Morris Udall Papers. That Johnson was assigned the task of writing the letters and in fact completed them is confirmed within these two memos.

52. George Rocha to "Friend," n.d., folder 5, box 4, CAP/89, John Rhodes Papers; and L. M. Alexander, "Memorandum—A Lobbying Plan," 8 June 1966; see also L. M. Alexander, "Subject: A Lobbying Plan (Ref. June 8, 1966 Memo)," 6 July 1966, folder 5, box 477, Morris Udall Papers. Though the Rocha letter is undated, comparable letters to Brower, LBJ, the National Council of Churches, and all congressmen were sent on 24 June 1966, and the memoranda cited above confirm that the letter to "Indian friends" was, in fact, sent.

53. Henry Dobyns to Representative Richard Ottinger, 3 August 1966, folder 5, box 477, Morris Udall Papers.

54. Bradley to Brower re: list of names, 4 June 1966, folder 11, box 21, SCMP; and Bradley to Brower, 12 April 1966, folder 33, box 19, SCMP; see also letters from Bradley to Charles Morton, editor, 3 April, 10 May, 27 August, 1966, folder "Atlantic," box 1 "Grand Canyon Dams," Richard Bradley Papers.

55. Mandell to Brower, 4 June 1966, folder 34, box 19, SCMP.

56. Colorado Open Space Coordinating Council Inc., "Activity Highlights 1965–1966: Future Goals, 24 September 1966, folder "Colorado Mountain Club," box 1 "Grand Canyon Dams," Richard Bradley Papers; and Joy Coombs to Stewart Brandborg, 23 June 1966, folder "Colorado River 1966," box 106, Wilderness Society Papers.

57. Cohen, *History of the Sierra Club*, 355.

58. Mander's comments are recalled by Brower in David Brower, "Environmental Activist, Publicist, and Prophet," 146; and David Brower's handwritten notes of 8, 23 May 1966, folder 46 "Notes 1966," box 15, SCMP; see also David Brower, interview by author, 27 July 1997.

Chapter 6

1. Please see chapter 1.

2. For a good example, please see Department of the Interior, *Lake Powell: Jewel of the Colorado*, passim.

3. Runte, *National Parks*, 190; and Fox, *American Conservation Movement*, 302.

4. W. L. Minckley, *Fishes of Arizona* (Phoenix: Sims Printing Company, 1973), 119–25.

5. Runte, *National Parks*, 190–91.

6. *New York Times*, 9 June 1966. The advertisements also appeared in the *Washington Post*, *San Francisco Chronicle*, and the *Los Angeles Times* the same day.

7. U.S. Congress, House, Speech of Morris K. Udall, "Flooding the Grand Canyon: A Phony Issue," *Congressional Record* (9 June 1966), 12315–17.

8. Ibid. Udall quoted from Brower's letter in this same speech; and *New York Times*, 9 June 1966; see also "Dam the Canyon?," *Newsweek*, 30 May 1966, 27.

9. U.S. Congress, House, Speech of Morris K. Udall, "Flooding the Grand Canyon: A Phony Issue," *Congressional Record* (9 June 1966), 12315–17.

10. Edgar Wayburn, "Sierra Club Statesman," 29; and *Arizona Republic*, 12 June 1966.

11. Brower, "Environmental Activist, Publicist, and Prophet," 146; and Wayburn, "Sierra Club Statesman," 293.

12. Floyd Dominy, interview by author, 1 November 1996.

13. Stewart Udall, *Quiet Crisis and the Next Generation*, 210.

14. Roy Elson, "Administrative Assistant to Senator Carl Hayden and Candidate for the United States Senate, 1955–1969," interviews by Donald Richie (27 April–21 August 1990), 203 (Senate Historical Office, Washington, D.C.), John F. Kennedy Library.

15. U.S. Congress, House, Subcommittee on Irrigation and Reclamation of the Committee on Interior and Insular Affairs, *Lower Colorado Basin Project: Hearings before the Subcommittee on Irrigation and Reclamation of the Committee on Interior and Insular Affairs*, 89th Cong., 1st sess., 23–31 August, 1 September 1965, 757–58, 803; and U.S. Congress, House, Subcommittee on Irrigation and Reclamation of the Committee on Interior and Insular Affairs, *Lower Colorado Basin Project: Hearings before the Subcommittee on Irrigation and Reclamation of the Committee on Interior and Insular Affairs*, 89th Cong., 2d sess., 9–13, 18 May 1966, 1492–93.

16. William E. Siri, "Reflections on the Sierra Club, the Environment, and Mountaineering, 1950s–1970s," interview by Ann Lage (Sierra Club History Series, 11 February 1976), 56, Regional Oral History Office, University of California Berkeley.

17. Morris Udall to Sheldon Cohen, 10 June 1966, folder 2, box 477 Morris Udall Papers.

18. For a recent reiteration of this argument, see Tom Turner, "The Grand Undammed," *Sierra*, July-August 1992, 18. None of the Sierra Club Oral History Series interviews examined by the author at the Bancroft Library are precise in describing a date or time that Mo Udall's alleged "admission" took place. David Brower indicated in his oral history as well as in an interview with the author that Udall admitted to precipitating the IRS revocation during a meeting in his congressional office; however, this account is not confirmed either by other witnesses or within the documentary record.

19. Please see chapter 1 for a discussion of the events leading up to and including the formation of the Sierra Club Foundation in 1960.

20. Cohen, *History of the Sierra Club*, 362.

21. *Congressional Quarterly*, 1 November 1966, 3024.

22. Orren Beaty to William Welsh, assistant to the vice president, 16 October 1966, pt 6, box 124, CCF/D of I.

23. Morris Udall, *Too Funny to Be President*, 56.

24. Reisner, *Cadillac Desert*, 297, in which he quotes former Bureau of Reclamation official Daniel Dreyfus.

25. Accurate tallies of the number of letters are difficult to come by. However, in

his examination of an estimated two thousand letters held in various archives, the author feels confident in making the following generalizations about the content of these letters and how that content shifted as a result of the IRS investigation.

26. A good example of this type of letter is John Cohan to Leo Irwin, chief counsel of the House Ways and Means Committee, 11 August 1966, folder 2, box 20, SCMP. Cohan writes that he is concerned that the IRS clouded the Sierra Club's tax status before holding a hearing or conducting an investigation, a violation of "due process." Cohan also cites revelations that the IRS had recently used electronic eavesdropping devices as evidence that it habitually went "beyond the proper course of conduct."

27. *Bakersfield Californian*, 28 June 1966; and *New York Times*, 17 June 1966.

28. Hartzog to All Regional Directors, 20 October 1965, folder 4, box 190, Stewart Udall Papers.

29. H. N. Smith to Superintendent, 7 June 1966, "Colorado River Dam Proposals Collection, 1931–1968," #2670, GCNPMC. Judging from the sarcastic language in communications between Stricklin and other superintendents, it appears as though they felt constrained from discussing the Grand Canyon dams even after this date. Please see Superintendent, Fort Clascop, to Superintendent, Grand Canyon, 7 September 1966, "Colorado River Dam Proposals Collection, 1931–1968," #2670, GCNPMC.

30. Superintendent, Yosemite, to Director, 21 June 1966; and George Marshall, president, to George Hartzog, 21 June 1966; see also George Marshall to George Hartzog, 30 June 1966; and Hartzog to Marshall, 1 July 1966, in folder 5, box 9, George Hartzog Papers.

31. Merrill Beal, interview by Julie Russell, 20 July 1981, (Grand Canyon National Park Oral History Project), GCNPMC.

32. Despite the efforts to repress Park Service opposition, there are occasional glimpses of it. On 7 June 1966 Regional Director Dan Beard lauded the efforts of David Brower and the Sierra Club, as well as those of *New York Times* editor John Oakes. Please see Beard to John Osseward, 7 June 1966, fiche 7423, "Dams on the Colorado River, 1954–1966," GCNPRL.

33. David Brower, interview by author, 27 July 1997.

34. Ibid., and *New York Times*, 25 July 1966. The Sierra Club also ran these ads in many other national publications during the summer of 1966, including *Harper's*, *Saturday Review*, *Ramparts*, *National Review*, and *Scientific American*. For Brower's thoughts on the advertising campaign, please see David Brower to Frank Masland, 28 December 1966, folder 36, box 19, SCMP.

35. U.S. Congress, House, Speech of George Senner, "Letter from White Mountain Apache Tribe," *Congressional Record* (2 August 1966), A-4075; and *Oakland Tribune*, 16 July 1966; see also *Arizona Republic*, 16 July 1966; and *Riverside Daily Enterprise*, 20 July 1966.

36. *Washington Post*, 14 August 1966.

37. Mrs. E. M. Bredwell, to Mrs. E. P. Pierce, 1 August 1966, folder 5, box 4, CAP/89, John Rhodes Papers.

38. *Arizona Republic,* 27 July 1966; and Robin Way to a Mr. Frederick Kellerman, and attached television listing from the *New York Times,* 17 August 1966, folder 73, box 218, SCMP.

39. A Mr. Rawson to Robin Way, small note attached to *Arizona Daily Citizen,* 10 August 1966; and Way to Rawson, 17 August 1966, folder 73, box 218, SCMP.

40. *Rocky Mountain News,* 11 August 1966; see also Assistant Commissioner to Commissioner, Bureau of Reclamation, 1 July 1966, folder 23, box 483, Morris Udall Papers.

41. John Rhodes to James O'Malley, 25 August 1966, folder 5, box 4, CAP/89, John Rhodes Papers; and *Arizona Republic,* 19 June 1966.

42. Morris K. Udall, "Memo to CAP," 22 August 1966, folder 11, box 480, Morris Udall Papers.

43. *New York Times,* 11 June 1966.

44. Water for the West, "Progress Report," 1 July 1966, folder 2, box 476, Morris Udall Papers; and *New York Times,* 28 July 1966. Water for the West was a joint Arizona/California-based western reclamation lobbying organization.

45. J. A. Riggens, "Memorandum to the Files Re: July 20, 1966," 21 July 1966; J. A. Riggens, "Memorandum for the Files Re: July 21, 1966, folder 2, box 476, Morris Udall Papers. It is important to distinguish between the three stages of the process by which a Bureau of Reclamation project gains congressional approval. The initial step is for the Bureau to make a "reconnaissance" study, which is a basic determination of whether the proposal should be considered further. The next step is called a "feasibility" study, where the Bureau sends geologists, engineers, and other experts into the field to do an in-depth analysis. The reports that result from feasibility studies are then used as the basis to draft legislation. When a bill is ready to be introduced before Congress, this final step is called an "authorization." The timing of these steps is critical: the reconnaissance phase takes two years, feasibility takes five more, and, consequently, it may be seven or more years between the time a reconnaissance study is initiated and congressional debate begins. California's objection arose because of the additional time it would add to the authorization process and because it was much easier to block a reconnaissance study than a feasibility study, once the latter was undertaken.

46. Rich Johnson, Memorandum, 22 July 1966; and J. A. Riggins, "Memorandum to the Files," 26 July 1966, folder 2, box 476, Morris Udall Papers.

47. *Wall Street Journal,* 29 July 1966; and J. A. Riggens, "Memorandum to the Files," 26 July 1966; see also Morris Udall to "Honorable ____," 27 July 1966, folder 2, box 476, Morris Udall Papers.

48. *New York Times,* 25 July 1966. The most famous ad of the campaign, released during August of 1966, asked the question: "Should we flood the Sistine Chapel so

tourists can float nearer the ceiling?" in response to the Bureau's arguments that the reservoir would make remote reaches of the canyon more accessible. This phrase appears in small type in the 25 July ad as well. Sierra Club historian Michael Cohen credits Ansel Adams for originating this phrase. Please see Cohen, *History of the Sierra Club*, 363.

49. *Arizona Republic*, 29 July 1966; and *New York Times*, 21 July 1966.

50. "Rules Headcount," 2 May 1966, folder 11, box 480, Morris Udall Papers. Udall's poll revealed eleven in favor or probably in favor, with four undecided.

51. Udall to Les Alexander and John Rhodes, 22 August 1966, folder 11, box 480, Morris Udall Papers.

52. Morris Udall to Les Alexander, 23 August 1966, folder 11, box 482, Morris Udall Papers.

53. Richard Bradley, "Ruin for the Grand Canyon," *Town Hall* 28, no. 28, (Los Angeles: Town Hall, 12 July 1966). Bradley spoke during the July 19 meeting.

54. Colorado Open Space Coordinating Council Inc., "Grand Canyon Workshop: Activity Highlights 1965–1966: Future Goals," 24 September 1966, folder "Colorado Mountain Club," box 1 "Grand Canyon Dams," Richard Bradley Papers.

55. *Sierra Club Bulletin*, July-August 1966, front cover.

56. Mrs. Helen Skelton to David Brower, 5 August 1966; and Robin Way to Mrs. Helen Skelton, 10 August 1966, folder 73, box 218, SCMP.

57. Jett to author, 28 December 1997; and Dr. Steven Jett, "Navajos Enter Fight against Grand Canyon Dams," August 1966, pp. 1–10, copy in author's possession; see also *Gallup Independent*, 4 August 1966; and Orren Beaty, "Notes to SLU," 5 September 1966; see also T. W. Taylor, BIA acting commissioner to Secretary Udall, 5 August 1966, folder 1, box 127, Stewart Udall Papers.

58. *Arizona Republic*, 16 August 1966.

59. These figures are derived from an examination of the *Congressional Record* for the year 1966. An analysis of the congressional floor debate from April to October 1966 over the Grand Canyon dams reveals that during this period, representatives against the dams delivered 43 speeches, while those in favor of the project spoke 28 times. In addition, 37 of the 43 antidam speeches were delivered by John Saylor of Pennsylvania; John Dingell of Michigan; Henry Reuss of Wisconsin; and Silvio Conte of Massachusetts. Morris Udall and John Rhodes delivered 14 of the 28 pro-dam speeches during the same period. Thus, the vast majority of floor activity was done by 6 out of 435 representatives. In comparison, 7 speeches in favor and 2 against took place in the Senate during this same time. Of course these figures do not account for all lobbying activities, such as Morris Udall's "steak offensive" of early June.

60. L. M. Alexander, "Memo to the CAP Files," 26 August 1966, folder 4, box 477, Morris Udall Papers; and "Report from Les Alexander," 19 August 1966, folder 2, box 476, Morris Udall Papers.

61. L. M. Alexander, "Memo to the CAP Files," 26 August 1966, folder 4, box

477, Morris Udall Papers; and L. M. Alexander, "Memo to the CAP files," 30 August 1966, folder 2, box 476, Morris Udall Papers.

62. MHR to MKU, "Memo," 29 August 1966, folder 11, box 480, Morris Udall Papers. This poll reveals that those in support had grown to 170. The pollster, possibly one of Udall's staff, prognosticated that if they added one-half of the probables (67), one-third of the undecided (30) and one-third of those uninformed (46) to the 170 certain votes, a relatively conservative assessment, the bill would pass with a total of 228 votes.

63. Ozell Trask and Ralph Hunsaker to Task Force, 30 August 1966, folder 2, box 476, Morris Udall Papers.

64. *Arizona Republic*, 27 August 1966; and *Arizona Republic*, 1 September 1966; see also "News of Conservation and the Club," *Sierra Club Bulletin*, September 1966, 2; and *Arizona Republic*, 17 September 1966.

65. Nash, *Wilderness*, 228–36; and Runte, *National Parks*, 191, which originated as a dissertation under the direction of Dr. Nash; see also Fradkin, *A River No More*, 228–34; and Martin, *Story That Stands Like A Dam*, 250–74; and Fox, *American Conservation Movement*, 319–20; see also Reisner, *Cadillac Desert*, 295–300.

66. L. M. Alexander to CAP Files, 26 August 1966, folder 4, box 477, Morris Udall Papers.

67. "Confidential Report from Les Alexander," 19 August, 1966, folder 2, box 476, Morris Udall Papers.

68. L. M. Alexander to CAP Task Force Members and Congressional Delegation, 15 September 1966, folder 1, box 481, Morris Udall Papers.

69. Reisner, *Cadillac Desert*, 267–68.

70. Johnson, *Central Arizona Project*, 162–63.

71. L. M. Alexander, "memo to CAP Files," 26 August 1966, folder 4, box 477, Morris Udall Papers.

72. MKU to John Rhodes, 7 September 1966, folder 2, box 476, Morris Udall Papers.

73. L. M. Alexander, "Memo to CAP Files," 30 August 1966, folder 2, box 476, Morris Udall Papers.

74. Rich Johnson, "Press Release," 31 August 1966, folder 1, box 4, CAP/89, John Rhodes Papers.

75. *Arizona Republic*, 11 September 1966; and *Arizona Republic*, 15 September 1966.

76. *Arizona Republic*, 8 September 1966.

77. Wayne Aspinall, "Colorado's Involvement in Westwide Water Planning," remarks made before the annual meeting of the Colorado State Grange, Cortez, Colorado, 1 October 1966, folder 2, box 4, CAP/89, John Rhodes Papers.

78. McFarland to the President, 1 August 1966; and McFarland to Les Alexander, in which he recalled his telephone conversation with LBJ, 1 August 1966, folder 1, box 4, CAP/89, John Rhodes Papers.

79. Orren Beaty, "Notes to SLU," 5 August 1966, folder 1, box 127, Stewart Udall Papers.

80. Sharon Francis, interview by author, 14 August 1997.

81. Beaty, "Note to SLU," 16 July 1966, folder 1, box 127, Stewart Udall Papers.

82. Mrs. Johnson's comments are recalled by Sharon Francis in a letter to Stewart Udall, 18 August 1966, folder 2, box 145, Stewart Udall Papers.

83. Sharon Francis, interview by author, 14 August 1997. Francis recalled in another interview an incident that illustrates how influential Mrs. Johnson may have been within the White House. Mike Manatos, of LBJ's staff and a former Wyoming congressman, tried to take Francis to task over the replies to the Grand Canyon letters that had gone out over Mrs. Johnson's signature. Francis recalled that Manatos backed off immediately when he determined that Francis's actions were in line with the desires of the First Lady. See Sharon Francis, interview by Dorothy Pierce McSweeney, 20 May 1969, AC 81-68, Lyndon Baines Johnson Library, Austin Texas.

84. Sharon Francis, interview with author, 14 August 1997.

85. Hayden's views are recalled in: Ben Cole, "Want to Know How to Pass CAP, Ask Carl," *Arizona Republic*, 16 September 1966. Rhodes, Udall, and Senner gave their general assessment in *Arizona Republic*, 8 September 1966. Perhaps the most revealing source about why the LCRBP bill failed was expressed in a detailed memorandum Mo Udall wrote to Rhodes on 22 September 1966. Udall assessed potential supporters of a 1967 CAP bill, labeling them as either "indispensable" or placing them into a lesser category he labeled "important." It is revealing to note that the five indispensable "power centers" Udall cites include: Senators Hayden, Jackson, and Anderson, along with Aspinall and LBJ; while those who are "important" include: Saylor, the preservationists, and Southern California. Apparently, Mo Udall believed, even after the national outcry of summer 1966, that he could obtain House passage of a bill over the objections of preservationists and Southern California, provided that the latter could be split away from Aspinall. Please see Morris Udall to John Rhodes, "The Power Centers," 22 September 1966, folder 2, box 476, Morris Udall Papers.

86. Assistant Secretary to Secretary, 12 September 1966, folder 4, box 168, Stewart Udall Papers; and "Weekly Report to the President from the Secretary of the Interior," 8 August 1966, folder 9, box 126, Stewart Udall Papers.

87. *Arizona Republic*, 18 September 1966; Governor Goddard also stated that while he still desired a federally funded CAP, he would be remiss not to explore the alternative of Arizona "going it alone."

88. *Arizona Republic*, 8, 17, 21 September 1966; and Orren Beaty to Stewart Udall, 6 April 1966, folder 1, box 127, Stewart Udall Papers.

89. *Arizona Republic*, 18 October 1966.

90. See for example, Samuel Hays, *Beauty, Health, and Permanence: Environmental Politics in the United States, 1955–1985* (New York: Cambridge University Press, 1987), 52–58.

91. Cohen, *History of the Sierra Club*, 387–88; and Byron Pearson, "Salvation for Grand Canyon," *Journal of the Southwest* 36, no. 2 (summer 1994), 159–75; see also Nash, *Wilderness*, 233; and Reisner, *Cadillac Desert*, 299–300. Reisner and Nash infer that preservationist pressure caused Udall to change his mind.

92. Stewart Udall, interview by author, 13 March 1997; see also "News of Conservation and the Club," *Sierra Club Bulletin*, September 1966, 2; and *New York Times*, 9 October 1966; see also *Arizona Republic*, 14, 18 October 1966. In autumn of 1966, Lyndon Johnson had not yet announced that he would not run for a second elected term. However, Stewart Udall was considering a run for Hayden's Senate seat that would become vacant in 1968, and so he anticipated leaving his post as interior secretary at the end of LBJ's first term.

93. Assistant Secretary to Secretary, 12 September 1966, folder 4, box 168, Stewart Udall Papers; and "Weekly Report to the President from the Secretary of the Interior," 8 August 1966, folder 9, box 126, Stewart Udall Papers; see also Sam Hughes to Stew Udall, 15 August 1966, folder 3, box 169, Stewart Udall Papers.

94. Stewart Udall, interview by author, 13 March 1997.

95. Frank Gregg, former assistant director of the Isaak Walton League, contended that Brower knew that nuclear power was dangerous early on but continued to tout it to draw congressional attention away from the Grand Canyon dams, an argument with which Brower agrees. Please see David Brower, interview by author, 27 July 1997.

96. "The Great Grand Canyon Subsidy Machine," *Sierra Club Bulletin*, October 1967, 89–94; and Cohen, *History of the Sierra Club*, 282–83. Rich Johnson of the Central Arizona Project Association noticed that the Sierra Club leadership had subtly backed away from nuclear power during a debate between Brower and him in July of 1966. To Johnson it appeared as though Brower was getting "nervous," about atomic energy as a possible alternative. See Johnson to Les Alexander, 5 July 1966, folder 1, box 4, CAP/89, John Rhodes Papers. See also Gregg interview by author, 15 October 1996.

97. Stewart Udall, interview by author, 13 March 1997. Udall continued to advocate in favor of the Southern California nuclear desalinization plant, and incredibly, the proposal passed Congress, only to be rejected at the last minute by the Metropolitan Water District of Los Angeles in 1969. Stewart Udall also flirted briefly with physicist Edward Teller's "Plowshare" theories about using underground nuclear detonations to increase Arizona's groundwater yield. Please see Science Advisor to the Secretary, 17 May 1968, folder 3, box 139, Stewart Udall Papers; and *Arizona Republic*, 1 June 1968.

98. *New York Times*, 9 October 1966; and "Weekly Report to the President from the Secretary of the Interior," 6 December 1966, folder 7, box 126, Stewart Udall Papers; see also Assistant Secretary—Water and Power to Secretary of the Interior, 26 January 1967, folder 7, box 169, Stewart Udall Papers. If we judge by his report to Pres-

ident Johnson of 6 December 1966, Udall had apparently made a definitive decision against the dams by this date.

99. Aspinall is quoted in *Denver Post*, 19 November 1966; see also *Arizona Republic*, 7 December 1966.

100. "News of Conservation and the Club," *Sierra Club Bulletin*, March 1967, 3.

101. RL to MKU, 28 March 1967, folder 7, box 481, Morris Udall Papers; and *Arizona Republic*, 22 January 1967.

102. *Arizona Republic*, 3 February 1967.

103. *Arizona Republic*, 2 February 1967.

104. *New York Times*, 2 February 1967; and *Arizona Republic*, 2 February 1967.

105. *Arizona Republic*, 8, 16 February, 8 August 1967; and *New York Times*, August 4, 8 1967.

106. "News of Conservation and the Club," *Sierra Club Bulletin*, March 1967, 2–3; see also *New York Times*, 13 March 1967; see also *Arizona Republic*, 7 March 1967.

107. U.S. Congress, House, Subcommittee on Irrigation and Reclamation of the Committee on Interior and Insular Affairs, *Lower Colorado Basin Project: Hearings before the Subcommittee on Irrigation and Reclamation of the Committee on Interior and Insular Affairs*, 90th Cong., 1st sess., 13–17 March 1967, 322–23, 506–10, 552.

108. *New York Times*, 14 March, 20 June 1967; and *Arizona Republic*, 14 March 1967.

109. RCO to MKU, 2 August 1967, folder 12, box 481, Morris Udall Papers.

110. Stewart Udall, "Wilderness Rivers: Shooting the Wild Colorado," *Venture*, February 1968, 62–71. Udall stated, however, that if a dam were built it should be a high dam to maximize the power potential of the site.

111. *Arizona Republic*, 4 October 1967.

112. O. M. Trask to Paul Fannin, 5 August 1967; and O. M. Trask to Mo and John, 5 August 1967, folder 12, box 481, Morris Udall Papers; Morris Udall, "Memo to the Files," 28 September 1967, folder 13, box 481, Morris Udall Papers.

113. Though an unusual move, precedent existed for Hayden's action including, ironically, the approval of the Big Thompson Project in Aspinall's home state. Having obtained a suspension of the rules, Hayden attached the CAP rider to the appropriations bill. After Senate passage of the bill, selected members of the House and Senate would meet in conference committee to iron out the differences in the two bills, and given the CAP's overwhelming popularity in autumn of 1967, it is unlikely that the conference committee would have deleted the provision. The committee would then release the bill to the floors of both houses for a final vote, thus bypassing Wayne Aspinall and the Interior Committee completely.

114. *New York Times*, 11 October 1967; and *Arizona Republic*, 28, 29 September, 11 October 1967.

115. Morris Udall to Honorable _____, 11 March 1968, folder 2, box 6, CAP/90, John Rhodes Papers; and *Arizona Republic*, 30 January, 27 March, 8, 16 May, 2

August, 6, 13 September, 1 October 1968; see also *New York Times*, 17 May 1968. LBJ endorsed the CAP in his message on conservation delivered to Congress on 8 March 1968, referenced in the Udall letter.

116. *Colorado River Basin Project*, U.S. Code, vol. 43, sec. 1555; and *Arizona Republic*, 4 September 1969; 5 March 1974; 8 April, 1 August 1974; 25 February 1985; see also *The Grand Canyon National Park Enlargement Act*, U.S. Code, vol. 16, sec. 228, *et seq*; and John McComb, "Regional Rep's Report: Southwest," *Sierra Club Bulletin*, June 1972, 20–21.

Chapter 7

1. Nash, *Grand Canyon*, passim.

2. Nash, *Wilderness*, 3d ed., 235.

3. For examples of these arguments please see Nash, *Wilderness*, 3d ed., 227–37; and Nash, *Grand Canyon*, 99–107; see also Runte, *National Parks*, 191, which originated as a dissertation under the direction of Dr. Nash; and Fradkin, *A River No More*, 228–34; see also Martin, *Story That Stands Like A Dam*, 250–74. Fradkin cites both *Wilderness and the American Mind*, and *Grand Canyon of the Living Colorado*, as support for his argument, while Martin cites *Wilderness*, and Fradkin. Stephen Fox also cites *Wilderness*, along with some primary sources in *American Conservation Movement*, 320, but holds to Nash's conclusion that the Sierra Club stopped the dams.

Marc Reisner's *Cadillac Desert*, 281–301, though a more journalistic account, also discusses the political aspects of the controversy in much greater detail than the aforementioned historiography. However, Reisner too, concludes that the dams were deleted because of the Sierra Club's campaign. See also Rothman, *Greening of a Nation?* 75–79; and Opie, *Nature's Nation*, 393–94, both of whom echo Nash's arguments. See also Ingram, *Water Politics*, 55–56, 59; and Cohen, *History of the Sierra Club*, 178, 315, 357–65. Possibly the only publication that does not credit the Sierra Club with the victory is Johnson's *Central Arizona Project*, an account of Johnson's own experiences while fighting for the CAP.

4. Reisner, *Cadillac Desert*, 295, is the most prominent example, and the quote is taken from his narrative. See also McPhee, *Encounters with the Archdruid*.

5. Stewart Udall, interview by author, 13 March 1997. Udall, illustrating the power Aspinall wielded as Interior Committee chair, called him a "one-man committee" in this interview.

6. Morris Udall to William Matthews, editor, *Arizona Daily Star*, 12 October 1967. Mo Udall stated in this letter that Arizona now had the votes to "run over California."

7. Floyd Dominy, interview by author, 1 November 1996. The Colorado River Storage Project was virtually the only exception to the "no new starts" policy during Eisenhower's tenure.

8. MKU to John Rhodes, 7 September 1966, folder 2, box 476, Morris Udall Papers. According to Mo Udall, Saylor's proposal was "written in Saylor's own hand."

9. The closest they came is when Dominy stated that the project would be "theo-retically possible" without the Grand Canyon dams. Please see U.S. Congress, House, Subcommittee on Irrigation and Reclamation of the Committee on Interior and Insu-lar Affairs, *Lower Colorado Basin Project: Hearings before the Subcommittee on Irrigation and Reclamation of the Committee on Interior and Insular Affairs,* 89th Cong., 2d sess., 9–13, 18 May 1966, 1073.

10. Harvey, *Symbol of Wilderness,* 271.

11. Thomas Kimball to all members of Congress, 24 March 1967, folder 2, box 5 CAP/90, John Rhodes Papers.

12. Brower to Kimball, 30 June 1967, folder 37, box 19, SCMP. The National Wildlife Federation also remained opposed to the enlargement of Grand Canyon National Park because of its effect upon deer hunting in the North Kaibab National Forest.

13. Harvey, *Symbol of Wilderness,* 273–84; 220.

14. "Firing Begins in Dinosaur Fight," *Sierra Club Bulletin,* March 1954, 30.

15. Harvey, *Symbol of Wilderness,* 291.

16. *Scenic Hudson Preservation Conference v Federal Power Commission,* 354 F.2d 608 (2d Cir. 1965).

17. Runte, *National Parks,* 191–92.

18. Fox, *American Conservation Movement,* 291–327, passim.

19. Stegner's quotation from his Wilderness letter is referenced in Cohen, *History of the Sierra Club,* 261.

20. Harvey, *Symbol of Wilderness,* 291.

21. David Brower to Harry Harrow, 29 December 1966, folder 36, box 19, SCMP; and "Atlantic Chapter—Sierra Club, Annual Report—1966," folder 11, box 56, SCMP; see also Fox, *American Conservation Movement,* 315; and Cohen, *History of the Sierra Club,* 432. Stephen Fox includes an informative chart that tracks from 1966 to 1975 the growth of five major conservation organizations: The National Wildlife Fed-eration; Sierra Club; Wilderness Society; Audubon Society; and the Izaak Walton League. David Brower claimed that the Sierra Club gained 3,000 new members from January to May of 1966, and 9,000 from June to December, and he attributed most of the growth in the second half of 1966 to public reaction to the IRS revocation. The club's Atlantic Chapter alone almost doubled in size during 1966, most of the growth coming after the IRS revocation, while the Sierra Club's aggregate membership, which grew at a moderate rate between 1960 and 1965, suddenly exploded. In 1966 the membership totaled 33,000; the next year 45,000; and 58,000 in 1968. This phe-nomenal growth rate continued through 1971, when the membership totaled 135,000, before leveling off. The Sierra Club's growth rate far exceeds that of any other major conservation organization during the same period, and it demonstrates that the public identified with the club's activism and distinguished the club from Brower, for the rate of growth continued undiminished for three years after Brower left the Sierra Club in May of 1969.

22. *Bakersfield Californian*, 28 June 1966. This quote typifies newspaper editorials printed about the IRS action. Many newspapers across the nation, from the *New York Times* down to small local weeklies, used similar rhetoric when criticizing the IRS revocation, including many papers like the *Californian*, which supported the construction of dams in Grand Canyon but opposed the heavy-handed tactics used by the Sierra Club's opponents.

23. Many historians have entered the debate over whether Native Americans were the first "environmentalists." Two prominent and controversial examples are Calvin Martin, *Keepers of the Game: Indian-Animal Relationships and the Fur Trade* (Berkeley: University of California Press, 1978); and Shepard Krech III, *The Ecological Indian: Myth and History* (New York: W. W. Norton, 1999).

24. Environmental historians credit David Brower with this phrase, but Brower attributes it to Gabrielson. See David Brower, interview by author, 27 July 1997.

① Selected Bibliography

I. PRIMARY SOURCES

Archival Materials

Sierra Club Members Papers
David Brower Papers, Bancroft Library, University of California, Berkeley.
Francis Farquhar Papers, Bancroft Library, University of California, Berkeley.
John Flannery Papers, Bancroft Library, University of California, Berkeley.
Richard Leonard Papers, Bancroft Library, University of California, Berkeley.
Martin Litton Papers, Bancroft Library, University of California, Berkeley.
Charlotte Mauk Papers, Bancroft Library, University of California, Berkeley.
Tom Turner Papers, Bancroft Library, University of California, Berkeley.
Francis Walcott Papers, Bancroft Library, University of California, Berkeley.
Robin Way Papers, Bancroft Library, University of California, Berkeley.

Sierra Club Records
Sierra Club Records, Financial, Bancroft Library, University of California, Berkeley.
Sierra Club Records, Membership Activity, Bancroft Library, University of California, Berkeley.
Sierra Club Records, Minutes, Board of Directors Meetings 1946–1969, Bancroft Library, University of California, Berkeley.
Sierra Club Records, Minutes, Executive Committee Meetings (selected) 1946–1969, Bancroft Library, University of California, Berkeley.
Sierra Club Records, Publications, Bancroft Library, University of California, Berkeley.

Other
Richard C. Bradley Papers, Western History Department, Denver Public Library, Denver, Colorado.
Frederick Dellenbaugh Papers, Department of Special Collections, University of Arizona, Tucson, Arizona.

Federal Records Center, Denver, Colorado
> Record Group 79, Records of the National Park Service
> Record Group 115, Records of the Bureau of Reclamation

Lemuel Garrison Papers, Special Collections, Clemson, University, Clemson, South Carolina.

Barry Goldwater Papers, Department of Archives and Manuscripts, Arizona State University, Tempe, Arizona.

Grand Canyon National Park Museum Collection, Microfiche: GRCA numbers: 04363; 04848; 14811; 32364; 48906; 50706; 55367; 63107; 66943; 66944. These include park superintendents reports, correspondence files and many items about Grand Canyon dam proposals from 1900–1985.

Grand Canyon National Park Research Library, Microfiche:
> Dams on the Colorado River 1938–1954, (L7423, 1–5)
> Bridge Canyon Dam 1948–1954, (L7423, 1–4)
> Bridge Canyon Dam 1950, (L7423, 1)
> Bridge Canyon Dam 1954–1966, (L7423, 1–4)
> Marble Canyon, Reference File, (L7423, 1)
> Marble Canyon–Kanab Creek Project 1961–1962, (L7423, 1–4)
> Marble Canyon–Kanab Creek Project 1963, (L7423, 1–5)

Letters, memos, and assorted documents, Bridge Canyon Dam Project, Marble Canyon Dam Projects u. d., (L7423, 1)

George B. Hartzog Papers, Special Collections, Clemson University, Clemson, South Carolina.

Carl Trumbull Hayden Papers, Department of Archives and Manuscripts, Arizona State University, Tempe, Arizona.

Emery Kolb Papers, Special Collections, Cline Library, Northern Arizona University, Flagstaff, Arizona.

National Archives, College Park Maryland
> Record Group 48, Records of the Department of the Interior

Central Classified Files of the Secretary of the Interior, 1940–1966
> Office Files of Secretary Stewart L. Udall, 1960–1966
> Record Group 79, Records of the National Park Service
> Central Classified Files
> Newton Drury Records
> Conrad Wirth Records

John Jacob Rhodes Papers, Department of Archives and Manuscripts, Arizona State University, Tempe, Arizona.

John Saylor Papers, Special Collections, Indiana University of Pennsylvania, Indiana, Pennsylvania.

George Senner Papers, Special Collections, Cline Library, Northern Arizona University, Flagstaff, Arizona.

Morris K. Udall Papers, Department of Special Collections, University of Arizona, Tucson, Arizona.

Stewart Lee Udall Papers, Department of Special Collections, University of Arizona, Tucson, Arizona.

Wilderness Society Papers, Western History Department, Denver Public Library, Denver, Colorado.

Interviews and Oral Histories

Albright, Horace. Interview by Julie Russell. Grand Canyon National Park Oral History Project. Grand Canyon National Park Museum, 7 April 1981.

Beal, Merrill. Interview by Julie Russell. Grand Canyon National Park Oral History Project. Grand Canyon National Park Museum, 20 July 1981.

Beaty, Orren. Interview with author. Vienna, Virginia, 19 March 1997.

Brower, David. Interview by Susan Schrepfer. "Environmental Activist, Publicist and Prophet." Regional Oral History Office, Bancroft Library, University of California Berkeley, 1974–1978.

Brower, David. Interview with author. Berkeley, California, 27 July 1997.

Brower, David. "Brower at Dam Site." undated cassette recording, Grand Canyon National Park Museum Collection.

Cameron, Bert. Interview by William E. Austin. Grand Canyon National Park Research Library, 21 June 1939.

Carver, John. Interview with author. Denver, Colorado, 20 August 1997.

Dominy, Floyd. Interview by Charles Coate by telephone. 14, July 1997.

Dominy, Floyd. Interview with author. Bellview Farm, Virginia, 1 November 1996.

Drury, Newton B. Interview by Amelia Fry and Susan Schrepfer. "Parks and Redwoods, 1919–1971." Regional Oral History Office, Bancroft Library, University of California Berkeley, 1983.

Elson, Roy. Interviews by Donald Richie. "Administrative Assistant to Senator Carl Hayden and Candidate for the United States Senate." John F. Kennedy Library, Boston, Massachusetts, 6 July 1990.

Francis, Sharon. Interview by Dorothy Pierce McSweeny. AC 81-68. Lyndon Baines Johnson Library, Austin, Texas, 20 May 1969.

Francis, Sharon. Interview with author by telephone. 14 August 1997.

Greg, Frank. Interview with author by telephone. 15 October 1996.

Hartzog, George. Interview with author. McLean, Virginia, 2 November 1996.

Ingram, Jeff. Interview with author. Tucson, Arizona, 12 March 1998.

Leonard, Richard. Interview by Susan Schrepfer. "Mountaineer, Lawyer, Environmentalist." Regional Oral History Office, Bancroft Library, University of California Berkeley, 1975.

Litton, Martin. Interview by Ann Lage. "Sierra Club Director and Uncompromising Preservationist, 1950s–1970s." Regional Oral History Office, Bancroft Library, University of California Berkeley, 1980–1981.

Robinson, Bestor. Interview by Susan R. Schrepfer. "Thoughts on Conservation and the Sierra Club." Regional Oral History Office, Bancroft Library, University of California Berkeley, 1974.

Siri, William E. Interview by Ann Lage. "Reflections on the Sierra Club, the Environment, and Mountaineering, 1950s–1970s." Regional Oral History Office, Bancroft Library, University of California Berkeley, 1976.

Steck, George. Interview by Michael Quinn. Grand Canyon National Park Oral History Project, Grand Canyon National Park Museum. 3 September 1995.

Stricklin, Howard. Interview by Julie Russell. Grand Canyon National Park Oral History Project. Grand Canyon National Park Museum. 26, August 1981.

Udall, Stewart. Interview with author. Tucson, Arizona, 13 March 1997.

Udall, Stewart. Interview with Charles Coate, Santa Fe New Mexico, 23 April 1997.

Udall, Stewart. Interview with W. W. Moss. John F. Kennedy Library, Boston Massachusetts 12 January 1970.

Wayburn, Edgar. Interview by Ann Lage and Susan Schrepfer. "Sierra Club Statesman, Leader of the Parks and Wilderness Movement: Gaining Protection for Alaska, the Redwoods, and Golden Gate Parklands." Regional Oral History Office, University of California Berkeley, 1976–1981.

II. NEWSPAPERS

Arizona Daily Star (Tucson), 1945–65.

Arizona Daily Sun (Flagstaff, Arizona), 1958–66.

Arizona Republic (Phoenix), 1948–85.

Bakersfield Californian, 1966.

Chicago Daily News, 1951.

Coconino Sun (Flagstaff, Arizona), 1901–12.

Denver Post, 1964–66.

Gallup Independent, 1966.

Kingman Miner (Arizona), 1902.

Los Angeles Times, 1945–64.

Oakland Tribune, 1966.

New York Sun, 1923.

New York Times, 1963–75.

New York Daily Tribune, 1923.

Phoenix Gazette, 1952–65.

Phoenix Republican, 1902.

Portland Oregonian, 1962–65.

Riverside Daily Enterprise (California), 1966.

Rocky Mountain News (Colorado), 1966.

Salt Lake City Tribune, 1893.

San Francisco Chronicle, 1921.

Wall Street Journal, 1966.

Washington Post, 1923–, 1966.

Williams News, 1956.

III. SECONDARY SOURCES

Abbey, Edward. *Desert Solitaire: A Season in the Wilderness*. New York: Simon and Schuster, 1968.

Berkman, Richard, and Kip Vicusi. *Damming the West: Ralph Nader's Study Group on the Bureau of Reclamation*. New York: Grossman Publishers, 1973.

"Blueprint for an Area Short of Water." *U.S. News And World Report*, 9 September 1963, 3.

Bradley, Richard C. "Attack on Grand Canyon." *Living Wilderness*, winter 1964–65, 3–6.

———. "Grand Canyon of the Controversial Colorado." *Sierra Club Bulletin*, December 1964, 73–78.

———. "Ruin for the Grand Canyon." *Audubon*, January–February 1966, 34–41.

———. "Ruin for the Grand Canyon." *Readers Digest*, April 1966, 193–98.

———. "Ruin for the Grand Canyon." *Town Hall* (Los Angeles) 28, no. 28, (12 July 1966).

Brower, David. *For Earth's Sake: The Life and Times of David R. Brower*. Salt Lake City: Peregrine Smith Books, 1990.

———. "The New Threat to Grand Canyon: Action Needed." *Sierra Club Bulletin*, January 1964, 18.

———. "Gigantic Southwest Water Plan Offers More Reservoirs Than Water." *Sierra Club Bulletin*, September 1964, 12–13.

———. "The Chips Are Down for Grand Canyon." *Sierra Club Bulletin*, February 1965, 2a–2b; 26a–26b.

———. "Grand Canyon: Department of Amplification." *Sierra Club Bulletin*, December 1965, 14–15.

———. *Work in Progress*. Salt Lake City: Peregrine Smith Books, 1991.

Burns, Stewart. *Social Movements of the 1960s*. Boston: Twayne Publisher, 1990.

Caro, Robert. *The Years of Lyndon Johnson. Vol. 1, The Path to Power*. New York: Alfred Knopf, 1982; New York: Random House Vintage Books, 1990.

———. *The Years of Lyndon Johnson. Vol. 2, Means of Ascent*. New York: Alfred Knopf, 1990.

Carothers, Steven W., and Brian T. Brown. *The Colorado River Through Grand Canyon: Natural History and Human Change*. Tucson: University of Arizona Press, 1991.

Cohen, Michael P. *The History of the Sierra Club, 1892–1970*. San Francisco: Sierra Club Books, 1988.

Colter, Fred. *The Highline Book*. Phoenix, Arizona: By the author, 1934.

"Compromise the Grand Canyon." *Sierra Club Bulletin*, March 1967, 4.

Dallek, Robert. *Lone Star Rising: Lyndon Johnson and His Times, 1908–1960*. New York, Oxford: Oxford University Press, 1991.

"Dam the Canyon?" *Newsweek*, 30 May 1966, 27.

"Dams vs. Scenery (Again)." *Izaak Walton Magazine*, March 1965, 15.

Dean, Robert. "'Dam building still had some magic then': Stewart Udall, the Central Arizona Project and the Evolution of the Pacific Southwest Water Plan, 1963–1968. *Pacific Historical Review* 66 (February 1997): 81–99.

DeVoto, Bernard. "Shall We Let Them Ruin Our National Parks?" *Reader's Digest*, November 1950, 18–24.

Farmer, Jared. *Glen Canyon Dammed: Inventing Lake Powell & the Canyon Country*. Tucson: University of Arizona Press, 1999.

"Firing Begins in Dinosaur Fight." *Sierra Club Bulletin*, March 1954, 30.

Foresta, Ronald A. *America's National Parks and Their Keepers*. Washington, D.C.: Resources for the Future, 1984.

Fox, Stephen. *The American Conservation Movement: John Muir and His Legacy*. Madison: University of Wisconsin Press, 1981.

Fradkin, Philip L. *A River No More*. Tucson: University of Arizona Press, 1981.

———. *Fallout: An American Nuclear Tragedy*. Tucson: University of Arizona Press, 1989.

Frome, Michael. *Regreening the National Parks*. Tucson: University of Arizona Press, 1992.

Gitlin, Todd. *The Sixties: Years of Hope, Days of Rage*. New York: Bantam Books, 1987.

Gould, Lewis. *Lady Bird Johnson and the Environment*. Lawrence: University of Kansas Press, 1988.

"Grand Canyon Cash Registers." *Life*, 7 May 1965, 4.

"Grand Canyon, Colorado Dams Debated." *Science*, 17 June 1966, 1–7.

Gunther, Gerald. *Constitutional Law*. 11th ed. Mineola, N. Y.: Foundation Press, 1985.

Hartzog, George B. *Battling for the National Parks*. Mt. Kisco, N. Y.: Moyer Bell Limited, 1988.

Harvey, Mark, W. T. *A Symbol of Wilderness: Echo Park and the American Conservation Movement*. Albuquerque: University of New Mexico Press, 1994.

———. "Paying the Taxpayer: The Internal Revenue Service and the Environmental Movement." Paper delivered at the American Society of Environmental History convention, Baltimore, Maryland, 6 March 1997.

———. "Defending the Park System: The Controversy over Rainbow Bridge." *New Mexico Historical Review* 73 (January 1998): 45–67.

Hays, Samuel P. *Conservation and the Gospel of Efficiency: The Progressive Conservation Movement, 1890–1920*. Cambridge: Harvard University Press, 1959.

———. "From Conservation to Environment: Environmental Politics Since World War Two." *Environmental Review* 6 (fall 1982): 14–41.

———. *Beauty, Health, and Permanence: Environmental Politics in the United States, 1955–1985*. Cambridge: Cambridge University Press, 1987.

Heald, Weldon. "Colorado River of the West." *National Parks Magazine*, October 1963, 4–9.

Hobbes, Thomas. *Leviathan*. New York: Penguin Books, 1985.

Hoxie, Frederick, ed. *Indians in American History*. Arlington Heights, Ill.: Harlan Davidson, 1988.

"How to Save the Grand Canyon and Water the Desert Too." *U.S. News And World Report*, 24 October 1966, 1–3.

Hughes, J. Donald. *In the House of Stone and Light*. Grand Canyon Natural History Association, 1978.

Humlum, J. *Water Development and Planning in the Southwestern United States*. Copenhagen, Denmark: Carlsberg Foundation, 1969.

Hundley, Norris. *Dividing the Waters: A Century of Controversy between the United States and Mexico*. Berkeley and Los Angeles: University of California Press, 1966.

———. *Water and the West*. Berkeley and Los Angeles: University of California Press, 1975.

———. *The Great Thirst: Californians and Water, 1770s–1990s*. Berkeley and Los Angeles: University of California Press, 1992.

Ingram, Helen. *Patterns of Politics in Water Resource Development*. Tucson: University of Arizona Press, 1969.

———. *Water Politics, Continuity and Change*. Albuquerque: University of New Mexico Press, 1990.

"Internal Revenue Service Used as a Weapon against the Sierra Club—and against Grand Canyon." *Sierra Club Bulletin*, July-August 1966, 5–7.

Jefferson, Thomas. "Notes on Virginia." In *The Life and Selected Writings of Thomas Jefferson*. New York: Random House, 1972.

Johnson, Rich. *The Central Arizona Project: 1918–1968*. Tucson: University of Arizona Press, 1977.

Jones, Holoway R. *John Muir and the Sierra Club: The Battle for Yosemite*. San Francisco: Sierra Club, 1965.

Keller, Robert H., Jr., and Michael F. Turek. *American Indians and National Parks*. Tucson: University of Arizona Press, 1998.

Kirwin, Jerome. *Federal Water Power Legislation*. New York: Columbia University Press, 1926.

Krech, Shepard, III. *The Ecological Indian: Myth and History*. New York: W. W. Norton, 1999.

Leopold, Aldo. *A Sand County Almanac and Sketches Here and There*. New York: Oxford University Press, 1949.

Leopold, Madelyn. "Disillusioning Dams and the Value of Beauty." *Sierra Club Bulletin*, October 1965, 12.

Leydet, Francois. *Time and the River Flowing*. San Francisco: Sierra Club, 1964.

Mann, Dean. *The Politics of Water in Arizona.* Tucson: University of Arizona Press, 1963.

Martin, Calvin. *Keepers of the Game: Indian-Animal Relationships and the Fur Trade.* Berkeley and Los Angeles: University of California Press, 1978.

Martin, Russell. *A Story That Stands Like a Dam: Glen Canyon and the Struggle for the Soul of the West.* New York: Henry Holt, 1989.

Mayo, Dwight Eugene. "Arizona and the Colorado River Compact." Master's thesis, Arizona State University, 1964.

McComb, John. "Regional Rep's Report, Southwest." *Sierra Club Bulletin,* June 1972, 20–21.

———. "Regional Rep's Report, Southwest: Grand Canyon National Park Diminution Act." *Sierra Club Bulletin,* February 1975, 18–19.

McPhee, John. *Encounters with the Archdruid.* New York: Farrar, Straus, and Giroux, 1971.

Minckley, W. L. *Fishes of Arizona.* Phoenix: Sims Printing Company, 1973.

Morehouse, Barbara. *A Place Called Grand Canyon: Contested Geographies.* Tucson: University of Arizona Press, 1996.

Nash, Roderick, ed. *Wilderness and the American Mind.* New Haven: Yale University Press, 1967.

———. *Grand Canyon of the Living Colorado.* New York: Ballentine Books, 1970.

———. *Wilderness and the American Mind.* 3d ed. New Haven: Yale University Press, 1982.

Neel, Susan Rhoades. "Irreconcilable Differences: Reclamation, Preservation, and the Origins of the Echo Park Dam Controversy." Ph.D. diss., University of California at Los Angeles, 1990.

"News of Conservation and the Club." *Sierra Club Bulletin,* September 1966, 2.

"News of Conservation and the Club." *Sierra Club Bulletin,* March 1967, 2.

"News of Conservation and the Club." *Sierra Club Bulletin,* February 1968, 3.

O'Neil, William. *Coming Apart: An Informal History of America in the 1960s.* New York: Times Books, 1971.

———. *American High: The Years of Confidence, 1945–1960.* New York: Macmillan, 1986.

Opie, John. *Nature's Nation: An Environmental History of the United States.* New York: Harcourt Brace, 1998.

Packard, Fred. "Grand Canyon National Monument in Danger." *National Parks Magazine,* July-September 1949, 3–8.

———. "Grand Canyon Park and Dinosaur Monument in Danger." *National Parks Magazine,* October–December 1949, 11–13.

Pearson, Byron. "Salvation for Grand Canyon." *Journal of the Southwest* 36, no. 2 (summer 1994): 159–75.

———. "The Marble Canyon–Kanab Creek Project." *Locus* 8, no. 1 (fall 1995): 65–80.

———. "People above Scenery, the Struggle over the Grand Canyon Dams, 1963–1968." Ph.D. diss., University of Arizona, 1998.

———. "Newton Drury of the National Park Service, A Reappraisal." *Pacific Historical Review* 68, no. 3 (August 1999): 397–424.

———. "We Have Almost Forgotten How to Hope": The Hualapai, the Navajo, and the Fight for the Central Arizona Project, 1944–1968." *Western Historical Quarterly* 31 (autumn 2000): 297–316.

Pinchot, Gifford. *The Fight for Conservation.* Garden City, N. Y.: Harcourt Brace, 1910.

Pisani, Donald, J. *To Reclaim a Divided West: Water Law and Public Policy, 1848–1902.* Albuquerque: University of New Mexico Press, 1992.

Porter, Eliot. *The Place No One Knew.* San Francisco: Sierra Club Books, 1963.

Powell, John Wesley. *The Exploration of the Colorado River and Its Canyons.* New York: Dover Publications, 1961.

———. *Report on the Arid Region of the United States.* 2d ed. Cambridge: Harvard University Press, 1962.

Ragsdale, John. "Anno Dominy MCMLXVI." *Biophilist* (March–April 1966): 1:7–8.

Raushenbush, Stephen. "A Bridge Canyon Dam Is Not Necessary." *National Parks Magazine*, April 1964, 4–8.

"*Reader's Digest* Enlists in the Fight to Save Grand Canyon." *Sierra Club Bulletin,* May 1966, 6–7.

"Reclaimed by Man." *Razz Review,* June 1975, 20–21, 34.

Reisner, Marc. *Cadillac Desert.* New York: Penguin Books, 1987.

———. *Cadillac Desert: An American Nile.* Chicago, Ill.: Home Vision Select, 1997. Videocassette.

Richardson, Elmo. "Federal Park Policy in Utah: The Escalante National Monument Controversy of 1935–1940." *Utah Historical Quarterly* 33 (spring 1965): 109–33.

Robinson, Michael C. *Water for the West: The Bureau of Reclamation, 1902–1977.* Chicago: Public Works Historical Society, 1979.

Rothman, Hal. *Preserving Different Pasts: The American National Monuments.* Urbana: University of Illinois Press, 1989.

———. *The Greening of a Nation?.* New York: Harcourt Brace Inc., 1998.

Runte, Alfred. *National Parks: The American Experience.* 2d ed. Lincoln: University of Nebraska Press, 1987.

Satchell, Michael. "Power and the Glory." *U.S. News and World Report,* 21 January 1991, 70–71.

Shankland, Robert. *Stephen Mather of the National Parks.* New York: Alfred Knopf, 1970.

Smith, Anthony Wayne. "Attack on Grand Canyon." *National Parks Magazine,* January 1962, 2.

———. "The Mighty Colorado." *National Parks Magazine,* October 1963, 2.

———. "The Editorial Page." *National Parks Magazine,* April 1964, 2.

"Southwest Gropes for New Ways to End Water Shortage." *U.S. News And World Report,* 12 December 1966, 59–61.

Stevens, Joseph E. *Hoover Dam.* Norman: University of Oklahoma Press, 1988.

Stevens, Larry. *The Colorado River in Grand Canyon: A Guide.* 3d ed. Flagstaff, Ariz.: Red Lake Books, 1990.

Stewart, Bruce. "Think Big." *Harper's,* August 1965, 62–63.

"Strong Words Betray a Weak Case." *Sierra Club Bulletin,* July-August 1966, 4.

Terrell, John U. *The Western Web: A Chronological Narrative of the Case against the State of Arizona and the Bureau of Reclamation in the Long Fight to Defeat the Proposed Multi–billion Dollar Central Arizona Project.* Vols.1 and 2. Los Angeles, Calif.: Colorado River Association, 1949–1952.

"The Entire Grand Canyon Must Be Protected." *Sierra Club Bulletin,* May 1966, 8–9.

Thomas, Clyde. "The Last Days of Grand Canyon Too?" *Sierra Club Bulletin,* October 1963, 2–3.

Thompson, Robert H. "Decision at Rainbow Bridge." *Sierra Club Bulletin,* May 1973, 20–21.

"Trouble at the Bridge." *National Parks Magazine,* April 1960, 19.

Turner, Tom. "The Grand Undammed." *Sierra,* July-August 1992, 18–19.

Udall, Morris K. *Education of a Congressman: The Newsletters of Morris K. Udall.* New York: Bobbs-Merrill, 1972.

———. *Too Funny to Be President.* New York: Henry Holt, 1988.

Udall, Stewart L. *The Quiet Crisis.* New York: Avon Books, 1963.

———. "Wilderness Rivers: Shooting the Wild Colorado." *Venture.* February 1968, 62–70.

———. *The Quiet Crisis and the Next Generation.* 2d ed. Salt Lake City: Peregrine Smith Books, 1988.

———. *The Myths of August: A Personal Exploration of Our Tragic Cold War Affair with the Atom.* New York: Random House, 1994.

Warne, William E. *The Bureau of Reclamation.* New York: Praeger, 1973.

Webb, Roy. *If We Had a Boat.* Salt Lake City: University of Utah Press, 1986.

White, Richard. *"It's Your Misfortune and None of My Own": A New History of the American West.* Norman: University of Oklahoma Press, 1991.

Wiley, Peter, and Roger Gotlieb. *Empires in the Sun: The Rise of the New American West.* Tucson: University of Arizona Press, 1982.

Wirth, Conrad. *Parks, Politics, and the People.* Norman: University of Oklahoma Press, 1980.

"Wild by Law." *The American Experience Series.* 35 min. Corporation for Public Broadcasting, 1991. Videocassette.

Worster, Donald. *Rivers of Empire: Water, Aridity and the Growth of the American West.* New York: Pantheon Books, 1985.

IV. UNITED STATES GOVERNMENT DOCUMENTS, PUBLICATIONS, AND REPORTS

Congressional Quarterly. 1965, 1966. Washington, D.C.

Congressional Record. 1919, 1960–1968. Washington, D.C.

Ives, Joseph C. *Report upon the Colorado River of the West,* Washington: Government Printing Office, 1861.

La Rue, E. C. *Colorado River and Its Utilization: Water Supply Paper 395.* Washington: Government Printing Office, 1916.

————. *Water and Flood Control of Colorado River below Green River Utah: Water Supply Paper 556.* Washington: Government Printing Office, 1925.

Leopold, Luna. *USGS Circular 410: Probability Analysis Applied to a Water Problem.* Washington, D.C.: Government Printing Office, 1958.

National Academy of Sciences. *Water and Choice in the Colorado Basin: An Example of Alternatives in Water Management.* Washington, D.C.: Printing and Publishing Office, National Academy of Sciences, 1968.

U.S. Congress. House. Subcommittee on Irrigation and Reclamation of the Committee on Interior and Insular Affairs. *Central Arizona Project: Hearings before the Subcommittee on Irrigation and Reclamation of the Committee on Interior and Insular Affairs.* 81st Cong. 1st sess., 1949.

U.S. Congress. House. Committee on Interior and Insular Affairs. *Central Arizona Project: Hearings before the Committee on Interior and Insular Affairs.* 82d Cong. 1st sess., 1951.

U.S. Congress. House. Subcommittee on Irrigation and Reclamation of the Committee on Interior and Insular Affairs. *Colorado River Storage Project: Hearings before the Subcommittee on Irrigation and Reclamation of the Committee on Interior and Insular Affairs.* 84th Cong. 1st sess., 1955.

U.S. Congress. House. Subcommittee on Irrigation and Reclamation of the Committee on Interior and Insular Affairs. *Lower Colorado Basin Project: Hearings before the Subcommittee on Irrigation and Reclamation of the Committee on Interior and Insular Affairs.* 89th Cong. 1st sess., 1965.

U.S. Congress. House. Subcommittee on Irrigation and Reclamation of the Committee on Interior and Insular Affairs. *Lower Colorado Basin Project: Hearings before the Subcommittee on Irrigation and Reclamation of the Committee on Interior and Insular Affairs.* 89th Cong. 2d sess., 1966.

U.S. Congress. House. Subcommittee on Irrigation and Reclamation of the Committee on Interior and Insular Affairs. *Lower Colorado Basin Project: Hearings before the Subcommittee on Irrigation and Reclamation of the Committee on Interior and Insular Affairs.* 90th Cong. 1st sess., 1967.

U.S. Congress. House. Committee on Interior and Insular Affairs. *Colorado River Basin Project.* 90th Cong. 2d sess., 1968, Report No. 1312.

U.S. Congress. Senate. Subcommittee on Public Lands of the Committee on Interior and Insular Affairs. *Bridge Canyon Dam and Central Arizona Project: Hearings before the Subcommittee on Public Lands of the Committee on Interior and Insular Affairs.* 80th Cong. 1st sess., 1947.

U.S. Congress. Senate. Subcommittee on Irrigation and Reclamation of the Committee on Interior and Insular Affairs. *Colorado River Storage Project: Hearings before the Subcommittee on Irrigation and Reclamation of the Committee on Interior and Insular Affairs.* 84th Cong. 1st sess., 1955.

U.S. Congress. Senate. S. 75. *A Bill Authorizing the Construction, Operation and Maintenance of a Dam and Incidental Works in the Main Stream of the Colorado River at Bridge Canyon, Together with Certain Appurtenant Dams and Canals, and for Other Purposes.* 82d Cong., 1st sess., 1951.

U.S. Department of the Interior. "National Park Service Appendix to Pacific Southwest Water Plan." August 1963.

———. "Pacific Southwest Water Plan Report." January 1964.

———. *Lake Powell: Jewel of the Colorado.* Washington, D.C.: Government Printing Office, 1965.

U.S. Department of the Interior. Bureau of Reclamation. "Preliminary Report on Colorado River–Phoenix Diversion Project, Arizona." March 1944.

———. *The Colorado River: A Natural Menace Becomes a National Resource: A Comprehensive Report on the Development of the Water Resources of the Colorado River Basin for Irrigation, Power Production, and Other Beneficial Uses in Arizona, California, Colorado, Nevada, New Mexico, Utah, and Wyoming.* March 1946.

———. U.S. Department of the Interior. Bureau of Reclamation. "Memorandum Report on Reconnaissance Studies, Marble Canyon–Kanab Creek Power Development." Boulder City, Nevada, October 1961.

———. "Bridge and Marble Canyon Dams and Their Relationship to Grand Canyon National Park and Monument." 1964.

U.S. Department of the Interior. Information Service. "Mathematics Applied to United States Water Supply Problems." 19 July 1959.

V. UNPUBLISHED SOURCES

Brower, Barbara. Correspondence with author. 19 December 1997; 9 January 1998.

Harza Engineering Company. "Preliminary Planning Report: Colorado River Development within the State of Arizona: Colorado River Projects." Chicago, 15 December 1958.

Harvey, Mark. "Paying the Taxpayer: The Internal Revenue Service and the Environmental Movement." Paper delivered at the biannual conference of the American Society for Environmental History, Baltimore, Maryland, 6 March 1997.

Jett, Stephen. Correspondence with author. 28 December 1997; 6 February 1998.

———. "Navajos Enter Fight against Grand Canyon Dams." August 1966. Manuscript, copy in author's possession.

Index

① About the Author

B yron Pearson, an Arizona native, is an assistant professor of history on the faculty of West Texas A&M University. Pearson graduated from the University of San Diego School of Law with the degree of Juris Doctor in 1988; he received an M.A. in history from Northern Arizona University in 1992, and his Ph.D. in history from the University of Arizona in 1998.

Pearson has won several awards for his teaching and scholarship. In 2000, he was named to the 2000 edition of *Who's Who Among America's Teachers*. He also received the Westerner's International Dissertation Prize from Phi Alpha Theta, the national history honor society, for the dissertation from which this book is largely derived. Additionally, the Pacific Coast Branch of the American Historical Association recognized his revisionist interpretation of the tenure of former Park Service Director Newton Drury, published in the fall 1999 *Pacific Historical Review*, by awarding him the W. Turrentine Jackson Prize.

Currently, Pearson is exploring early state and federal Grand Canyon dam proposals within the political and social context of the twentieth century prior to 1963, in order to provide a detailed historical foundation for the controversy discussed in this book. He is also working on an analysis of Thomas Jefferson's environmental consciousness and how it relates to his expertise in the law.